GUERNICA
and
Other Plays

Fernando Arrabal

Guernica · The Labyrinth ·
The Tricycle · Picnic on the
Battlefield · And They Put
Handcuffs on the Flowers ·
The Architect and the
Emperor of Assyria ·
Garden of Delights

GROVE PRESS, INC., NEW YORK

CONTENTS

GUERNICA

The tree of liberty in Guernica escaped
the massacre of the town, and still stands.

translated from the French
by Barbara Wright

CHARACTERS

FANCHOU   *An old Basque man*
LIRA   *An old Basque woman*

Also taking part in the play:

A Woman and her 10 year old daughter
A Journalist
A Writer
An Officer

Guernica *was performed in German by the Schloss-theater company at Celle, which presented the play in Paris in June 1961 at the Théâtre du Vieux-Colombier.*

GUERNICA

The sound of the boots of marching troops is heard for some ten seconds. Then the sound of an air raid: aeroplanes and exploding bombs. The curtain rises when the raid is over. The interior of a bombed house: crumbling walls, debris, stones. FANCHOU *is in the house, near a table, in despair.*

FANCHOU: My precious, my lamb.
He searches a pile of rubble on his right, unsuccessfully.
Where are you, my lamb?
He goes on searching.
LIRA'S VOICE [*plaintively*]: Darling.
FANCHOU: Have you finished peeing?
LIRA'S VOICE: I can't get out. I'm stuck. Everything's collapsed.
FANCHOU *climbs on to the table with some difficulty, trying to see* LIRA. *He raises himself on tiptoe. He sees her, and looks pleased.*
FANCHOU: Look at me.
He stands on tiptoe again.
LIRA'S VOICE: Are you there?
FANCHOU: Go carefully, my precious.
LIRA'S VOICE: Ow, ouch.
She moans like a child.
FANCHOU: Have you hurt yourself?
Pause. FANCHOU *looks anxious.*
LIRA'S VOICE [*plaintively*]: Yes. All the stones fell on top of me.
FANCHOU: Try and stand up.
LIRA'S VOICE: There's no point, I won't be able to get out.
FANCHOU: Make an effort.

9

LIRA'S VOICE: Tell me you still love me.

FANCHOU: Of course, you know I do. [*Pause.*] You'll see, when you get out we'll do all sorts of lovely dirty things.

LIRA'S VOICE: Of course we will. [*Sounding pleased.*] You'll never change.

> *Sound of aeroplanes. Bombs start falling again for a few seconds. The raid stops.*

FANCHOU: Have any more stones fallen on you?

LIRA'S VOICE: No. Have they on you, my precious?

FANCHOU: No. Make an effort and get out of there.

LIRA'S VOICE: I can't. [*Pause.*] Look and see if they've hit the tree.

> FANCHOU *gets down off the table with difficulty. He goes over to the left. He has to clear a lot of rubble out of the way. Part of the window appears.* FANCHOU *looks out of it. He seems pleased. He comes back. He climbs on to the·table again.*

FANCHOU: No, they haven't hit it, it's still there.

> *Pause.*

LIRA'S VOICE [*plaintively*]: What am I going to do?

FANCHOU: Try and stand up carefully, very carefully.

LIRA'S VOICE: I can't.

FANCHOU: Make an effort.

LIRA'S VOICE: I'll try.

FANCHOU [*speaking slowly*]: Carefully does it, that's right, very carefully.

> *There is a sound of falling rubble. Plaintive moans from* LIRA.

Have you hurt yourself? [*Silence.*] What's happening? Say something. Have you hurt yourself?

> *Plaintive moans from* LIRA.

Have you really hurt yourself?

LIRA'S VOICE [*sadly*]: Yes. [*She whimpers like a child.*] Some stones fell on my arm; it's bleeding.

FANCHOU: Bleeding?

LIRA'S VOICE: Yes.

FANCHOU: A lot?

LIRA'S VOICE: Yes, a lot.

FANCHOU: Is it a scratch or a wound?

LIRA'S VOICE: It's a scratch, but there's a lot of blood.

FANCHOU: I'll go and get you some cotton wool.

FANCHOU *searches the rubble. He shifts some of the debris, but more and more rubble falls. He gives up. He goes back and gets up on the table again.*

The wardrobe's buried in rubble.

LIRA *whimpers like a child.*

Don't cry. Put a bit of saliva on your arm and tie your handkerchief round it.

LIRA *groans. Enter right, the* JOURNALIST *and the* WRITER. *The* JOURNALIST *has a notebook in his hand. The* WRITER *walks round* FANCHOU *inquisitively and examines him carefully. He suddenly stops for a moment in the middle of the stage.*

WRITER [*to the* JOURNALIST]: And you can say, too that I'm writing a novel, and perhaps a film, on the Spanish civil war.

The WRITER *and the* JOURNALIST *walk towards the left.*

WRITER [*confidently*]: This heroic and paradoxical people, which reflects the spirit of Lorca's poems, Goya's paintings, and Buñuel's films, is demonstrating, in this dreadful war, its courage, its capacity for suffering, its . . .

The WRITER *and the* JOURNALIST *go out, left. The* WRITER'*s voice fades away in the distance.*

FANCHOU: Do you feel any better?

LIRA'S VOICE: A bit. [*Pause. Plaintive voice.*] But not much.

FANCHOU: Would you like me to tell you a nice story so it doesn't hurt any more?

LIRA'S VOICE: You're no good at telling stories.

FANCHOU: Would you like me to tell you the one about the woman who was in the lavatory and who got buried in the rubble? [*Pause.*] Don't you like that one?

LIRA'S VOICE: It hurts a lot.

FANCHOU: It'll soon be better, you'll see. I'll act the clown and make you laugh.

FANCHOU *does an awkward dance and pulls all kinds of faces. Then he bursts out laughing.*

11

FANCHOU: Did you like it?

LIRA'S VOICE: I can't see you.

Sound of aeroplanes. Raid. While this is going on a woman and her little girl cross the stage from right to left, looking angry and helpless (see the Picasso painting). The raid ends.

FANCHOU: Are you all right, my lamb?

Long pause.

LIRA'S VOICE: Darling, I feel terrible. I'm going to die.

FANCHOU: You're going to die? [*Pause.*] Are you really and truly going to die? D'you want me to tell the family?

LIRA'S VOICE [*irritable*]: What d'you mean, the family?

FANCHOU: Isn't that what people say?

LIRA'S VOICE: What a rotten memory you've got. Don't you remember we haven't got a family any more?

FANCHOU: Hm! Nor we have! [*He cogitates.*] What about Joséchou?

LIRA'S VOICE: You must be dreaming! Have you really forgotten that he was shot at Burgos?

FANCHOU: Well you can't say it was my fault. I always told you I didn't want a boy. Whenever a war crops up they get killed. Whereas if we'd had a girl the house would be nice and tidy now.

LIRA'S VOICE: That's it, nothing but reproaches. It wasn't my fault.

FANCHOU: Don't be cross, my love, I didn't mean to hurt your feelings.

LIRA'S VOICE: You're never a bit sorry for me.

FANCHOU: Oh yes I am. When you get out of there I'll give you another one, if you like, just to show that I don't hold it against you.

LIRA'S VOICE: But you can't any more.

FANCHOU: That's right, now tell me I'm not a man any more, go on.

LIRA'S VOICE: No, it's not that, it's just that you can't get an erection any more.

FANCHOU: I can't, can't I? Well, you're the only one who says that. Don't you remember that Saturday?

12

LIRA'S VOICE: Which Saturday?

FANCHOU: Which Saturday d'you think? You'll tell me you've forgotten that, next.

LIRA'S VOICE: Are you going to start boasting all over again?

FANCHOU: I'm not boasting. It's just the plain, honest truth, but you don't want to admit it. [*Pause.*]

LIRA'S VOICE: Have another look and see if they've got the tree.

FANCHOU gets off the table. He goes over to the window. He opens it. An OFFICER *appears on the other side of it. They look at each other very gravely for quite some time.* FANCHOU *hangs his head apprehensively. The* OFFICER *laughs mirthlessly and plays with a pair of handcuffs he is holding.* FANCHOU, *still hanging his head, shuts the window. He comes back looking terrified. He gets up on the table.*

Well?

Pause.

Well? Is it still there?

FANCHOU: I don't know.

LIRA'S VOICE: What d'you mean, you don't know?

FANCHOU: I couldn't see it.

LIRA'S VOICE [*plaintively*]: That's fine—here I am, stuck, all I ask you to do is look and see if they've hit the tree and you won't even do that.

FANCHOU: I couldn't.

LIRA'S VOICE [*plaintively*]: All right, have it your own way.

FANCHOU gets down from the table. Fearfully, he goes over to the window. He opens it anxiously. He looks out of it. He goes back to the table and climbs on to it. He raises himself up on tiptoe, looking pleased.

FANCHOU: It's still there.

LIRA'S VOICE [*proudly*]: I told you it would be. [*Pause. Very sadly.*] Help me a bit, though. Don't leave me all by myself.

FANCHOU: What d'you want me to do?

LIRA'S VOICE [*plaintively*]: Can't you think of anything? How

13

you've changed. It's quite obvious that you don't love me any more.

FANCHOU: But I do, my lamb. Try and stand up. Stretch your arm out, I'll try and reach it.

> FANCHOU *raises himself as high as he can and stretches out his arm towards the rubble. While* FANCHOU *is trying to grasp* LIRA's *hand, the* OFFICER *enters, right. The* OFFICER *looks at* FANCHOU, *who has his back to him.*

Make an effort. If you can stretch just a little bit further I'll be able to reach you. A bit more. There. There.

> FANCHOU *is on tiptoe. The* OFFICER *pushes him from behind and makes him fall over. The* OFFICER *immediately goes out, right.* FANCHOU *laboriously gets up again. He looks towards the right. The* OFFICER *appears at the window. He laughs mirthlessly and plays with his handcuffs.* FANCHOU *looks at the window apprehensively. When their eyes meet the* OFFICER *stops laughing and playing with the handcuffs. They look at each other gravely.* FANCHOU *hangs his head. The* OFFICER *again starts laughing mirthlessly and playing with the handcuffs. He finally disappears.* FANCHOU *raises his head and looks over towards the window; he seems relieved.*

LIRA'S VOICE: Ow, ouch, why've you gone and left me?

FANCHOU: I slipped. Have you hurt yourself, my lamb?

LIRA'S VOICE: Some more stones have fallen on me. Ouch.

FANCHOU: I'm sorry.

LIRA'S VOICE: I can't rely on you.

FANCHOU: Oh yes you can. I've got a surprise for you: a present.

> FANCHOU *takes a piece of string and a flabby object out of his pocket. He inflates it with his mouth. It's a blue balloon. He ties it with the string. He attaches a stone to the end of the string.*

[*Very pleased*]:Catch this stone I'm throwing over. [*He throws it over the wall.*] Have you got it?

LIRA'S VOICE: Yes.

FANCHOU: Pull the string.

LIRA *does so. The balloon settles over her head.*
Look up in the air. Can you see it?
Sound of aeroplanes. Raid. A deafening row. While it is going on the woman and the little girl cross from right to left. They are pushing a wheelbarrow. On it is a packing case on which the word DINAMITA *is written. They look angry and helpless. The raid ends.*
My lamb! [*Pause. Worried.*] My lamb!
The balloon moves up and down.
Are you all right?
The balloon moves up and down.
Say something.
Long silence.
Won't you say something to me? Are you cross with me? It's not my fault. [*Pause.*] Now if only *I* had a hand in things. [*Pause.*] *I* didn't destroy the houses. [*Pleased.*] In any case, they haven't got the tree. [*Suddenly.*] Are you going to be cross for ever and ever? [*Silence.*] Are you mortally offended? [*Silence.*] So that's the way you love me. All right. Have it your own way. [*He looks the other way, obstinately, as if he doesn't care. He crosses his arms.*] You heard me, I suppose? Have it your own way, it's all the same to me. [*Pause.*] And don't turn round afterwards and tell me that I started it and that I'm so difficult. This time it's obvious; I haven't done a thing, you're the one that's refusing to talk. I saw what you were up to— you started by saying that I couldn't make it, that Saturday, and now you refuse to talk to me. [*Pause.*] Don't you even want to play with the balloon?
FANCHOU *turns round to have a look. The balloon is moving gently up and down.*
Ah! Her ladyship can't talk, she's tired, she only deigns to play with the balloon. Right—two can play at that game. [*Pause.*] But say something, tell me what you want, even if it's something horrid, but say something. [*Long silence.*] Oh, very well.
Once again he adopts a sulky look. He crosses his arms and looks in the opposite direction. Enter, right, the

WRITER *and the* JOURNALIST, *still holding his notebook.*
FANCHOU *is terrified, and takes refuge under the table.*
The WRITER *smells him out. He examines him from every*
angle and prevents him from moving.

WRITER [*to the* JOURNALIST]: What a complex, heart-rending
people! Put that down—no, say that the complexity of
this heart-rending people flourishes in a spontaneous
fashion in this cruel and fratricidal war. [*Pleased with
himself.*] Not bad, eh? [*He hesitates.*] No, no, leave out
that sentence. Too emphatic; I must find something more
definitive, more restrained. [*He considers.*] It'll come,
it'll come.

FANCHOU *is still lying on the ground, under the table,*
terrified. The WRITER *and the* JOURNALIST *go out, left.*
The WRITER'S *voice fades away in the distance.*

WRITER'S VOICE: What a novel I shall make out of all this.
What a novel! Or a play, perhaps, and even a film. And
what a film!

LIRA'S VOICE: Who were you talking to?

FANCHOU: Her ladyship has found her tongue. She's not
dumb any more. Well, I may as well tell you that now it's
my turn to refuse to talk.

LIRA'S VOICE: [*plaintively*]: Darling, it hurts, it hurts terribly.
You aren't a bit sorry for me.

FANCHOU [*anxiously*]: What's the matter—are you ill?

LIRA'S VOICE: Can't you see I'm covered in stones and I
can't move.

FANCHOU: I wasn't thinking about it.

LIRA'S VOICE: You never do think about me.

FANCHOU: Nor I do. I ought to tie a knot in my handkerchief.

LIRA'S VOICE: What would become of you without me?
You're so irresponsible.

FANCHOU [*angry and boastful*]: That's what you always say.
Right then, I'll marry someone else. I can still turn
people's heads, you know. You ought to see the way the
baker's wife looks at me when I go and fetch the bread
every morning.

LIRA'S VOICE: That's fine. So you deceive me with the first

16

performing dog you meet, now. I knew I couldn't trust you.

FANCHOU: *She* looks at *me*. I just ignore her.

LIRA'S VOICE: That's what *you* say. I'd like to see you.

FANCHOU: I haven't done anything, I swear.

LIRA'S VOICE: More of your drunkard's oaths. You always promised you'd take me away on a honeymoon.

FANCHOU: I haven't forgotten. The moment the war's over we'll go for a holiday. I'll take you to Paris.

LIRA'S VOICE: Huh yes, Paris. You want to have a good time.

FANCHOU: You see the way you are: you never agree with me.

LIRA'S VOICE [*plaintively*]: Ouch. Some more stones are falling on me.

FANCHOU [*worried*]: Did they hurt a lot? [LIRA *groans*.] Oh dear, this war business is really very annoying.

LIRA'S VOICE: Do something for me.

FANCHOU: What shall I do?

LIRA'S VOICE: Get a doctor.

FANCHOU: They've sent them all away.

LIRA'S VOICE: You might as well say straight out that you don't want to do anything to help me.

FANCHOU: But you don't seem to realise that there's a war on.

LIRA'S VOICE: We haven't done anyone any harm.

FANCHOU: That doesn't count. The next thing you'll be saying is that I'm the one who forgets everything. You've already forgotten how these things are.

LIRA'S VOICE: They might at least make an exception for us; we're old.

FANCHOU: What *are* you thinking of? War is a serious business. It's quite obvious you never had any education.

LIRA'S VOICE: That's right, now you're going to insult me. You might as well say straight out that you don't love me.

FANCHOU [*tenderly*]: I didn't mean to hurt you, my love.

LIRA'S VOICE: You didn't mean to hurt me, but you did.

17

How you've changed! In the old days, nothing was too good for me.

FANCHOU: It's just the same now.

LIRA'S VOICE: And this business of education. Don't you think I've got feelings too?

FANCHOU: But I said it just like that, without thinking.

LIRA'S VOICE: Take it back.

FANCHOU: I take it back.

LIRA'S VOICE: No mental reservations?

FANCHOU: No, I swear.

LIRA'S VOICE: What on?

FANCHOU: Same as usual.

LIRA'S VOICE: Right. I hope you aren't going to start all over again.

Pause.

FANCHOU: Can't you stand up, and try and get out of there?

LIRA'S VOICE: But whenever I move, stones start falling.

FANCHOU: We must do something.

Sound of aeroplanes. Raid. While it is going on the mother and daughter cross from right to left. The mother is carrying some sporting guns. The daughter has three. LIRA's *balloon bursts. The raid ends.*

LIRA'S VOICE [*plaintively*]: They've busted my balloon.

FANCHOU: The brutes! They shoot just anyhow, without aiming.

LIRA'S VOICE: They did it on purpose.

FANCHOU: No, but they shoot without aiming, they don't bother.

LIRA'S VOICE: The brutes! First they demolish our house and then, to crown it all, they bust our balloon.

FANCHOU: They're impossible.

LIRA'S VOICE: See if they've hit the tree.

FANCHOU *gets down off the table. He goes over to the window. The* OFFICER *appears on the other side of it. The* OFFICER *looks gravely at* FANCHOU. FANCHOU *is terrified and hangs his head. The* OFFICER *laughs mirthlessly and plays with the handcuffs with one finger. The* OFFICER

18

disappears from the window. FANCHOU *raises his head.
He can't see anyone. He puts his head cautiously out of
the window. He looks at the tree. He seems pleased.
Laughter behind him, to his right. He turns round to the
right. The* OFFICER'S *sneering face appears, and then
immediately disappears.* FANCHOU *is frightened and
doesn't know what to do. Laughter to his left. He turns
round. The* OFFICER'S *sneering face appears on his left.
It immediately disappears.* FANCHOU *is frightened and
doesn't know where to look. Laughter on his left, then
on his right, then left, then right, then left, then right.*
FANCHOU *is terrified and doesn't budge. The* OFFICER
*enters, right. Looking serious and observant. He seems
very much concerned with* FANCHOU. *He pulls a sandwich
out of his pocket, and starts gnawing at the bread, all the
time keeping his eyes glued on him. He goes over and
stands near* FANCHOU. FANCHOU *retreats. The* OFFICER
moves again and stands right by him. FANCHOU *timidly
tries to escape. The* OFFICER *sticks to him, doesn't take
his eyes off him, and finally drives him into a corner.*
FANCHOU *can't move, now. He keeps his eyes fixed on the
ground. The* OFFICER *extends his elbows and bars the
way to him. The* OFFICER *goes on calmly gnawing at his
bread and doesn't take his eyes off him.
Long silence.*

LIRA'S VOICE: What on earth are you doing?
    FANCHOU *can't move, and doesn't answer.*
That's right, now you're going to leave me alone.
    The OFFICER *munches his sandwich impassively, still
keeping* FANCHOU *a prisoner.*
[*Tenderly.*] Come on, my love.
    The OFFICER *stops eating and grimaces: he bares all his
teeth and looks as if he is laughing, but makes no sound.*
FANCHOU *looks sheepish and hangs his head even lower.
Then the* OFFICER *stops laughing and starts eating again.*
Are you angry? [*Pause.*] All right then—it *is* true that
you could, that Saturday. [*Pause.*] Now are you satisfied?
    The OFFICER *stops eating and grimaces. He bares all his*

19

teeth and looks as if he is laughing, but makes no sound.
FANCHOU looks sheepish and hangs his head even lower.
Then the OFFICER stops laughing and starts eating again.
I do realise that you're a great success with the ladies—
and specially with the baker's wife.

Same business. Then the OFFICER carefully disposes of
the remains of the sandwich: he wraps it up in newspaper.
He wipes his mouth meticulously with the sleeves of
FANCHOU'S jacket. He polishes his boots with the bottom
of FANCHOU'S jacket. Then he turns round and goes off,
right, looking very martial. FANCHOU laughs merrily and
puts out his tongue. Then he quickly checks himself, and
looks terrified. He looks all around him. He makes sure
that no one can see him. He puts out his tongue and makes
a long nose several times. He laughs merrily and climbs
back on to the table.

FANCHOU: The tree's still there, my lamb.

LIRA'S VOICE: Did it take you all this time to find *that*
out?

FANCHOU: I like to do things properly.

LIRA'S VOICE: You haven't been to see the baker's wife, by
any chance?

FANCHOU: Who d'you take me for? Do you think I'd go
having affairs in the middle of a war?

Air raid. Aeroplanes, bombs. During which the woman
and her daughter cross the stage from right to left,
pushing a pram piled high with cartridges. The raid ends.
Long silence.

My own Lira!

Long silence.

LIRA'S VOICE: What?

FANCHOU: Why didn't you ever have lovers?

LIRA'S VOICE: Lovers? [*A short laugh.*]

FANCHOU: Yes, lovers. [*He laughs. Then he stops.*]

LIRA'S VOICE: *Me*? [*A short laugh.*]

FANCHOU: Yes, you.

LIRA'S VOICE: I never thought of it.

FANCHOU: You never think about *me*. I could have played

tricks on them. [*Pause.*] You ought to have had a least
one. [*He considers the matter.*] A colonel.
LIRA'S VOICE: Oh yes, a colonel, that's the way you love me.
FANCHOU: You're always behind the times.
LIRA'S VOICE: Go on, insult me, as well.
FANCHOU: No, my lamb. [*Pause. Obstinately.*] But every
self-respecting woman has lovers. [*Pause.*] You never
wanted to do anything to help me: when I undress you so
that my friends can touch you you always make a fuss.
LIRA'S VOICE: Because I catch a cold.
FANCHOU: You find excuses for everything you do.
LIRA'S VOICE: And you never think about anyone but
yourself: you're an egoist.
FANCHOU: But I do it for *you*. [*He seems pleased with him-
self—he's had a good idea.*] You'll be able to write your
autobiography later on.
LIRA'S VOICE: Ow! [*Pause.*] The stones are falling on me
again. [*She groans.*] I'll never be able to move my feet
again.
FANCHOU: Make an effort.
LIRA'S VOICE [*plaintively*]: They're buried!
FANCHOU: Things really are going from bad to worse.
LIRA'S VOICE: Is that all you can think of to say? You never
worry about me.
FANCHOU: Yes I do, I'm worrying now. [*Suddenly.*] Do you
want me to cry?
LIRA'S VOICE: I know what you're up to: you're going to play
another trick of me.
FANCHOU: No I'm not—you'll see; I can really cry properly
when I want to.
LIRA'S VOICE: I know *you*. It'd be all the same to you if I
died.
FANCHOU: That's what *you* say. When you're dead I'll . . .
[*He considers.*] I'll sleep with you three times running.
LIRA'S VOICE: Still bragging.
FANCHOU: Don't say you've already forgotten . . .
LIRA'S VOICE [*interrupting him indignantly*]: Oh yes, *I* know:
that famous Saturday when . . .

21

FANCHOU [*angry*]: Next thing'll be that you'll be saying that *I'm* the one that's nasty to *you*.
> *More stones fall.*

LIRA'S VOICE: Ow, ow. [*Her groans increase.*] I really am going to die.

FANCHOU: Shall I get a priest?

LIRA'S VOICE: What d'you mean, a priest?

FANCHOU: Isn't that what people say?

LIRA'S VOICE: What a rotten memory you've got: Don't you remember we aren't religious any more?

FANCHOU [*terrified*]: Who? Us?

LIRA'S VOICE: But you were the one who decided. Don't you remember?

FANCHOU [*who doesn't remember anything*]: Ah yes!

LIRA'S VOICE: You said that then we'd be . . . [*Pause. Emphatically.*] more mature.

FANCHOU [*surprised*]: Mature? Us?

LIRA'S VOICE: Of course.

FANCHOU: Now we're in a fine mess: you're going to die and you'll go to hell.

LIRA'S VOICE: For ever and ever?

FANCHOU: Naturally, for ever and ever. And the tortures! You'll see some fine ones. He does things properly, he does.

LIRA'S VOICE: Who d'you mean, he?

FANCHOU: Well, God.

LIRA'S VOICE: God?
> *A short laugh.*

FANCHOU: Yes, God.
> *A short laugh.*
> *They both laugh nervously in chorus.*
> *Air raid. The sound of aeroplanes and bombs falling, during which the woman and her little girl cross from right to left. On her back the woman is carrying a bag full of makeshift ammunition. The child helps her as best she can. The raid ends.*

LIRA'S VOICE: Ow, ow.

FANCHOU: What's happened?

LIRA'S VOICE: I'll never get out of here, now.

FANCHOU: Don't give up hope.

LIRA'S VOICE: The stones are up to my waist.

FANCHOU: Don't worry. You'll see, I'll find some way of getting you out.

LIRA'S VOICE: We really don't have any luck.

FANCHOU: It's all your fault, you and your passion for reading in the lavatory. You spend hours and hours there. What's happened to you doesn't surprise me in the least.

LIRA'S VOICE: Everything's always my fault.

FANCHOU: Don't take it like that, I didn't mean to hurt you. *Silence.*

LIRA'S VOICE: Why've they demolished the house?

FANCHOU: You have to be told the same thing over and over. [*Sounding each syllable separately.*] They're trying out high explosives and incendiary bombs. Next thing you'll be saying that I'm the one that forgets things.

LIRA'S VOICE: Couldn't they try them out somewhere else

FANCHOU: You seem to think everything's so easy. They ha· to try them out on a town, after all.

LIRA'S VOICE: Why?

FANCHOU: You'll say that I'm making fun of you again, but it's quite obvious that you've never had the slightest bit of education. Why! Why! Why d'you think, except to find out whether they work.

LIRA'S VOICE: And then what?

FANCHOU: And then what? And then what? You're being stupid on purpose: if a bomb kills a lot of people, then it's a good bomb and they make some more, but if it doesn't kill anyone, it's no good and they don't make any more.

LIRA'S VOICE: Oh!

FANCHOU: You have to have everything explained to you.

LIRA'S VOICE [*annoyed*]: I don't see why you have to talk like that. I know very well I didn't have as much schooling as you did.

FANCHOU [*swollen with pride*]: I know everything, eh? People really might think I'd been to a university.

23

[*Pause. He looks pleased with himself. He's had a good idea.*] Anyone might take me for a professor, don't you think?

LIRA'S VOICE [*bored and sceptical*]: Yes, of course.

FANCHOU: In which case you'd be a professor's wife. And when people saw us in the street, they'd say: 'look at the professors.' [*Pause.*] We'd be one up on them. We'd have visiting cards and we'd go to conferences. All I need is the umbrella. And anyway, you're pretty well educated, with all you've read in the lavatory!

LIRA'S VOICE: Are you starting all over again?

FANCHOU: Don't you agree?

LIRA'S VOICE: Us? Professors?

FANCHOU: You never agree with my ideas. It's always been the same. If you're going to start again, right, I'm off for good. [*Irritated.*] I don't want you to live with a man who talks nonsense. Goodbye!

FANCHOU *crouches down and makes a noise on the table so that it sounds as if he's going away.*

LIRA'S VOICE: Darling! Are you going to leave me all alone?

LIRA *groans.* FANCHOU *doesn't move. He's still squatting.* Come back, darling!

Long silence. FANCHOU *doesn't move, he's still squatting.* But it was just a joke. [*Pause.*] You know very well how much I admire you. [*Long pause.*] You'd make a magnificent professor. [*Pause.*] When people hear you talk they take you for a captain, or even an antique dealer.

Long silence. FANCHOU *looks proud.*

Darling! [*Pause.*] Are you going to leave me all alone? [*Pause.*] Come over here!

Long pause. Same business.

LIRA'S VOICE: Ow, ow. [*She weeps.*] The stones have started falling again.

FANCHOU [*standing up, anxious*]: What's happening, my angel? Have you hurt yourself?

LIRA'S VOICE: I'll soon be completely buried. And that's the moment you choose to leave me. You're just heartless.

FANCHOU: Well, you started it.

LIRA'S VOICE: It was just a joke.

FANCHOU: Swear you won't do it any more.

LIRA'S VOICE: I swear.

FANCHOU: What on?

LIRA'S VOICE: The usual.

FANCHOU: No mental reservations?

LIRA'S VOICE: No mental reservations.

FANCHOU: Right. I hope you won't start again.

> Air raid. *Sound of bombs and aeroplanes, during which the woman and her daughter cross from right to left pulling a little handcart full of old rifles. The raid ends.*

LIRA'S VOICE: Ow, ow. Now I can't move my arms.

FANCHOU: Don't worry, I'll get you out.

LIRA'S VOICE: But the stones are up to my neck.

FANCHOU: Don't worry. You'll see, I'll think of something.

LIRA'S VOICE: I'm going to die.

FANCHOU: Do you want me to get a lawyer for your will?

LIRA'S VOICE: What d'you mean, my will?

FANCHOU: Isn't that what people say?

LIRA'S VOICE: Are you going to start all over again?

FANCHOU [*flattered*]: You ought to make one. I'd show it to the neighbours.

LIRA'S VOICE: All you ever think of is showing off.

FANCHOU: But I'm doing it for you. That's what all great ladies do. You ought to be making your will and thinking up your last words.

LIRA'S VOICE: What d'you mean . . . my last words?

FANCHOU: The ones people say before they die. D'you want me to prompt you? You could say something about . . . [*He thinks, and then says quickly.*] life, or humanity . . .

LIRA'S VOICE [*interrupting him*]: Stop it, you're talking nonsense.

FANCHOU: D'you call that nonsense? Well you *are* frivolous!

LIRA'S VOICE [*plaintively*]: Are you going to start insulting me again?

FANCHOU: No, my little lamb.

LIRA'S VOICE: I can't move at all now. [*Plaintively.*] But when is this war going to be over?

FANCHOU: That's right, now her ladyship wants the war to be over when it suits *her* convenience.

LIRA'S VOICE [*whimpering*]: Can't they stop it?

FANCHOU: Of course they can't. The general said he wouldn't stop until he's occupied the whole country.

LIRA'S VOICE: All of it?

FANCHOU: Yes, of course, all of it.

LIRA'S VOICE: That's going a bit far.

FANCHOU: Generals don't do things by halves: it's all or nothing.

LIRA'S VOICE: What about the people?

FANCHOU: The people don't know anything about making wars. And in any case, the general is getting an awful lot of help.

LIRA'S VOICE: Then it's not a game any more!

FANCHOU: You don't suppose the general cares, do you?

LIRA'S VOICE: I can't move at all, now. If any more stones start falling I shall be completely buried.

FANCHOU: What a bore. Don't worry. You'll see, the raids will soon be over.

LIRA'S VOICE: For good?

FANCHOU: For good.

LIRA'S VOICE: How d'you know?

FANCHOU [*cut to the quick*]: Do you doubt my word?

LIRA'S VOICE: No. [*Sceptically.*] Why d'you suppose I should doubt it?

> *Three shells explode. A ghastly noise.*

[*Weeping bitterly.*] Darling, I'm completely buried, come and rescue me.

FANCHOU: I'm coming this minute, my little lamb. You'll see, I'll get you out.

> FANCHOU *goes over and climbs laboriously on to the* debris. LIRA *weeps.*

LIRA'S VOICE: This time I really am going to die.

FANCHOU: Don't panic. I'm coming.

FANCHOU *moves laboriously over the debris. He reaches the place where* LIRA *is.*

My little lamb. Here I am. Give me your hand.

LIRA'S VOICE: Can't you see I'm covered in stones?

FANCHOU: I'll get you free this minute. You just wait, I'll get you out.

Long raid. More stones fall. FANCHOU *too is buried under the rubble.*

As the long raid is just coming to an end, the woman crosses from right to left. The little girl isn't with her this time. She is carrying a small coffin on her shoulder. She looks angry and helpless (see the Picasso painting). She disappears, left.

In the background: the tree of liberty can be seen above the debris of the walls. The raid is over: there is now nothing but debris on the stage. Long silence.

Two coloured balloons float gently upwards from the exact spot where FANCHOU *and* LIRA *disappeared. Enter the* OFFICER, *who fires at them with his Lewis gun but doesn't hit them. The balloons disappear into the sky. The* OFFICER *fires again. From above,* FANCHOU *and* LIRA *can be heard laughing happily. The* OFFICER *is terrified, looks all round him, and goes out, right, quickly. Enter the* WRITER. *He gets up on to the table. He examines the place where* FANCHOU *and* LIRA *were. He looks pleased. He gets down from the table. He goes out, left, almost running, quite delighted, saying:*

WRITER'S VOICE: I shall make an extraordinary novel out of all this. A magnificent novel! What a novel! . . .

His voice fades away in the distance. Pause. The sound of the boots of marching soldiers is heard close by. Further away, very softly, a group of men is singing 'Guernikako arbola'. The group gradually becomes more numerous and the voices gradually louder. Now a whole crowd is singing 'Guernikako arbola', which finally completely drowns the sound of the boots, as the curtain falls.

THE LABYRINTH

The great Theatre of Oklahoma calls
you! Today only and never again! If you
miss your chance now you miss it for ever!

Franz Kafka

translated from the French
by Barbara Wright

CHARACTERS

ETIENNE
BRUNO
MICAELA
JUSTIN
THE JUDGE

THE LABYRINTH

A labyrinth of blankets takes up almost the whole of the stage. The blankets, like washing hung out to dry, are pegged on to wires which criss-cross over the stage in all directions.

On the right, a very small latrine, dark and dirty. It has a small window with an iron grating looking on to the space left by the blankets in the middle of the stage.

All this—all that the audience can see, that is—is only a minute part of the immense park-labyrinth formed by the blankets.

In the latrine, lying on the ground, are BRUNO *and* ETIENNE. *They are manacled together by their ankles.* BRUNO *is very ill and can hardly move. He is also very dirty and has several days' growth of beard.* ETIENNE *is dressed in a fairly clean suit; he seems in good health.* ETIENNE *is filing the manacles attaching him to* BRUNO.

BRUNO: I'm thirsty. [*Pause. It is an effort for him to speak.*] Give me some water.

    ETIENNE *continues his filing, trying to cut through the manacles.*

[*In a very faint voice*]: I'm very thirsty.

    ETIENNE *is annoyed, but drags himself over to the lavatory bowl.* BRUNO *utters a loud cry.* ETIENNE *pulls the chain, gets a little water in his cupped hands and gives it to* BRUNO. *He then immediately returns to the task of freeing himself. He is making great efforts; all this is obviously painful for* BRUNO, *as* ETIENNE *is pulling on the manacles with some force.* BRUNO *groans.*

ETIENNE: Don't groan so much.

    He gets on with his work. BRUNO *groans again.*

31

Is that the way you help me? [*Pause.*] Make a bit of an effort, let me try and get away. [*Pause.*] It's the only way we've got left of getting some sort of justice. [*Pause.*] As soon as I've got free I'll go to the court and insist on their going into our case in detail. I won't tell them we're angels, of course, that'd be telling a lie, but I'll make them see that we've been victimised and that it's unjust.

BRUNO: I'm thirsty.

ETIENNE: Again!

BRUNO [*exhausted*]: I'm very thirsty.

ETIENNE: Wait till I've finished. When I'm free I'll give you all the water you want.

BRUNO *groans.* ETIENNE *concentrates hard on his work, because it looks as though the manacles are about to give.* BRUNO *groans more loudly and, in spite of his weakness, starts kicking* ETIENNE *with his free leg.*

[*Extremely annoyed*]: Don't start that! Just leave me alone and stop kicking me.

BRUNO: I'm thirsty.

ETIENNE: Wait a minute.

ETIENNE *goes on filing the manacles. Now and then he gives them a sharp tug.* BRUNO *groans more and more and kicks him.*

How can I explain? Let me get on with it. It's the only chance we've got left. Or would you rather rot in this hole for the rest of your life?

BRUNO: I'm thirsty.

ETIENNE [*annoyed*]: Oh, all right. [ETIENNE *pulls the chain and gives him some water*]. Now are you going to keep quiet? [*He goes on filing. Groan from* BRUNO.] It's almost through. [*Joyfully.*] One last effort and I'll be free.

BRUNO *kicks him more and more, which considerably hinders* ETIENNE. *He defends himself with his head and goes on filing joyfully. Groan from* BRUNO.

BRUNO: I'm very thirsty.

ETIENNE: Just a moment.

BRUNO *is hindering him more and more.* ETIENNE *goes*

on filing. He finally manages to file through the manacles. He's free.

BRUNO: I'm thirsty.

ETIENNE gives him some water and then immediately goes out of the latrine. In spite of his weakness, BRUNO *lifts up his hands to him to stop him.*

I'm very thirsty.

BRUNO remains stretched out in the latrine. ETIENNE, *in the park, pauses. He finally decides to penetrate into the labyrinth of blankets. So he disappears. Silence. He reappears. He goes over to the latrine window. He looks inside.* BRUNO *makes an effort and sits up with great difficulty.*

I'm thirsty.

ETIENNE is terrified, and flees. But before he penetrates into the labyrinth of blankets he pauses. He finally makes up his mind. Silence. He reappears again, quite out of breath. He looks through the bars. BRUNO *makes a great effort and sits up with difficulty.*

I'm thirsty.

ETIENNE is horrified, and flees. He goes towards the labyrinth of blankets. He hesitates, and then plunges into it. He disappears. Silence. He reappears. He goes up to the window. BRUNO *sits up.*

Hesitation. He disappears. Silence. He reappears. He repeats the operation and once again reappears, out of breath.

Silence. MICAELA *appears from the blankets.*

MICAELA: What are you doing in my park?

ETIENNE: I got lost. I'm trying to get out. [*Pause.*] I can't find the way out. I keep going round the park in between the blankets and every time I think I've found it I'm always back in the same place.

MICAELA: It's not surprising. When my father decided to hang up the washing in the park we all thought that as it was so big it would turn into a labyrinth; all the more so as they don't hang up anything but blankets.

ETIENNE: But *you'll* be able to tell me how to get out of here.

MICAELA: I'd be delighted to—if I only knew the way. Unfortunately, though, and in spite of all my efforts to get to know all the exits, I still haven't managed to find my way around.

ETIENNE: Why did you come as far as this then?

MICAELA: If you knew my house you wouldn't be in the least surprised. My father is a very right-minded sort of man but he was brought up very strictly, which means that everyone in the house has to be much too submissive. That's why I venture out into the park from time to time—to get away from the atmosphere in the house, even if it's only for a moment. I can tell you, to give you some idea, that everyone in the house has to dress very formally, that we are only allowed to speak in whispers, that we have to bow to him—to my father—every time we see him, that we aren't allowed to look out of the windows, that we aren't ever allowed to laugh, etc. etc. So you'll understand why I like to go for a walk in the park from time to time.

ETIENNE: But how can such a well-organised man have thought up this terrifying labyrinth of blankets?

MICAELA: You're quite right; it seems absurd, at first, but when you know the precise reasons you'll see that it isn't really so absurd. I'll tell you: this park, which is enormous, miles and miles, started off by being a playground where we could all amuse ourselves in any way we liked. The idea of turning it into a place to dry the washing occurred to my father in the most plausible way, I might almost say in the most necessary way. It was a long time since anyone had washed any of the blankets in the house—which contains, as you may know, a large number of rooms. These things start in the most ordinary way. My father had decided that each time a dirty blanket had to be changed it would be done in the simplest fashion: that is, the dirty blanket would be changed for a clean blanket and the dirty one would be put in the cellar. My father thought it would be better to wait till there were enough dirty blankets to wash them all in one go, which would be cheaper. Time went on and the blankets were gradually accumulating in the cellar. My father was horrified. He started looking for some workmen to wash the blankets but unfortunately there weren't enough in the neighbourhood at that time. So he decided to consult his friends in the capital and they immediately started looking for some workmen, while the dirty blankets, as there wasn't any more room in the cellar, started to invade the best bedrooms on the first floor. The situation was getting worse daily, there was a real danger of the blankets taking possession of the whole of the first floor, which would have been an enormous hindrance to us, because then we'd have had to have a fire escape built outside. Well, as I was saying, as the situation was daily getting worse, my father decided to go to the capital himself to engage some workmen. But unfortunately the workmen were on strike and no one was interested in my father's offer. So then he decided to promise them double pay, which didn't really satisfy them, not that the wages seemed insufficient to them but they were afraid of the anger of their comrades. In the meantime I was looking after the house and I was trying to stow the blankets in the most rational possible way, so they'd take up less room, but unfortunately, in spite of all my efforts, they went on accumulating more and more and, worst of all, there was a danger of their blocking the main staircase. I reported all this to my father in several letters, which weren't answered. I was surprised by this silence, and at his staying away so long, and telephoned him at the hotel where he was living, but they told me he'd disappeared some days before without leaving any address. This news dismayed me, all the more so as the blankets were already beginning to invade the main staircase, and the staircase that had been built to give direct access to the second floor was very unsafe and could easily collapse one fine day, which wouldn't have been so tragic if one of us had been in the road at the time, but which would have been serious if we'd all been on the second floor, because then no one would have been able to build a new staircase to replace the old one. The situation, as you must see, was becoming more and more tragic. A few days later the blankets had invaded the main staircase and deprived us of half our communications, and they were seriously threatening the second floor. It was then that my father reappeared with about a hundred men, though we never found out where he'd got them from. It was odd—they were all in chains. My father explained that what with all the strikes these days it was better to force workmen to work. He immediately had some enormous boilers installed and for the next few months the workmen washed the blankets. My father thought it would be a good idea to put them in the park to dry, as it was big enough for them all to be hung up. To start with, the workmen hung them in a certain order, parallel to the boilers, but unfortunately there were so many blankets that they took up all the vacant space, so that very gradually, in a meticulous sort of way, this kind of labyrinth of blankets that the park has become came into being. And although the workmen were chained up to start with, my father took off their chains later; as the labyrinth was such a great distance between the boilers and the last clothes lines, they'd have needed exceptionally long chains, which were impossible to find. So that gradually, one by one, under cover of the night, they went away, and there wasn't a single one left. The present situation is very critical for my father: the blankets are hanging up but we can't get them taken down because of a shortage of labour. And what's more, they make a labyrinth in front of the house which almost completely stops us going out, or at least means that we have to run the risk of getting lost in it and dying of thirst, fatigue, and exhaustion. And then, for the moment, we can't count on recruiting the necessary workmen (a hundred, two hundred, maybe a thousand or more, my father is the only one who knows) to take down the blankets and pile them up properly so they don't start getting in our way again. As you can see, there's nothing

at all pleasant about this situation, especially for us who
have to suffer the direct consequences of it. But you're
only passing through here and you can't realise what it's
all like.

*A pause. She stares ostentatiously at the manacle round
his ankle.*

Unless you're here for good.

ETIENNE [*awkwardly hiding the manacle with his other leg*]:
Of course I'm not, I'm not here for good.

MICAELA: I hope that's how it is. It would be very surprising
if you were to be at the house or in the park for good
without my knowing you. Because my father knows
everyone who lives in the house very well, but I think I
can say without fear of being mistaken that I know them
all, too—or nearly all.

BRUNO [*who is still lying on the latrine floor, says plaintively*]:
I'm very thirsty. [*Pause.*] Give me some water, Etienne.

ETIENNE *is obviously nervous, and tries to pretend.*
MICAELA *has heard* BRUNO'S *voice. She looks perfectly
natural and doesn't seem at all surprised.*

MICAELA: We have to take my father's perfect organisation
into account. We can be quite sure that nothing happens in
the house or in this park that he doesn't know about.
There only needs to be one blanket missing, only one—
and just think, there must be millions and millions in the
park—for him to notice at once, and if he doesn't
immediately, in person, take the matter up with whoever
has stolen it, it's simply because at that moment his time
is very precious, he's busy with other, much more
important things. But there isn't the slightest doubt that
sooner or later, according to an order which is too
complicated for me, and incomprehensible, he will deal
with the matter and settle it with perfect impartiality,
taking into consideration, one by one, all the circumstances which either incriminate or vindicate the accused.
That's why . . .

BRUNO [*interrupting her*]: I'm very thirsty.

Silence. ETIENNE *is nervous.* MICAELA *is completely calm.*

MICAELA: As I was saying, that's why things here may appear to be in some disorder, but it is an apparent disorder which only throws into relief the existence of a superior order which is much more complex and exigent than any we can imagine. My father controls it with a skill which is of exceptional efficiency.

ETIENNE: Then how do you explain this labyrinth of blankets, which came into being, according to what you say, because your father showed such a lack of foresight that he let the blankets pile up in the cellar, and even obstruct the entrance to the house?

BRUNO: I'm thirsty.

Same business.

MICAELA: I consider that a fair question, and I would have asked myself the same thing a thousand times if I didn't know my father, but the solution is much simpler than that. I've already told you that my father observes a strict order in the affairs he deals with, which sometimes leads him to solve some problems which seem insignificant to us but which must be seen to before others, which we imagine to be more important. This is merely a consequence of the difference between our scale of values and that of my father. For instance, I told you that when the pile of blankets had risen so dangerously up to the first floor, I telephoned his hotel, where they told me that he was away. Gone without leaving an address. After making detailed enquiries, I heard, though perhaps it wasn't correct, that my father had spent a month in a town a long way away, forgetting the business of the blankets, and completely absorbed in picking certain herbs reputed to cure chilblains. I mean it when I say that I'm not sure of the accuracy of the facts, because my father's life is a real mystery, but there's a good chance of them being true. In any case, this way of behaving is peculiarly his own, and I could give you a thousand other examples of the same sort. The case I've told you of is a perfect illustration of what I was trying to prove to you, which is that my father has a scale of values which is different from ours and that his priorities obey a rigorous and impenetrable system which, in spite of its absurdity, turns out to be the best in the long run, as I've been able to observe a thousand times.

BRUNO: I'm very thirsty.

Silence. MICAELA *gets up and goes over to the latrine.*

ETIENNE: Where are you going?

MICAELA: There.

She points to the latrine.

ETIENNE: I don't think that's necessary. Is something worrying you? Tell me what's surprising you and I'll explain everything.

MICAELA: I don't see why anything should be surprising me. Why d'you think I should be surprised?

ETIENNE: No reason, no reason.

ETIENNE *tries awkwardly to stop* MICAELA *going over to the latrine; he even goes so far as to grab her by the arm.* MICAELA *manages to free herself and goes into the latrine.* ETIENNE *anxiously watches her through the latrine window.* MICAELA *pulls the chain. She watches the water flow with profound satisfaction.* BRUNO *sits up a bit with a painful effort, and in spite of his suffering and his thirst, says nothing.* MICAELA *goes out of the latrine. She avoids walking on* BRUNO, *who is by the entrance. She goes back to* ETIENNE.

MICAELA [*continuing the conversation*]: As I was saying, my father's order is a complete enigma for us. How could anyone justify spending his time picking herbs for chilblains when the situation in the house was becoming tragic because of the blankets, especially if you take into account the fact that no one in the house ever has chilblains and that, on the other hand, the efficacy of these herbs has been denied in the most categorical fashion by the best doctors, who even go so far as to state that the value of these herbs is based on superstition and witchcraft.

ETIENNE: Yes. [*Worried.*] But how shall I be able to get out of here?

MICAELA: Unless you're very lucky, or get direct help from my father, you needn't hope to get out.

ETIENNE: I could get out of here with you.

MICAELA [*with a compassionate smile*]: Impossible; unfortunately, it's impossible.

ETIENNE: Can't you get out either, then?

MICAELA: Of course I can. Would I venture into the labyrinth if I couldn't get out again?

ETIENNE: Well then—when you leave here, let me come with you.

MICAELA: That's something I couldn't do for you, even if it was what I wanted most in all the world. My father, who, as I've told you, has organised everything to perfection, has managed to work out a very cunning scheme to enable me to get back to the house even if I happen to be in the remotest part of the labyrinth. This scheme, like all my father's schemes, by the way, is simple but effective. It's this bell [*she produces a little bell*]—every time I want to go back I ring it until one of the servants who knows the labyrinth appears. A servant who is dumb, and so can't reveal its secret to anyone.

ETIENNE: How many servants are there?

MICAELA: That's something I've never been able to find out. So far it's always been a different servant who's come and fetched me, which means that there must be more than a thousand, maybe even more, but maybe less—my calculations in these matters are only guesswork, which means that I may well be wrong; in any case they're all dumb, and none of them has ever been able to tell me the secret of the way back to the house, a secret my father must have revealed to them.

ETIENNE: But none of this stops me coming with you.

MICAELA: Let me finish my explanation. Your questions, as always, are reasonable. That's why I have to explain to you in detail—well, with all the precision I'm capable of —every little factor of every problem, to arrive at an accurate and comprehensible solution. As I told you,

40

when I ring the bell a servant arrives in a surprisingly short time, sometimes ten minutes, sometimes just a few seconds, while I'll have been walking in the labyrinth for hours and hours, and he leads me to the house. It's all the same to me whether you come with me or not, but there are insuperable obstacles. In the first place you have to take into account the extreme susceptibility of the servant, who is prepared to serve the people who belong to the house but not strangers, which is logical. How do you suppose I could make him serve you—*you*, an outsider? I could, of course, *try* to ask him, just to do you a favour, even though I know beforehand that the chances of his accepting such a responsibility are extremely remote. But that's not the worst. As the labyrinth is tortuous, and the blankets are almost touching each other, they're so close together—you must have noticed that you can only make any progress by moving them one at a time—it's absolutely impossible for the servant to guide two people. Every time I've tried it the person with me has disappeared very shortly after starting to walk between the blankets and, later on, the servants have found his dead body. As you'll realise, it means taking a completely useless risk: if you come with me you won't have the slightest chance of getting out of the labyrinth but, on the other hand, there'll be every likelihood of your dying of thirst and fatigue. If you try to get out on your own, the difficulties are the same but the risks less, because as people have a natural sense of direction they manage to come back to their point of departure, that's to say to this sort of island, without running the risk of dying of hunger in the labyrinth. But if you follow the servant you'll make so much headway in a few seconds— I've already told you that he can travel a surprising distance in a few seconds, because of my father's system, I suppose—that when you've got lost you won't be able to find this refuge again. It's the only privileged place in the labyrinth, and it's exactly in the centre of the park, as you may perhaps know.

BRUNO: I'm thirsty.

Silence.

MICAELA: As you'll have been able to realise, this business of the blankets has caused us nothing but trouble from the very beginning, and, unfortunately, there's extremely little likelihood of the situation getting any better.

BRUNO: I'm thirsty.

MICAELA *goes into the latrine, trying to avoid* BRUNO. *Pulls the chain. She watches the water flow with profound satisfaction.* ETIENNE *watches her through the window.* BRUNO *makes a supreme effort and raises himself very slightly. He says nothing.* MICAELA *goes out of the latrine. She goes back to* ETIENNE.

MICAELA: We really haven't had much luck; things have gradually got more and more complicated in a simple, but implacable fashion.

She stares ostentatiously at the manacle round ETIENNE'S *ankle.* ETIENNE *hides it awkwardly by putting his other leg on top of it.*

You've managed to break the chain, at least.

ETIENNE: What chain?

MICAELA: What chain do you think? The one you were tied up by over there.

ETIENNE [*after a pause, anxiously*]: Yes.

MICAELA: It's always the same. I'm sick and tired of telling him that that method's no good, that it's easy to file through manacles, but he never listens to me. Well, after all, it's all the same to me. Whether manacles can be filed through or not, whether it's a good method or not, doesn't matter much. [*Pause.*] And, naturally, you want to get out of here as soon as possible.

ETIENNE: Yes.

MICAELA: That's logical. [*Pause.*] But it seems to me to be very difficult. As I've already explained.

ETIENNE: It's not impossible, then?

MICAELA: Impossible, really impossible . . . everything in life is possible.

BRUNO: I'm very thirsty.

MICAELA, *slightly annoyed, as if she's had enough, gets up. She goes to the latrine. She avoids* BRUNO *as she goes in. She pulls the chain. She watches the water flow with profound satisfaction.* ETIENNE *watches her through the window.* BRUNO *tries to sit up. He says nothing.* MICAELA *goes out of the latrine. She comes back to* ETIENNE.

MICAELA: As I say, it's quite obvious that nothing in life is impossible, but what you want to do is one of the most difficult things to put into practice. To prove my good faith, and the sincerity of my offers, I'm going to do everything it's in my power to do for you: call my father, so that he can find the best solution for you himself.

MICAELA *produces a little bell and makes a very faint sound with it twice.*

ETIENNE: Do you think they'll have heard the bell at the house?

MICAELA: Of course not. Even if the bell rang much more loudly they wouldn't hear it from the house. The distance between us and them is immense! But to remedy this drawback my father has invented a rather ingenious system: he's posted a series of servants all along the park —I've never seen them, you must realise—who pass on, from one to the other, until it gets to the house, the call, or it might be the information, that my father wants to hear. All this is done with fantastic speed, so that my father knows what is going on at the remotest parts of the labyrinth without the slightest delay. The whole thing, now, is to find out whether he wants to come immediately or whether we'll have to wait long for him. If you climb up on to my shoulders you'll be able to find out; you'll see over the blankets whether he's coming or not. Unfortunately the blankets get higher and higher, so you won't be able to see anything beyond a radius of a hundred yards. Come on, then.

ETIENNE: You want me to climb on to your shoulders?

MICAELA: Yes, you'll see whether my father's coming.

ETIENNE: I'm heavy.

43

MICAELA: Doesn't matter, I'm used to it. The last time there was a flood my father made me carry all the servants to safety on my shoulders. At first this work seemed exhausting; I had to carry each servant nearly two miles, leave him in the shelter and then rush back to the house to get the next one. But I got used to it in the end, and at the end of a month I can say that I didn't feel the weight any more.

MICAELA *grabs* ETIENNE *roughly by the arm and pulls him over to the latrine.*

Climb on my shoulders.

ETIENNE *climbs on to* MICAELA'S *shoulders and leans against the wall.*

Can you see anything?

ETIENNE: No.

MICAELA: Look again.

ETIENNE [*anxiously*]: But . . . who is it?

MICAELA: It must be my father, it can't be anyone else.

ETIENNE [*full of anxiety*]: But that's the man who put me in the lavatory and put the manacles on me.

ETIENNE *tries to escape.* MICAELA *brutally grabs his legs, paralysing them with her arms.*

[*In anguish*]: Let me escape. Do let me.

MICAELA [*calmly, but without releasing* ETIENNE'S *legs*]: You see my father's meticulous organisation. I called him a few minutes ago and here he is already. One really can say that there is not the slightest doubt that he controls absolutely everything that goes on in the park.

Enter the Father. ETIENNE *gets down from* MICAELA'S *shoulders.* JUSTIN, *the father, kisses his daughter* MICAELA *ceremoniously on the forehead.* ETIENNE *is absolutely terrified and doesn't know what to do or say. He hesitates. Then, as* JUSTIN *and* MICAELA *seem to be looking the other way for a moment, he tries to escape.* MICAELA *brutally holds him back by the arm.* JUSTIN *who, up till then, had appeared not to have noticed* ETIENNE'S *presence, goes over to him calmly and courteously.*

JUSTIN: What do you want, young man?

MICAELA: He must have been shut up in the lavatory, look at the manacle still hanging from his ankle—[ETIENNE *tries awkwardly to hide it*] he's managed to break it. Now he wants at all costs to escape from the park, and he's tried to buy me in every possible way to achieve his end. First of all he promised me a vast sum of money if I'd help him get out of the park.

  ETIENNE *tries to protest.* JUSTIN *takes not the slightest notice of what he does. Nor does* MICAELA.

Then he proposed marriage to me, he tried to seduce me in the most lamentable fashion, and finally he submitted to me a plan of rebellion against your authority in which the two of us would seize the house and park.

ETIENNE [*excitedly*]: Monsieur, please don't believe . . .

  No one is listening to him.

JUSTIN: And what was the young man's plan?

MICAELA: You can imagine it: a piece of rank stupidity, devoid of the most elementary common sense. He wanted me to help him set fire to the park, because he maintained that as blankets burn very easily the fire would soon assume gigantic proportions and the park and house would be completely destroyed. And when everything was razed to the ground and the servants, and everyone else in the house, dead—and you too, of course —we could sell most of the park and, with the money we'd get for it, build a new house where he and I and a few servants would live.

JUSTIN: Yes, it really is lamentable.

ETIENNE: But, Monsieur . . .

MICAELA: Naturally I didn't listen to any of his suggestions, and I was all the time trying to dissuade him from them.

JUSTIN: You did well; individuals of this sort are very dangerous, especially when one allows oneself to be deceived by their appearance of being so calm and good, which conceals their perfidious intentions. Leave him to me, my girl, his punishment will fit his crime. I shall deal with this matter personally. [*Pause.*] Now, if you like, you may go and see your fiancé.

> JUSTIN *kisses her ceremoniously on the forehead.* MICAELA *goes into the latrine where* BRUNO *is. She sits down by him and caresses him passionately.* BRUNO *takes absolutely no notice of her.* JUSTIN *and* ETIENNE *remain in the middle of the stage.*

I must ask you, young man, to excuse my daughter. Take it in good part. [*He sighs.*] There's nothing that can be done about it, all I ask is that you don't contradict her, so as not to aggravate her mental imbalance. In any case, as a rule everything she says is of very little importance; her evidence has almost no chance of being accepted by any court.

ETIENNE: If that's the case, Monsieur, I completely absolve her, but I can assure you that while she was inventing all those tales against me I couldn't stop myself hating her with all my heart.

JUSTIN: I'm very grateful to you for being so understanding about her.

ETIENNE: Was it all lies too then, what she told me about the labyrinth?

JUSTIN: It was and it wasn't. She made some colossal mistakes which could have misled you, not out of malice or because she needs to tell lies, but because she doesn't remember things very well. Her memory is very poor and she forgets all the most important details, or else changes them, and substitutes other very precise facts for them. For instance, she told you that I spent a month in a town a long way away, while the blankets were piling up and becoming dangerous, picking herbs to cure chilblains. That's completely untrue: actually I spent a month in that town picking herbs to cure corns, and not chilblains, as she twice asserted. That's why we must excuse her, we must take a generous view of what she says, and never get angry. That's what I do, and what I'm asking you to do too.

ETIENNE [*very humbly*]: Yes, I promise you I won't get cross.

46

JUSTIN: Well, now we've cleared up the first important point, let's move on to the next. You want to get out of the park, don't you?

ETIENNE: Yes, Monsieur.

JUSTIN: My daughter has already explained to you the rather unusual circumstances we are in because of the blankets. You can't imagine how much I regret that you should be a victim, even temporarily, of this situation. Believe me, I deplore it even more than you do. Do you realise the delicate situation I am in in relation to my guests, my prisoners, my servants, and the friends who come to the house? There's not the slightest doubt that that's one of my gravest worries at the moment.

ETIENNE: I can understand you.

JUSTIN: I don't know if you are aware of it, but every day thousands and thousands of people pass through my house, guests, prisoners . . . [*a pause.* ETIENNE *looks absolutely terrified.* JUSTIN *goes on calmly*] . . . friends, clients.

Silence.

MICAELA [*to* BRUNO]: Kiss me, my love.

MICAELA *is sprawling in an obscene fashion by* BRUNO'S *side in the latrine. He is still lying down, and takes no notice. She caresses him.*

[*To* BRUNO]: Caress me, caress my breasts, Bruno. My body belongs to you.

In the park, JUSTIN *watches his daughter through the window with a certain satisfaction.* ETIENNE *is near* JUSTIN, *and also watches what is going on. In the latrine,* MICAELA *is still obscenely sprawling all over* BRUNO, *who still takes no notice.* MICAELA *tries to excite* BRUNO *by obscene imprecations. She kisses him on his mouth and on his belly.*

JUSTIN: [*very satisfied, to* ETIENNE]: You can't imagine how delighted I am at my daughter's romantic behaviour. [*He is still watching the scene. Groans from* MICAELA. *Kisses. Caresses.*] She's a child, she doesn't see any harm in it, she's just a child. I'm completely satisfied. I'm lucky to have a daughter like that. Especially these days, when everything's so unstable. [*With great enthusiasm.*] A child. Just a child! Innocence personified. [MICAELA *obscene*, BRUNO *impassive, etc.*] It's such a touching love story. All the more so if you take into account the highly unusual circumstances that have, and still do, beset them. But let's not change the subject. It's a real problem getting out of the park, as you know very well, but there is, fortunately, a solution to it. It's very complicated, it's true, but still it's a solution. In principle your case has to be dealt with by a judge who represents the Supreme Tribunal, given that you have that manacle on your ankle, which doesn't make matters any easier for you, as I might as well tell you from the start.

ETIENNE: But I'm wearing this manacle, not because I've done anything wrong, or committed any crime, but just because . . . [*he hesitates*] . . . just as an ornament.

JUSTIN: You needn't worry in the slightest. In actual fact you'll appear before the Supreme Tribunal—I mean, of course, before the judge representing it—simply to comply with a bureaucratic formality. If, as you state, you aren't guilty, the judge, after a superficial investigation and after he's filled in the requisite forms, will immediately set you free, and allow you the help of the servants, who will do their best to lead you out of the labyrinth.

ETIENNE: I'd like to get out as soon as possible, because I'm in a hurry. Can't I avoid the court formalities?

Obscene gestures from MICAELA *in the latrine.*

MICAELA: Kiss me, I'm yours.

MICAELA *is obscene,* BRUNO *is impassive, and at death's door.* JUSTIN *looks pleased.*

JUSTIN: That's impossible—absolutely impossible. The judge has to carry out his investigation not only on account of that accursed manacle, which makes you suspect from the start, but also to comply with the regulations.

ETIENNE: I don't see the point.

JUSTIN: The judge has to give you an exit permit, after the

usual investigation; this has been the rule ever since they discovered how little the law was respected. Because, after considerable research, they managed to discover that, in a single year, eleven thousand people against whom proceedings were pending had got out of the park, and most of them were accused of very serious offences, what's more. This was because there had been no check on people coming into or going out of the park. I remember distinctly that in those days you only had to ask for an exit permit to get one immediately. Fortunately they've put a stop to all that: now everyone coming into and going out of the park has to be investigated by the judge.

ETIENNE: And do I have to be investigated by the judge too?

JUSTIN: Naturally. There are no exceptions. I've already told you that there was a great deal of abuse, that's why the judges are so severe now. Perhaps a bit too much so, but however you look at it, it's necessary. What I can do for you is speed up the proceedings.

ETIENNE: How d'you mean, speed up the proceedings?

JUSTIN: I mean that I can try and arrange for your hearing to take place as soon as possible. In general you have to wait at least a month.

ETIENNE: I can't wait that long.

JUSTIN: They nearly always say: I can't wait that long. But what do you suppose they can do, when the number of trials is increasing all the time? Do you imagine they can settle them all just like that?

ETIENNE: It's not my fault if there are more trials.

JUSTIN: No, in theory, it's not your fault. And yet, if we were to examine the problem a little more closely, we should come to the conclusion in the end that, like all the other individuals who have passed through the park, you *are* guilty—indirectly, if you like, of this state of affairs. You are neither more nor less than one more link in the chain that has been formed, is being formed, and will continue to be formed, out of the increasing number of cases investigated by the tribunal. I told you I'd try and have your case dealt with as soon as possible.

There's a trick I'll play. [*Pause.* JUSTIN's *expression is ironic.*] A trick which, naturally enough, is perfectly legal, because you will quite understand that I wouldn't break the law, even to help you. I'll explain. The judges have had very strict orders that they are always to deal with these matters in strict chronological order. Exceptions can be made, though, if I remember rightly, in the following case: if the individuals found in the park are thought liable to be subject to another tribunal, then they may appear immediately. And this, precisely, applies in your case: the manacle round your ankle makes you particularly suspect. Thanks to this detail you'll be able, legally, to be dealt with by the tribunal before your turn.

ETIENNE: Good. That's what I want.

JUSTIN: I must warn you that this provision is a two-edged weapon, because the judges of the emergency tribunal who investigate cases like yours are very severe. They have some excuse: they're used to trying criminals of the worst type, who maintain their innocence with the greatest cynicism. That's why they tend to be suspicious at first, I might even go so far as to say that they take no notice of the testimony of the accused. But after all, it isn't too serious if they make a mistake because the accused goes on afterwards to the higher tribunal, and they do consider the evidence when they try him.

ETIENNE: I've nothing to be afraid of.

JUSTIN: Quite: we shouldn't exaggerate. And anyway, this first tribunal, as I told you, is only concerned with fact-finding, and it's very rare for it to condemn the accused directly.

ETIENNE: But this tribunal *can* condemn people?

JUSTIN: I've already told you that in theory it only enquires into the facts of the case, but in certain cases, where there is absolutely no doubt of the accused's guilt, or when he is obviously dangerous, the tribunal takes it upon itself to decide to punish him without reference to the higher tribunal. The punishment can sometimes, even, be the death penalty.

Silence. MICAELA, *in the latrine, is still obscenely wrapping herself round* BRUNO.

ETIENNE: Doesn't matter, I want to get out as quickly as possible.

JUSTIN: You can choose: either you wait your turn, or else you can be tried quickly by the emergency tribunal which will treat you, as I told you, very severely, all the more so as it will take your manacle into account. Tell me which you prefer.

ETIENNE: To be tried as soon as possible.

MICAELA [*still obscenely kissing* BRUNO *in the latrine*]: Kiss me, kiss my thighs.

JUSTIN *looks pleased.*

JUSTIN [*pointing to the latrine*]: Isn't that sweet? [*A pause.*] Excuse me, I get so easily sidetracked. We were saying . . . ah yes, you say you want to be tried by the emergency tribunal.

ETIENNE: Yes, Monsieur.

JUSTIN: Would you like me to go now and fetch the judge who investigates cases like yours?

ETIENNE: Yes, if you can.

JUSTIN: I'll go at once, then. I can't promise to come back immediately because the judge may not be in his office for the moment and I may have to wait for him. Anyway, I'll do my best to come back with him as soon as possible. [*Pause.*] You see how these things are—I too am curious about your case and I shall be interested to hear the verdict. So . . .

JUSTIN *looks delighted. He goes over to the latrine window, through which he watches* MICAELA, *still tangled up with* BRUNO.

Goodbye then, young man.

ETIENNE: Goodbye, Monsieur.

JUSTIN *gets lost among the blankets.* MICAELA *stops embracing* BRUNO *and smoothes down her clothes. She comes out of the latrine quickly and goes over to the blankets. She listens carefully. Silence.*

MICAELA: He's gone. [*She seems excited.*]

51

ETIENNE: But he said he'd be back very soon.

MICAELA: You never know.

ETIENNE: How d'you mean, you never know?

MICAELA: Yes, you never know for certain whether he'll be back at once or a long time after.

ETIENNE [*incredulous*]: Yes, of course.

MICAELA: Don't you believe me?

ETIENNE: Of course I believe you.

MICAELA: I'm not joking, I've known lots of cases like yours and I'm only too well aware of it.

ETIENNE: Naturally.

MICAELA: I can see you don't believe me.

ETIENNE: But I do—I do believe you.

MICAELA: No, don't pretend, I know what's going on. My father told you I was mad and that you must humour me. Didn't he? [*Silence.*] And anyway, you must resent my inventing all those bad things about you. Don't you? [*Silence.*] Tell me the truth.

ETIENNE: Naturally: do you suppose I liked it?

MICAELA: You mustn't attach so much importance to it.

ETIENNE: I don't attach the slightest importance to it.

MICAELA: You're quite right. It's not my fault. My father forces me to say all those things.

ETIENNE [*suspicious*]: Of course.

MICAELA: Don't say it like that. I'm telling you the truth. My father forces me to.

Silence. MICAELA *weeps.*

ETIENNE [*touched*]: Don't cry. [*Pause.*] What can I do for you? I tell you, I believe you.

MICAELA [*sighing*]: You're only trying to cheer me up.

Silence. ETIENNE *hesitates.*

My father forces me to tell all those unlikely tales so that afterwards he can show how generous he is, and that's how he gets everything he wants. People start by being suspicious of what I say, and then he passes for someone who loves his daughter dearly.

Silence. MICAELA *weeps. She bares her back. It is covered with blood and bears obvious marks of the whip.*

Look.

ETIENNE, *horrified, examines* MICAELA'S *back.*

MICAELA: Touch it, touch it.

MICAELA *makes* ETIENNE *touch her back. He gets blood on his hand.*

You see the blood.

ETIENNE [*impressed*]: Yes.

MICAELA: My father did that to me.

ETIENNE: He can't have.

MICAELA: He whips me every day. [*Sobbing.*] And he says he'll beat me more if I don't do everything he wants. That's why when he's there I have to say everything he's told me to say beforehand. This morning he made me pretend to be mad in front of you, I couldn't do anything but obey him. Otherwise he'd have beaten me worse than usual tonight.

ETIENNE [*deeply moved*]: It's intolerable.

MICAELA: Yes, but what can I do?

ETIENNE: Run away.

MICAELA: That's impossible.

ETIENNE: What d'you mean, impossible?

MICAELA: My father would stop me. And in any case I wouldn't know where to go. I'd starve to death. At least my father feeds me. [*She weeps.* ETIENNE *is moved.*] And in any case, he isn't my father. He makes me call him my father and he calls me his daughter when other people are there, but he isn't really my father. Everything he does is so as to get a good reputation.

ETIENNE [*resolutely*]: I'll get you out of here.

MICAELA [*sadly*]: It'll be very difficult. And anyway, you'll have enough trouble saving yourself.

ETIENNE: Why?

MICAELA: I heard my father telling you you'd be tried by the emergency tribunal judge. He's a very cruel judge who finds practically everyone who comes up before him guilty. During the hearing of the case he treats the accused with contempt and he's quite merciless. He hardly even allows them to speak or defend themselves;

he pees on them, sticks pins into them, belches into their mouths, ties them hand and foot, and even bites them, sometimes. It's true too, though, that in other circumstances he can be extremely polite to them, but this is rare. The worst thing is that no one, or practically no one, ever gets off.

ETIENNE: Ah, but *I* shall—I'm innocent. I haven't done anything wrong. [*Pause.*] When I'm free I shall get you out of here.

MICAELA [*touched*]: Thank you very much. You're very good to me.

ETIENNE: I can't allow your father to treat you like that.

> BRUNO, *in the latrine, gets up. He goes over to the lavatory chain.*

MICAELA: You mustn't worry about me, you must try and escape without bothering about me. You can see very well all the difficulties involved, you'll have your work cut out just trying to get away from here on your own.

> BRUNO, *in the latrine, has reached the chain. He hangs himself from it. The weight of his body makes the water in the tank overflow.* ETIENNE *and* MICAELA *are much affected, and say nothing for a moment.*

MICAELA: Did you hear that?

ETIENNE: Yes. [*He goes over to the latrine and looks at* BRUNO's *corpse in horror.*]

MICAELA: He's hanged himself. [*Silence.*] It was only to be expected. [*Silence.* MICAELA *suddenly goes over to the corpse.*] Help me.

> MICAELA *and* ETIENNE *between them take down the body. They carry the body to the centre of the stage. Silence. They contemplate the body. Silence.* MICAELA, *in meditative mood, respectfully takes one of* BRUNO's *hands. She kisses it. She may be crying. Silence.* MICAELA *covers* BRUNO's *face with a handkerchief.*

We must hide the body.

ETIENNE: Hide it. Why?

MICAELA: If the judge sees a corpse here he'll accuse you of murder. Help me.

ETIENNE: What d'you want me to do?

MICAELA: We'll put the corpse in the furthest possible place from here.

ETIENNE: Right, I'll help you.

MICAELA: That's the best way to make a body disappear. The park's so big that it'll be almost impossible for anyone to find it. Help me, take his legs.

ETIENNE: Let me take his shoulders, they're heavier.

MICAELA: No, do what I say.

They lift BRUNO *up, take him off and disappear among the blankets. Silence. No one on the stage.* ETIENNE *and* MICAELA *reappear.*

MICAELA: I don't think anyone will find him.

ETIENNE: And if someone does find him, what'll happen?

MICAELA: Your cause will be lost.

Silence.

ETIENNE: When did Bruno arrive in the lavatory?

MICAELA: I don't know. Every time I've been here I've found him tied up. Since I was a very small child.

ETIENNE: And weren't you sorry for him?

MICAELA: Yes, I was at first, I used to come here every morning and pee in front of him because he liked that. He looked quite happy when he watched me. Then we'd play together, I'd bring some buckets of sand and he'd bury my feet. [*Pause.*] But it was very difficult to play with him because he was always tied up and very ill.

ETIENNE: Has he always been ill?

MICAELA: Yes, always. He used to bleed all the time and no one ever changed his clothes. The blood used to dry on his shirt and suit. [*Pause.*] I used to bring him chocolate, and almonds, too, to give him a treat, and needles, lots of needles, especially.

ETIENNE: What did he want needles for?

MICAELA: To prick me with. When I was small he used to prick my legs, and when I became a woman he'd only prick my breasts and my stomach

ETIENNE: And you let him do it?

MICAELA: Of course, why not?

ETIENNE: But it must have been very painful.

MICAELA: Yes, very. It was almost unbearable. [*Pause.*] And then he wouldn't let me cry, or scream.

ETIENNE: But why did you go and see him?

MICAELA: I was terribly bored. When I was with him I got hurt, but at least I wasn't bored.

ETIENNE: He was a monster, then.

MICAELA: That wasn't the worst. The worst thing was that he used to tell my father all about it afterwards. [*Pause.*] My father had strictly forbidden me to go and see him, and particularly to take him anything. Well, he always used to tell, and my father would beat me.

ETIENNE: Your father told me you were his fiancée.

MICAELA: That's just a figure of speech. I wasn't really, but my father liked to tell everyone I was his fiancée, because, on the other hand, it wasn't completely false either. That's why he ordered me to kiss him and take him in my arms as passionately as possible when strangers were there. It was never passionate enough for his liking.

ETIENNE: And were you going to marry him?

MICAELA: No, not that. It wouldn't have been possible to marry him. He couldn't ever have left the lavatory.

ETIENNE: Why not?

MICAELA: Only my father knows that. My father told me that he came into the park one day like you did, and that he'd been here ever since.

ETIENNE: Was he found guilty by the judge?

MICAELA: I don't know. We never know much about that sort of thing.

ETIENNE: He told me that he was innocent and that I must intercede for him.

MICAELA: Yes, he used to say the same to everyone.

ETIENNE: How d'you mean, to everyone?

MICAELA: Yes, to everyone who spent a few days with him in the lavatory.

ETIENNE: He told me he'd always been on his own.

MICAELA: Yes, he had. That didn't stop him now and then

having a companion chained to him by the ankle, though. But all his companions always managed to file through the chain and escape, so he always got left on his own.

ETIENNE: And what happened to them?

MICAELA: My father will have dealt with them. I don't think any of them ever managed to get out.

Silence. ETIENNE *looks tragic.* MICAELA *pulls an enormous comb out of her pocket and combs her hair coquettishly.*

They were all extremely nice. [*Pause.*] They were sorry for me and promised to get me out of here. [*Pause.*] Always full of hope. It was a pleasure to come and have a chat with them.

Enter JUSTIN. *He doesn't speak. He waits, impassively.* MICAELA *has her back turned to her father; she makes fun of him and puts out her tongue at him.* ETIENNE *is scared and signals to* MICAELA *to stop making fun of him.* JUSTIN *intercepts his signals to* MICAELA *and stares at him reproachfully. Noises off: it seems that someone is moving some heavy furniture. The* JUDGE *appears; he comes in backwards, dragging after him a small table with a large drawer in it. Attached to the table, like railway carriages to an engine, are four chairs. The* JUDGE *has a bottle in one pocket; he is very dirty. He has a fairly long beard.* ETIENNE *studies him with animosity.* MICAELA *doesn't look at the* JUDGE, *but goes on putting out her tongue at her father. The* JUDGE, *fussily, but awkwardly, detaches the chairs. He sets out the table and chairs, in what are presumably their predetermined places (he does it with a great deal of care, guessing at the correct distances separating them, etc.).*

JUDGE: Take your seats.

ETIENNE *is about to sit down on one of the chairs.*

[*Violently*]:No, not yet.

ETIENNE *stands up again apprehensively. The* JUDGE *takes the chair* ETIENNE *was going to sit on, looks at him angrily—and puts it behind the table. He sits down on it. The table and chairs are distributed thus:*

	Judge's chair
	Table

Justin's chair   ⬜

Micaela's chair ⬜   ⬜   Etienne's chair

JUDGE: Take your seats.

No one sits down.

Didn't you hear what I said?

ETIENNE, *trembling, sits down on one of the chairs to the left. The* JUDGE, *furiously angry, gets up, grabs him violently by the jacket and moves him over to the chair on the right.* MICAELA *and* JUSTIN *then immediately sit down on the chairs on the left:* MICAELA *on the one furthest away from the* JUDGE *and* JUSTIN, *therefore, on the other. The* JUDGE *sits down on the chair behind the table. The* JUDGE *takes all sorts of papers out of his pockets and puts them methodically on the table: when he puts one in the wrong place he corrects his mistake. Then he brings a bottle of wine out of another pocket and puts it on the ground by his chair. Finally he brings out a big sausage sandwich wrapped in newspaper. During the whole of the hearing he eats his sandwich very slowly and monotonously. He nibbles at it, rather than eats it.*

JUDGE [*suddenly addresses* ETIENNE, *pointing his finger at him*]: I have been vaguely informed about your case. I hope you aren't going to make me waste too much time and that you'll state the facts as concisely as possible and with all the necessary exactitude.

ETIENNE *is about to speak.*

[*Interrupting him*]: If I tell you to state your case as concisely as possible it is because I wish sentence to be passed without delay. But if you need to call witnesses to support your evidence, have no fear; even if they are a long way away we shall have them brought here. The

motto of the emergency tribunal is: severity and justice.
ETIENNE *is comforted.*

Begin.

ETIENNE: In actual fact, your worship, I don't think there's any case for you to hear.

The JUDGE *is surprised and irritated, and sits up with a gesture of disapproval.* MICAELA *is very pleased and makes approving gestures.*

I simply got lost in the park, and I want to get out of it as soon as I can. I'm within my rights, I think. The master of the house has no option but to let me go. It's truly inconceivable—that anyone who owns this property should make difficulties when people get lost in one of his parks and want to get out.

JUSTIN *is hanging his head, and seems impressed.* MICAELA *encourages* ETIENNE. *She sends him kisses with her hand. The* JUDGE *nibbles at his sandwich.*

JUDGE: In principle, I have nothing against your request . . . [*he picks up his bottle and uncorks it*] . . . Which I should say is quite justified. [*He drinks a little wine out of the bottle.*] But there's one extremely serious detail; I am speaking, as you have probably guessed, of your manacle.

ETIENNE: The manacle . . . that's just for appearances. I wear it on my ankle like a piece of jewellery. What's surprising about that?

MICAELA *is full of enthusiasm and encourages* ETIENNE.

JUDGE: No, really, there's nothing surprising about that.

Pause. He nibbles. He shakes off the crumbs. His beard is full of them.

We've seen odder things than that. [*Pause.*] At my age, as you can imagine, I've seen just about everything.

Pause. He nibbles. He points at ETIENNE *and speaks in an accusing tone of voice.*

You didn't get lost in the park, you were put in the lavatory by the owner of the house [*pointing to* JUSTIN] who chained you up there with that manacle.

He calms down. He drinks a mouthful of wine. He nibbles. MICAELA *is sad,* JUSTIN *is pleased. Silence.*

ETIENNE: Yes, it's true. He chained me up.

JUDGE [*going through the same routine*]: Were you alone in the latrine?

ETIENNE: Yes.

JUDGE [*bored*]: You mean to say that no one was chained up with you?

ETIENNE: Yes. I was by myself. That was why I wanted to escape. I was terribly bored. He had no reason to chain me up, that was why I wanted to escape. [*Pause.*] I filed through the chain and I managed to escape;

JUDGE [*to himself*]: Those manacles are no good.

ETIENNE: It was very difficult.

JUDGE: Nothing was more natural than to try and escape. I'd have done the same, in your situation. Being chained up all by yourself in that latrine can't be very amusing. If you'd had a companion it would have been another matter. People can always find something to say to each other, can't they? [*Silence.*] I'm asking you whether you don't agree with me?

ETIENNE [*in a strangled voice*]: Yes.

The JUDGE *nibbles. He gets up from his chair and goes over to* ETIENNE. *He says to him, politely.*

JUDGE: Excuse me. Get up a moment.

The JUDGE *changes his position so that he is now directly facing him. He sits down again.*

[*After reading a few of the papers on his table*]: Your system won't get you anywhere.

ETIENNE: What system?

JUDGE: Your defence system. [*Pause.*] You lie too much. [*Pause. Aggressively.*] You were in the latrine with another man called Bruno, and you were manacled to him.

ETIENNE: But he was very ill, he didn't count.

JUDGE: Why did you escape on your own?

ETIENNE: I tell you, Bruno was very ill and he couldn't escape.

JUDGE: He didn't want to go with you?

ETIENNE: No, he couldn't have. He could hardly move. He was almost paralysed.

JUDGE [*interrupting him, shouts*]: Wait a minute.

> The JUDGE *makes a few notes with great care on a big sheet of white paper in gigantic handwriting. Holding the paper away from him he admires its effect with half-closed eyes.*

So he was paralysed then?

ETIENNE: Well, almost paralysed.

JUDGE: And he helped you run away?

ETIENNE: He couldn't.

JUDGE: Ah, of course not. But he didn't try to stop you, either?

ETIENNE: No, he didn't try to stop me.

JUDGE: And while you were filing through the chain you were hurting him.

ETIENNE: No, not at all.

JUDGE [*calmly*]: This business is going from bad to worse. [*Pause.*] Bruno wanted to escape but you didn't want to help him. On the other hand, he tried with all his might to stop you going, and what's more you hurt his ankles terribly while you were filing through the chain: he still bears the traces.

> The JUDGE *nibbles.* JUSTIN *is very pleased. The* JUDGE *drinks a mouthful of wine.*

Would you like us to go into the latrine and observe the traces?

ETIENNE: No.

JUDGE: You believe me, then?

ETIENNE: Yes.

JUDGE: You must have made poor Bruno suffer a lot.

JUSTIN [*getting up from his chair*]: Bruno isn't in the latrine. [*He sits down again.*]

JUDGE [*stopping his nibbling*]: Did you hear that?

ETIENNE: Yes.

JUDGE: Where is he, then?

ETIENNE: I've no idea.

JUDGE: You've no idea, and yet you were with him last. That's odd. Very odd.

ETIENNE: He must have escaped.

JUDGE: That's impossible. [*He looks for a paper on the table. He is holding in his hand a paper on which he has just written something.*] You've just told me that he could hardly move, that he was almost paralysed.

ETIENNE: He may have got better, though.

JUSTIN [*gets up again and speaks with great propriety. The* JUDGE *listens to him very attentively: he stops his nibbling*]: May I be permitted to inform you of certain facts which may throw some light on this case?

JUDGE: Please do.

JUSTIN: As you will have realised, your worship, the accused is adopting an attitude which might well deceive a tribunal that was inclined to be over-credulous. He is trying to make himself out an honourable man who is incapable of wrong-doing. Let us examine the facts with all the necessary accuracy: the accused was put in the latrine where he was chained to Bruno. He had been promised that he would be tried as soon as possible. But the accused, instead of quietly awaiting the day of his trial, forces the issue and escapes. Which can only be interpreted, purely and simply, as an inadmissible act of contempt of court. If the accused imagined that he was detained in the latrine for no reason, and even in a manner totally devoid of the most elementary courtesies as he gave us to understand at the beginning of the hearing, the only possible solution would have been for him to await the court's verdict, which is always in conformity with the law. I must stress this point: his lack of consideration towards the tribunal and his attempted escape must be interpreted as proof of his inadmissible attitude of contempt for the workings of justice and the law.

And now I have thrown some light on this first point, which may be considered as giving essential information about the attitude of the accused, I will pass on to others, of no less importance. The accused has admitted to having been lost in the park, to not knowing me, to having been chained to another person, etc. etc. That is to say that he has lied several times, and was trying, by his lies, to create the alibis necessary to conceal his wrong-doing. [*Pause.*] And I have been informed of some striking details by various people who, in these special circumstances, were witnesses to the events which took place in the latrine while the accused was confined there. The accused tortured Bruno with thirst; he was asking for water but the accused hardly ever took any notice. Then he had the idea of filing through the chain so that he could escape. The manacles were also secured round Bruno's ankles, since they were chained together, and the accused pulled so hard on Bruno's ankle that he made a deep wound. Bruno, overcome by pain and suffering, could do nothing to prevent the tortures the accused inflicted on him. The moment he was free he abandoned him without consideration for his thirst. [*Pause.*] But there is something even worse. [*Pause. Ceremonially.*] My servants have found Bruno's corpse in the park: he had been strangled. [*Pause.*] Although I am not aware of the precise details, I feel that all the circumstances prove that the accused strangled him.

ETIENNE [*violently*]: No. I didn't.

MICAELA *is distressed. The* JUDGE *starts eating again. He drinks a mouthful of wine and says in a calm voice.*

JUDGE: Well who did then? Are you going to accuse someone?

ETIENNE: He committed suicide.

JUDGE: How?

ETIENNE: With the lavatory chain.

JUDGE: You're contradicting yourself. You said at first that he could hardly move, that he was paralysed.

ETIENNE: He must have made a great effort.

JUSTIN: Don't forget that the body was found a long way from the latrine.

JUDGE: Yes. Can dead men walk?

ETIENNE *hesitates.*

ETIENNE: She and I [*pointing to* MICAELA] moved Bruno's body. We were afraid that if it was found I would be accused of murder.

JUSTIN [*very dignified*]: Your worship, I think it is useless to go any further. If the accused continues he will end by indicting us all. All the evidence points to his being the murderer, and as such he should be found guilty at once.

ETIENNE [*very angry*]: And who's he to talk about finding me guilty? He's the last one who can talk, he's the cruellest person I've ever met in all my life.

> *Silence.* MICAELA *encourages* ETIENNE *and blows kisses at him.* JUSTIN *seems disconcerted. The* JUDGE *listens carefully.*

This man brought me into the park for no good reason and had me shut up in the middle of the labyrinth in a filthy lavatory with a kind of living corpse. And all this for no reason at all: out of sheer cruelty. And he's so cruel he ill-treats his daughter every day, and whips her. [*Ironical.*] Look at him, the good father, the father who loves his daughter. And in any case, Micaela isn't his daughter, and he often takes advantage of her, at the same time passing himself off as a good father, when he's nothing but a veritable tyrant. Look, look at Micaela's back, you'll see the traces of blood from the whip-lashes her father gave her last night.

JUSTIN [*to the* JUDGE]: May I ask you to verify the truth of what this man says?

JUDGE: There's no point.

JUSTIN: I should be grateful.

> *The* JUDGE *bares* MICAELA'S *back. There's nothing wrong with it. It is white, and bears no trace of blood or scars.*

ETIENNE [*shouting*]: It's not possible.

> MICAELA *covers her back.*

JUDGE: So that's how you behave to the man who came and got me out of bed so that you could be tried at once and not have to wait, the man who has done you nothing but kindnesses, and protected you from all sorts of dangers.

ETIENNE [*obstinately*]: He's a criminal. He can fake up anything he likes.

JUDGE: How dare you treat him like that? [*Pause.*] Actually, I'm nothing but his slave, he has the right of life and death over me. And anyway he appointed me to try you—and I have the reputation of being the most lenient judge of all on the emergency tribunal—simply to show you how much he has your interests at heart. I don't need to hear any more: the way you attack him and insult him is quite enough to prove your guilt.

JUSTIN: No—I want the trial to be based only on the observed actions of the accused from the time he entered the labyrinth, without any account being taken of what he has said against me.

JUDGE: You can certainly think yourself lucky.

The JUDGE *starts looking through his papers, and then goes on to others. Silence.*

There is not the slightest doubt of the accused's guilt.

He drinks a mouthful of wine. He nibbles a bit of sandwich.

The accused, from the very beginning of the hearing, has told all sorts of lies that it would be idle to recall; still worse, he has questioned the legal proceedings and attempted to escape. And to crown this series of offences, he has tortured his companion in the latrine, strangled him, and tried to dispose of his body in the park. The accused is found guilty of murder. [*Pause. He drinks. He nibbles.*] I condemn him to death. [*Pause. He drinks. He nibbles.*] The guards will come to fetch him at once, to the sound of the drum.

The JUDGE *stuffs all his papers in his pockets at record speed. The bottle, too. He attaches the chairs to the table, as they were to start with. While he is doing this* MICAELA *has gone over to her father and is stroking his back tenderly; from time to time her father kisses her on the forehead with great devotion.* ETIENNE *is crushed and stands there motionless.*

[*To* ETIENNE]: You are not to move from here. The guards will come and fetch you with their drums.

The JUDGE *goes out, pulling the table after him.* JUSTIN *and* MICAELA *follow him.* JUSTIN *tenderly supports his daughter, putting his arm round her shoulder. They go out.* ETIENNE *is left alone on the stage. Silence. Drums in the distance.* ETIENNE *looks anxiously towards the blankets. He hesitates. He goes into the labyrinth. Leaves the stage. Pause. The sound of the drums comes nearer.* ETIENNE *reappears, out of breath. The sound of the drums comes nearer.* ETIENNE *hesitates. He lifts up a blanket, intending to go into the labyrinth.* BRUNO *appears behind it, in his death throes.*

BRUNO: I'm thirsty.

ETIENNE *starts back in anguish. The blanket hides* BRUNO. *The drums come closer.* ETIENNE *hesitates. Very carefully he lifts up a blanket, intending to go into the labyrinth. There's no one there. He goes into the labyrinth. Leaves the stage. Pause. The sound of the drums comes nearer.* ETIENNE *reappears, out of breath. The sound of the drums comes nearer.* ETIENNE *hesitates. He lifts up a blanket, intending to go into the labyrinth.* BRUNO *appears behind it, in his death throes.*

BRUNO: I'm thirsty.

ETIENNE *starts back in anguish, the blanket hides* BRUNO, *the drums come nearer.* ETIENNE *hesitates, etc.*

CURTAIN

THE TRICYCLE

**translated from the French
by Barbara Wright**

CHARACTERS

APAL
CLIMANDO
THE OLD FLUTE PLAYER
MITA
THE MAN WITH THE BANKNOTES
POLICEMAN
POLICE CHIEF

The action takes place on the banks of a river in a big town.

Iron rings along the quay. Path about 30 feet wide. Garden at the far end, separated from the path by a little wall, along the whole length of which runs a stone bench.

The Tricycle was performed in Spanish in Madrid in 1957, under the direction of Josefina Sanchez-Pedreño, and premièred in France on February 15, 1961 in Paris, at the Théâtre de Poche Montparnasse, directed by Olivier Hussenot, with scenic design by Georges Richard.

ACT ONE

Evening; it's not quite dark yet. APAL, *a poorly dressed individual, is lying on a bench.*

A VOICE: Apaaaal! . . . Apaaaal! . . . Apaaaal!
The voice is coming from the garden. Someone we can't see is crossing it, calling Apal. When he stops calling we can hear the tinkling of bells. The voice gradually dies away to nothing. Short silence. Then we again hear the voice and the bells.

THE VOICE: Apaaaal! . . . Apaaaal! . . . Apaaaal! . . .
The voice gets nearer and nearer, and CLIMANDO *finally enters, mounted on a rusty old box-tricycle. The box is decorated with characters from 'Alice in Wonderland' and is big enough to hold six children. It has a row of little bells on a crossbar.*

CLIMANDO [*getting down from the tricycle*]: Apal, Apal, wake up, mate.
He shakes him fairly roughly. APAL *wakes up and gets on to the tricycle, quickly, like an automaton.*
How come you aren't at the fountain?

APAL: I was sleepy.
APAL *goes off on the tricycle. After a moment or two he comes back. He gets off the tricycle and lies down on the bench again.*

CLIMANDO: But . . . aren't you going to the park, then?

APAL: I'm sleepy.

CLIMANDO: You've got a hell of a nerve.

APAL: Mmm . . .

CLIMANDO: And then, we've got to pay for the hire of the tricycle, and we haven't got a bean.

APAL: Let me sleep.

CLIMANDO: All right, all right. In any case you wouldn't have had much to do. Most of the kids have gone.

Enter the OLD FLUTE PLAYER.

OLD MAN: Hallo, boys! I'm going to sit down here, I don't feel I could walk another step.

CLIMANDO: That's just what I feel like too.

CLIMANDO *lies down by the river and the* OLD FLUTE PLAYER *sits down on the bench and stretches out his legs. Long pause.*

OLD MAN: It's because of the tricycle.

CLIMANDO: What is?

OLD MAN: Being so tired.

CLIMANDO: I'll say; I've spent the whole afternoon giving rides to kids. It hurts under my arms, more than anywhere else.

OLD MAN: It must be your espadrilles. Almost exactly the same thing happens to me; my knees hurt because I play the flute.

They both speak very quickly.

CLIMANDO: It must be your hat. Almost exactly the same thing happens to me; my nails hurt because I don't eat anything.

OLD MAN [*very cross*]: It must be the water you drink at the fountain. Almost exactly the same thing happens to me; my eyebrows hurt me because I wear trousers.

CLIMANDO [*aggressive*]: It must be your not being married. Almost exactly the same thing happens to me; the flies hurt me because I go to sleep.

OLD MAN [*violently*]: It must be your not buying lottery tickets. Almost exactly the same thing happens to me; all the hairs on my head hurt because I walk.

CLIMANDO [*very pleased*]: It's not true. It's not true!

OLD MAN: It's not true?

CLIMANDO: No, no, it's not true; all the hairs on your head can't possibly hurt you because you're bald.

OLD MAN: You're cheating.

CLIMANDO: No I'm not; we'll start again if you like.

OLD MAN: We can't; you reason better than I do, and reason always wins.

CLIMANDO: You won't go about saying I took unfair advantage of you, will you? I'll give you a ride on the tricycle, if you like.

OLD MAN [*relenting*]: A ride on the tricycle! And will you let me stroke the children?

CLIMANDO: Yes—so long as you don't steal their chocolate.

OLD MAN: You see how you dislike me? What's their chocolate got to do with it? You see? Eh?

    CLIMANDO *is ashamed*.

Don't hang your head—don't. [*Pleased*.] So you do realise how badly you treat me, eh?

CLIMANDO [*humbly*]: Yes. [*Justifying himself*.] But I did promise to give you a ride on the tricycle. I can't be any nicer than that.

OLD MAN [*softly*]: A ride on the tricycle . . . stroking the children. I'll put my hands on their heads and say . . . and say . . . [*aggressively*] Yes, but will you let me play the bells?

CLIMANDO: No, because you have to play the flute, and no one's ever been known to play two instruments at the same time.

OLD MAN: You won't let me because I haven't got any banknotes and I'm not good at reasoning. Goodbye! [*He goes off angrily as far as the end of the bench, and turns his back on* CLIMANDO.] And afterwards you won't say *pax*, or give me a sardine . . . or bring me a mouthful of water when I'm thirsty.

CLIMANDO: You take me for Father Christmas.

    CLIMANDO *sits down by the river and starts fishing. He throws a baited line into the water.*

CLIMANDO [*intoning, making each syllable very clear and detached*]: And then, Apal and I are going to be very pleased with ourselves because we've thought up a marvellous scheme. We shan't let anyone else into the secret.

OLD MAN [*also intoning*]: I'm going to be very pleased with myself on account of a different scheme. I shan't say a word to anyone, just to rile the idiots who won't let me have a ride on the tricycle.

    Pause.

CLIMANDO: We've discovered a way to stop anyone following us, so's we don't have to escape from one place to another, like we do now.

OLD MAN: I'd be mighty surprised if Apal had done something.

    APAL *wakes up for the second time. He runs round the stage twice. Then he starts slapping himself on the back, crossing his arms.*

[*Going off*]: Right, I'm off.

CLIMANDO [*to* APAL, *without looking at him*]: Are you cold?

APAL: Yes.

CLIMANDO: If you like, we'll go and sleep by the metro.

APAL: There's the cops. [*He always speaks as if it's a great effort.*]

CLIMANDO: That's true. Yes, but we could go and sleep near the kitchens of the Grand Hotel.

APAL: The porter.

CLIMANDO: Yes, that porter fellow doesn't care for us overmuch; the old goat chucks water over us. [*Pause.*] We could sneak into a cinema.

APAL: Very difficult.

CLIMANDO: And all because we aren't invisible. Ah! if only we were invisible! Apal, if I were invisible, I'd go and sleep in a box in the Green Palace. On the carpet! I'd be all right there! But what can we do to find somewhere warm to sleep?

APAL: Die!

CLIMANDO: Die?

APAL: We haven't got any money, so we'd go to hell.

CLIMANDO: But the thing is, I'm afraid.

APAL: So'm I.

CLIMANDO: We're not so poor as all that. We've got the tricycle. [*Pause.*] The trouble is that if we don't pay for its hire tomorrow they'll take it back. And we haven't got anything else.

APAL: We've been worse off before.

CLIMANDO: The worst of all is the cold. There's one thing we can do. We can sleep together, and when you say: 'Climando, my feet are cold,' I'll blow on them for you. And when I say: 'Apal, my hands are cold,' you can blow on my hands for me.

APAL: That's tiring.

CLIMANDO: No more than lifting your little finger.

APAL: I'm going to have a snooze.

CLIMANDO: You do nothing else all day.

> CLIMANDO *sits down by the river bank and whistles as he casts a line into the water in an attempt to catch some fish. Enter* MITA, *a young girl dressed in black rags.*

Hi, Mita!

MITA: Hi! [*She sits down near* CLIMANDO.]

CLIMANDO: You're terribly sad!

> MITA *makes a vague gesture.*

I ought to give you a kiss so's you won't be sad. [*Pause.*] I like your kisses better than the ovens in the patisserie in the avenue.

MITA: That's more or less how it is with me, about you. But we can't make a meal out of kisses.

CLIMANDO: Then you like cakes better than my kisses.

MITA: 'Course I do!

CLIMANDO: Well, I do too.

MITA: We're awfully alike.

CLIMANDO: We were born for each other. [*Gaily.*] We both like cakes better than kisses.

MITA: But I'm very sad.

CLIMANDO: What's happened?

MITA: Nothing.

CLIMANDO: Really nothing?

MITA: Yes, really, really nothing.

CLIMANDO: Oh my goodness, you must be sad!

MITA: I'd like to commit suicide, I'm so sad.

CLIMANDO: Really and truly?

73

MITA: Yes.

CLIMANDO: Why?

MITA: I don't know—no reason. Then I wouldn't be sad any more.

CLIMANDO: Oh, that's true, nor you would. I hadn't thought of that.

MITA: If only I had the courage!

CLIMANDO [*after a long moment's meditation*]: It's obvious. Commit suicide.

MITA: It's the best thing to do, don't you think?

CLIMANDO: Of course it's the best thing to do. I see it now. I was going to be sorry about it because I like you a lot— more than the tricycle—and then your kisses are almost better than anchovy sandwiches. But Mita, if you think you'll be happier committing suicide, commit suicide as soon as possible.

MITA: You're so good! You give me such good advice!

CLIMANDO: There's no doubt about it—you, and the old flute man, even though he is such a cross-patch, and Apal, are what I love most in the world. Commit suicide, Mita, don't be afraid.

MITA: Why don't you, too?

CLIMANDO: Well, I hadn't thought about it. And anyway, I've got to pay for the hire of the tricycle tomorrow. I can't commit suicide. Tell Apal, in case he wants to commit suicide too.

MITA: Not Apal. He's always asleep.

CLIMANDO: Tell the old man, then.

MITA: He's very old to think about suicide.

CLIMANDO: That's true, it's never happened yet. That'd be bad.

MITA: And anyway, he could only commit suicide with his flute; just think how ugly and difficult that'd be.

CLIMANDO: Yes, but he could climb on to a roof, though, and hide his eyes, and then just when he was least expecting it—woomph—and he'd be dead.

MITA: But what if he doesn't get giddy? When you're old you don't even get giddy any more.

74

CLIMANDO: That's a nuisance. [*Pause.*] And how are *you* going to commit suicide?

MITA: I've forgotten.

CLIMANDO: You always forget everything. Do you remember the day when you were walking down a little street arm in arm with Apal and you met a bus driver and said to him: 'Hey, don't go away, it's my birthday tomorrow,' and he didn't listen to you and went away?

MITA: That doesn't mean I forget everything.

CLIMANDO: Hm! Nor it does! [*Pause.*] The trouble is that when you've committed suicide I won't be able to stroke your knees.

MITA: You can stroke Cepina's—you know, the girl who sells pancakes.

CLIMANDO: And what is there to tell me that her knees are as pretty as yours?

MITA: I know my knees are pretty but hers aren't bad either. She washes them every morning with water and herbs.

CLIMANDO: They won't be like yours, I tell you . . . let me stroke them again.

> MITA *raises her skirts a little and* CLIMANDO *strokes her knees.*

I love your knees because they're soft, and smooth, and big and white, like a china plate only more velvety. And then they aren't wrinkled like mine. I'll show you how ugly they are.

> CLIMANDO *starts to take off one of his boots.*

MITA: Why do you take off your boot to show me your knee?

CLIMANDO: Er . . . my trouser leg has to be in my boot, you see, so I don't catch cold. [*He finally manages to take off his boots, and pulls his trousers up to his knees.*] Look— touch them, touch them and you'll see.

MITA [*touching them*]: Pooh! Aren't they ugly, aren't they wrinkled!

CLIMANDO: And what's more, you're seeing them on a day when I've eaten some bread soaked in tunny fish oil. You just ought to see them the other days.

MITA: And then, they're very dirty.

CLIMANDO: That's because I don't wash them.

MITA: Ah!

APAL *moves, probably trying to find a more comfortable
position.*

CLIMANDO: Apal, when on earth are you going to stop
sleeping?

APAL: Mmm. . . .

MITA: Leave him, Climando, you know very well he has to
sleep at least 18 hours a day.

CLIMANDO: Yes, but one of these days he'll die from sleeping
so much.

MITA: That doesn't worry him in the slightest. His dreams
must be much sweeter.

CLIMANDO: I'm sure he's dreaming that he's asleep.

MITA: That must be very pleasant.

CLIMANDO: Wonderful! And then, when he's awake, as he
never does anything, he can't be any happier. We're
much less happy than he is, we're always having to hide
from the cops, and porters, and men with money. And
worst of all is the fact that we haven't got any means of
paying for the hire of the tricycle. [*Pause.*] They'll put us
in prison.

MITA: In prison—that won't be much fun. They say they're
full of bugs, and the worst thing is that they keep on
having hunger strikes, so that if you don't look out you
die.

CLIMANDO: You needn't bother about that. The tricycle isn't
yours. . . . And anyway, you're going to commit suicide.

MITA: I'd forgotten all about it.

CLIMANDO: You see how you forget everything.

MITA: I'd only forgotten I was supposed to commit suicide.

CLIMANDO: And you needn't think I'm joking. That's how
people start. For instance—I had a friend who wore
braces on Sundays and a belt on every other day, and
that's why he drank more than usual on Sundays.

MITA: Yes, of course. But what do I have to do to remember
I've got to commit suicide?

76

CLIMANDO: Make a note of it, or else tie a knot in your handkerchief.

MITA: . . .

CLIMANDO: It's in your own interests. Just think that you won't be happy unless you commit suicide.

MITA: Really?

CLIMANDO: Of course. So you see—commit suicide as soon as possible.

MITA: And won't you be sorry?

CLIMANDO [*tenderly*]: Me, Mita? Yes, very, terribly. I love you so much. You and your kisses, your white, smooth, big knees.

MITA: I love you too, even though you're so incredibly ugly.

CLIMANDO: I'll let you take the tricycle back to the garage if you like, Mita.

MITA: Will you really?

    CLIMANDO *nods happily.*

What a bit of luck! [*Pause.*] And will you let me steer it with one hand?

CLIMANDO: Only one hand? [*He considers.*] Well, all right. [*He considers.*] And what'll you do with the other?

MITA: I'll put one of my fingers up my nose.

CLIMANDO: You are a one! You can do everything.

MITA [*enthusiastically*]: If you like I'll even steer with my eyes shut.

CLIMANDO: Oh no you don't. You'd fall in the water and the fishes would eat you.

MITA [*terrified*]: Oh my goodness!

CLIMANDO: You have to be told everything. What would become of you if I wasn't here?

MITA: All right. I'll take the tricycle back to the garage without shutting my eyes.

CLIMANDO: And come straight back. The garage is no distance, it'll only take you two minutes.

MITA: Don't worry.

CLIMANDO: And don't play about behind the trees watching the men peeing.

MITA: No, you'll see, I'll come straight back. See you.

CLIMANDO: See you.

> MITA *gets on to the tricycle and goes off. The bells can be heard.* CLIMANDO *hesitates. He walks up and down, thinking. He goes over to* APAL *and shakes him to wake him up.*

Apal, you've had your 18 hours.

APAL: Mmm. . . .

CLIMANDO: Come on Apal, wake up.

APAL: Mmm. . . .

CLIMANDO: You're just like a dormouse! Come on, chum, get up, wake up.

> APAL *slowly sits up.*

APAL: What's going on?

CLIMANDO: We've got to find the money for the hire of the tricycle.

APAL: Where?

CLIMANDO: That's just what I don't know.

APAL: Doesn't matter.

CLIMANDO: But they'll put us in prison.

APAL: Well, they can.

CLIMANDO: And they'll take the tricycle away from us.

APAL: Well, they can.

CLIMANDO: But what'll we do, you and I?

APAL: *I* shall sleep.

CLIMANDO: We must think of something.

APAL: Personally what I must do is sleep. When I think, I'm hungry and cold.

CLIMANDO: Yes, that's the trouble with thinking.

APAL: Especially if the things you think about are very worrying.

CLIMANDO: Why don't you tell yourself some nice stories?

APAL: I don't know.

CLIMANDO: That's very bad. [*Pause.*] And you can't think of any way of paying for the tricycle?

APAL: No.

> *Enter* MITA. APAL *takes advantage of her arrival to go to sleep.*

MITA [*to* CLIMANDO]: Look.

She points to someone we can't see on her right.

CLIMANDO: What a peculiar-looking chap! What's he doing here?

MITA: He's following me. *He* must like my knees, too.

CLIMANDO: No, not he. He looks peculiar: people like that don't like your knees.

MITA: But he's following me.

CLIMANDO: Don't be afraid. He won't dare take us both on. In any case, if he does, we'll call Apal to help us.

MITA: Can't you see he's asleep?

CLIMANDO: We'll wake him up.

MITA: Yes, we'd better.

CLIMANDO [*looking to the right*]: He's stopped.

MITA [*pointing to him*]: He's looking at us.

CLIMANDO: Did he say anything to you?

MITA: No, he just showed me his wallet.

CLIMANDO: Were there many notes in it?

MITA: It was full.

CLIMANDO: Then why's he following you? Greedy pig! The more you have the more you want. Just imagine, he not only has a wallet full of banknotes but he wants you, too.

MITA: Yes, he's going a bit far.

CLIMANDO: Well, I don't think much of his taste, considering how dirty you are today.

MITA: That's true—I *am* very dirty.

CLIMANDO: And he can't like you. He doesn't know your good sides. He can't know that you can walk in a barrel, or that you can draw in the sand with your toes, or that you make paper boats. So as he doesn't know anything about all that, he can't like you.

MITA: No, of course he can't.

CLIMANDO: Peculiar chap. [*Long pause.*] Don't you remember—I knew you when you were pulling posters off the walls to sell the paper. He'll never know such joy with you. I carried the bag half way to Sarpe's shop and you carried it the rest of the way. And afterwards we used the money to buy peanuts from old Simplicie. What does he want?

If he has so many banknotes all he has to do is buy enough peanuts to make him sick and then he'll be quite happy.

MITA: The trouble is that men who have banknotes wear very ugly suits and shave a lot, that's why their faces look like bits of silk. It's disgusting. And they can't breathe properly, which is even worse. And they're always getting tired. It's nauseating. If I had a lot of money I'd wear the same clothes as I do now and I'd eat lots of sardine sandwiches, and when the nights were cold I'd spend them in the warm, but in the summer I'd come and sleep by the river.

CLIMANDO: That's what you say now, but if you had a lot of money one day you'd only buy silly and ugly things which aren't any use.

MITA: Quite likely.

CLIMANDO: There's not the slightest doubt. People make a lot of promises and then they get rich and forget all about them. That little Vincent, for instance, Moscona's son— he got pneumonia when he was five months old and then when he was six years he fell downstairs.

MITA: Misfortunes seldom come singly.

CLIMANDO: The worst misfortune is to die of hunger, and hunger always comes by itself.

MITA: Huh! So it does.

CLIMANDO: That's why, when I die, I want them to throw my fishing line into the water for the fishes to eat, and I want the old flute player to play a sad or gay tune while they do it.

MITA [looking to the right]: Hey, d'you see how he's looking at us?

CLIMANDO: He is too. He must be a low type.

MITA: Does he think he's going to stay there all night?

CLIMANDO: People like him are very annoying. You'd think they'd nothing better to do. [Pause.] I feel almost sorry for him.

MITA: Yes of course, poor chap.

CLIMANDO: Naturally—poor chap. And all because he wants to kiss you, probably. [He stares at her.] Don't be nasty to him.

80

MITA [*touched*]: He's sad.

CLIMANDO: Yes, he is. And it's all your fault. Don't you feel sorry for him?

MITA: Yes, very sorry. But he's horribly ugly.

CLIMANDO: Then you ought to feel even sorrier for him.

MITA: Yes, but I feel even more disgusted.

CLIMANDO: Think it's me. If you shut your eyes you won't be able to tell the difference.

MITA: Won't I?

CLIMANDO: 'Course you won't.

MITA: But he's got some banknotes.

CLIMANDO: So he has; I'd forgotten.

MITA: If he's got some banknotes it'll be all the same to him whether he kisses me or someone else. You can buy what you like when you've got money, you can even buy a thousand tins of anchovies.

CLIMANDO: I've got an idea. Why couldn't we take the notes he's got in his wallet?

MITA: And what'd we do with so much money?

CLIMANDO: We'd take what we need to pay for the hire of the tricycle.

MITA: Is that all?

CLIMANDO: We could take enough to buy four sandwiches, too—one for Apal, one for the old man, one for you, and one for me.

MITA: And a brazier, too.

CLIMANDO: And . . . [*annoyed*] We can't ask for anything else or we'd get to be like tortoises.

MITA: That's the trouble, when you ask for things.

CLIMANDO: Yes but—how can we take the banknotes?

MITA: I don't know. You ought to know better than I do, you're a man.

CLIMANDO: I could say: 'Beg your pardon, sir, but what colour is your wallet?' And he'd say: 'Green', and I'd say: 'Red' until he has to take it out to prove it. And then we'd grab it and run away. As he's a rich man, either he won't be able to run or else he'll run like a duck and he'll never be able to catch us.

81

MITA: But what if his wallet is red?

CLIMANDO: Yes, then it's more serious.

MITA: We've got to think of everything.

CLIMANDO: Best thing would be to ask Apal what he thinks.

MITA: Yes, that'd be best.

CLIMANDO: Apal, Apal, Apal. [*He shakes him.*] You've had your 18 hours.

APAL: Mmm. . . .

CLIMANDO: Come on, Apal, wake up.

APAL *sits up.*

APAL: What is it?

CLIMANDO [*pointing*]: You see that chap?

APAL: Yes.

CLIMANDO: He's got a lot of banknotes.

APAL: Good.

CLIMANDO: We've got to take them from him to pay for the hire of the tricycle.

APAL: Mmm. . . .

CLIMANDO: How can we take them?

APAL: I don't know.

CLIMANDO: Can't you think of anything? Try really hard, like when you're looking for somewhere to sleep.

APAL [*after a pause*]. By killing him.

CLIMANDO: By killing him?

MITA: That's going too far.

CLIMANDO [*looking* MITA *in the eyes*]: Don't say you're scared. Or are you suddenly going to discover that you're superstitious, or that you're afraid of the dead? You wanted to commit suicide.

MITA: That's different.

CLIMANDO: You needn't think it's so very different. It's a question of death in both cases, when you really come down to it.

MITA: But in one case it was *my* death.

CLIMANDO: Even worse. I remember so well the day I fell downstairs.

MITA: Apal's going off to sleep again.

CLIMANDO: Apal—how do we kill him?

APAL: Very simple.

MITA: Of course—couldn't be more simple, there are three of us.

CLIMANDO: I don't very much like having to kill him. It's a terribly long way of robbing him.

MITA: It's the only way for no one to know. If we don't kill him the first thing he'll do is go and ask the judge to lock us up, and as he's sure to have some more banknotes at home he can do what he likes.

CLIMANDO: What a rotten sort of chap.

MITA: And anyway, he's sure to want to commit suicide.

CLIMANDO: I hadn't thought of that.

MITA: We'll be saving him the trouble.

CLIMANDO [*to* APAL]: Don't go to sleep now, mate.

APAL: I'm listening.

CLIMANDO: We agree; we'll kill him.

APAL: Good.

CLIMANDO: But how?

APAL [*pointing to the garden wall*]: Over there.

CLIMANDO: Do we throw ourselves on him?

APAL: Yes: Mita must stay here to attract his attention.

    CLIMANDO *and* APAL *start to go off.*

MITA: I'm scared.

CLIMANDO: Don't be daft, think about the tricycle and the anchovy sandwiches, and about how he wants to commit suicide. Don't move, don't move.

    He retreats, step by step, towards the wings, saying in a sing-song voice:

Don't move, watch for the birdie. Don't move.

    MITA *is left alone on the stage. She starts humming, to keep up her courage, and then pulls up the rags that cover her knees. Her voice becomes more and more assured as she sings. The man with the banknotes comes in slowly. Before he gets to* MITA *the lights gradually dim until there is complete darkness.*

CURTAIN

ACT TWO

MITA *can be heard singing. Then a short silence. The lights gradually come up again.* APAL *is back on the bench, asleep. The bench is covered with blood stains. Enter the* OLD FLUTE PLAYER.

OLD MAN: Hey, Apal, have you seen that? [*He points to the stains.*] What a mess! [*He follows the bloodstains and smells them.*] Someone must have killed an animal here, don't you think? [*Pause.*] Unless it was an elephant . . . What a lot of blood!

APAL [*without getting up*]: What's going on?

OLD MAN: Look, there's blood all over the place.

APAL: Don't disturb me.

OLD MAN: But my dear chap, can't you see all the blood?

APAL: Yes, of course I can.

OLD MAN: We must do something.

APAL: Leave me alone, I'm sleepy.

OLD MAN: Well you are a one! Right, I'm off, I don't want to know anything about it. Blood makes me thirsty and the water's very cold at the moment, and wine's very dear. Goodbye, Apal.

APAL: Mmm. . . .

The OLD FLUTE PLAYER *goes off.* APAL *runs round the stage twice, trying not to tread in the blood. Then he slaps himself on the back and lies down again. Silence. We hear the tricycle bells tinkling. Then* MITA *and* CLIMANDO *come in, riding on the tricycle.*

CLIMANDO [*loudly and happily*]: Apal, Apal, I've paid for the hire of the tricycle.

APAL: Aren't you going to let me sleep?

MITA: Of course we are; let him sleep, Climando, he did a lot of work yesterday.

CLIMANDO: So he did.

MITA: People always think it's dead easy to kill someone.

CLIMANDO: Personally I think he might have found somewhere else to sleep.

MITA: No, because blood's lucky.

CLIMANDO: No, it's salt that's lucky.

MITA: No no, I remember perfectly—blood on the ground brings luck to the chickens.

CLIMANDO: But Apal isn't a chicken.

MITA: It's a saying.

CLIMANDO: Oh.

MITA: We haven't given him the sandwich.

CLIMANDO: Nor we have.

MITA: Call him.

CLIMANDO: Apal, Apal!

APAL: What is it?

CLIMANDO: We've brought you a sandwich.

APAL: Thanks. [APAL *eats it.*]

CLIMANDO: Is it good?

APAL: Yes.

CLIMANDO: It didn't cost much.

APAL: That's good.

CLIMANDO: We've still got ten notes left.

MITA: And we've paid for the hire of the tricycle.

CLIMANDO: Now we'll be able to live in peace.

APAL: Maybe.

    Enter the OLD FLUTE PLAYER.

OLD MAN: There's a lot of cops over there.

    He points to his right.

CLIMANDO: Why?

OLD MAN: I don't know.

CLIMANDO: Perhaps there's a procession.

OLD MAN: No, because they have tanks in processions.

CLIMANDO: But you *can* have a procession without tanks.

OLD MAN: Not possible. They need tanks to make the ground level.

CLIMANDO: No, to level the ground in processions they have flags.

OLD MAN: Never, they have flags to hide the tall soldiers.

CLIMANDO: The tall ones wear short coats so's they don't look so tall.

OLD MAN: That's not right, either. They give short coats to the soldiers who haven't got any hair on their legs.

CLIMANDO: It's not true, it's not true. Soldiers who haven't got any hair on their legs aren't soldiers. They're soldieresses. And as there aren't any soldieresses, what you're saying isn't true.

OLD MAN: You're cheating again.

CLIMANDO: We'll start again if you like.

OLD MAN: No, because you reason better than I do and reason always wins.

CLIMANDO: You always say that but the truth is you're afraid and you're trying to find excuses for yourself.

OLD MAN: They're not excuses, they're truths. You cheat all the time.

CLIMANDO: No, no, no and no. Do you remember the fountain in the rue du Peigne? Yes—well, that fountain was flooded the other day when a hay cart fell into it.

OLD MAN: You just say that to impress me. But you know very well you're cheating.

CLIMANDO: I'll give you something to make up for it if you like.

OLD MAN: What?

CLIMANDO: Well um . . . um . . . um . . . [Silence.] Well . . . I don't know.

OLD MAN: You see—you don't want to give me anything. You see how you immediately climb down? You see how you dislike me? You see?

CLIMANDO is ashamed.

Don't hang your head—don't. [Pleased.] So you do realise now that you cheat and that you treat me terribly badly, do you? Tell me—do you realise?

CLIMANDO [very humbly]: Yes, I do.

OLD MAN: I knew it.

87

CLIMANDO [*becoming natural again*]: But I'd promised to give you something to make up for it . . . I know what I'll give you. I'll cut out two letters from every word you say.

OLD MAN: Two letters? [*The* OLD MAN *thinks for a few moments. Delighted.*] Two letters, eh? What about in the word *it*? And in the word *A*? And in the word SSS? And in the word TTT? And in the word ddd? And in the word ggg? And in the word E? And in the word fff? And worst of all, in the word . . .?

   No sound can be heard.

CLIMANDO: Which one?

OLD MAN: In the word . . . [*He looks as if he's saying something but no sound can be heard.*]

CLIMANDO: Which one?

MITA: Can't you hear it's the h in honour?

CLIMANDO: Oh!

OLD MAN: What've you got to say to that, eh? You were trying to cheat again. What were you thinking, eh? Answer me!

CLIMANDO: That you're older, and that as you'll die before I do, you're better at this sort of discussion than I am. Now you'll be able to win. But the most important thing is that you have a lot more experience than I have.

MITA: But you both argue very badly. As if you were half-fare passengers.

CLIMANDO: You keep out of this.

OLD MAN: You women, all you can do is make sewing machines.

   They are speaking very fast, and shouting.

CLIMANDO: And forks.

OLD MAN: Those, and forks, that's all you can produce.

CLIMANDO: And keys.

OLD MAN: Those, and keys, that's all you can produce.

CLIMANDO: And children that look like horses.

OLD MAN: Those, and children that look like horses. That's all you can produce.

CLIMANDO: And ashtrays.

OLD MAN: And ashtrays, that's right, that's all.

CLIMANDO: And wars.
OLD MAN: Those, and wars.
CLIMANDO: And blankets.
OLD MAN: Those, and blankets.
CLIMANDO: And weddings.
OLD MAN: Those, and weddings.
CLIMANDO: And ties.
OLD MAN: Those, and ties.
CLIMANDO: And emperors.
OLD MAN: Those, and emperors.
CLIMANDO: And lavatories.
OLD MAN: Those, and lavatories.
CLIMANDO: And banknotes.
OLD MAN: Those, and banknotes.
CLIMANDO: And banknotes.
OLD MAN: And banknotes.
CLIMANDO: And banknotes.
OLD MAN: And banknotes.
CLIMANDO: And banknotes.
OLD MAN: And banknotes.
CLIMANDO: And banknotes.
OLD MAN: And banknotes.
CLIMANDO: And banknotes.
OLD MAN: And banknotes.

> They go on saying 'and banknotes' *till they fall to the ground, exhausted.*

MITA: Of course, now you'll be able to boast of knowing how to conduct an argument.

OLD MAN [*trying to get up*]: She' . . . s . . .won.

MITA: Come on, pull yourselves together.

OLD MAN [*still on the ground*]: We . . . we . . . can't.

> MITA *brings her lips close to the old man's. Both he and* CLIMANDO *then make an effort and raise their hesitating heads to her. But* MITA *moves away. They fall back in despair. This is repeated several times.*

Lea . . . ve . . . us . . . a . . . lone . . . Mi . . . ta . . .

MITA [*sitting down on the bench*]: Come on, jump to it—last person up pays a forfeit.

CLIMANDO *and the* OLD FLUTE PLAYER *make a great effort and stand up.*

CLIMANDO [*in an imploring voice*]: Mita, why do you treat us so badly? What have we done to you? Mita, I love you very much.

OLD MAN: So do I—I love you too.

MITA: So do I—I love you both very much.

CLIMANDO: And Apal loves you, too.

OLD MAN: And so do the cops.

MITA: And so do I—I love Apal and the cops.

CLIMANDO: The cops?

MITA: Yes, the cops.

CLIMANDO: But what are they doing, the cops?

MITA: They're having a procession.

CLIMANDO [*to the* OLD MAN]: Go and see what the cops are doing.

OLD MAN: What'll you give me?

CLIMANDO: Nothing.

OLD MAN: Right: so long.
He goes out.

MITA: Aren't you going to the park today, to give rides to the kids?

CLIMANDO: No, it's not a holiday today.

MITA: If things go on like this you'll never have any money.

CLIMANDO: But I'll have lots of sun, and lots of sand to make castles with, and lots of leaves on the trees.

MITA: But you'll never be able to buy a potted plant.

CLIMANDO: What *I* like is sugar lumps. So white and so hard.
The OLD MAN *comes in, running.*

OLD MAN [*speaking very quickly*]: The cops are coming for you.

CLIMANDO: Us?

OLD MAN [*pointing to* APAL]: They're looking for you—you and Apal. They say you've got to stay here quietly until the chief comes.

CLIMANDO: Why?

MITA: You never listen to the cops.

CLIMANDO: But I never understand them.

MITA: Well—make an effort, then. I don't understand them either, and when I see one in one street I go down another. Yesterday, for instance, I was just picking up some papers when I suddenly saw an apple—well, I didn't waste a minute, I ate it. Not you, though. When you see a cop it doesn't make any difference to you either way, he's just like one of the family.

CLIMANDO: It's a habit.

MITA: And what a habit! Don't think that's any excuse.

OLD MAN: Of course it isn't.

CLIMANDO: But I behave nicely.

OLD MAN [*sing-song*]: Yes yes, you do. [*In his normal voice.*] And the way you cheat—what've you got to say about that?

CLIMANDO: Quite true. But I don't cheat to annoy you. If I wanted to annoy you I could pour water over your head when you're asleep, for instance.

OLD MAN: Yes yes, I agree—that would be more annoying.

MITA: But then, what *have* you done wrong? Try and remember.

CLIMANDO [*counting on his fingers*]: That business with the cops, cheating the old man, the time I . . . [*Silence.*] I can't think of anything else.

MITA: Make an effort, mate.

CLIMANDO: Ah! I remember. One day . . . [*He stops. Silence.*]

MITA: What?

OLD MAN: Go on—what? What?

MITA: Come on, be brave, Climando.

CLIMANDO: Well, one day . . .

The other two punctuate his words with nods.

. . . but that made me very sad.

MITA: Oh no, you mustn't let that make you sad.

OLD MAN: Now he claims to be sad. *You*—sad?

MITA: Well, yes, it could have made him sad.

OLD MAN: Don't you believe it. There's no reason. Does he like corn, by any chance? No—well then, how could he be sad?

MITA: He might, though—it could have made him sad. But who knows whether he writes with both hands?

OLD MAN: No one. Absolutely no one can know. Not even his own shoe. That's asking too much of us.

MITA: The thing is, you don't like Climando.

OLD MAN: Oh yes I do—very much.

MITA: Well, what have we decided? Does Climando make you sad or doesn't he?

OLD MAN: He does—very.

MITA [*to* CLIMANDO]: Climando, you make us very sad.

CLIMANDO [*with tears in his eyes*]: I make myself even sadder than I do you.

OLD MAN: Why?

CLIMANDO: I've forgotten.

OLD MAN: You've forgotten?

CLIMANDO: Yes, I've forgotten, d'you think I can't forget the things that make me sad?

OLD MAN: Of course.

MITA: But what *we* wanted to know was why the cops are looking for you.

CLIMANDO: Who?

OLD MAN: Apal and you.

CLIMANDO: Apal and me?

OLD MAN: Yes.

MITA: Yes.

CLIMANDO [*calling*] Apal, Apal.

APAL: Hmm. . . .

CLIMANDO: Apal, wake up, you've had your 18 hours.

APAL: What's going on?

CLIMANDO: The cops are looking for us.

APAL: Why?

CLIMANDO: I don't know. Don't *you* know?

APAL: Yes.

CLIMANDO: Why?

APAL: For the murder of the man with the banknotes.

MITA: Of course that's why.

CLIMANDO: But Apal, we haven't ever slept in the warm since then.

APAL: No.

92

CLIMANDO: And anyway, we didn't mean any harm when we killed him.

OLD MAN: And where's it all written down?

MITA: That's right, it has to be in writing.

OLD MAN: And signed by the most important chief in the district.

CLIMANDO: I haven't asked him.

MITA: He hasn't had time.

OLD MAN: And what d'you think's going to happen? That everything's going to fall into your lap?

CLIMANDO: But he wanted to commit suicide.

OLD MAN: The document.

MITA: You're sure to need to put that in writing, too.

CLIMANDO: I can say I've left it at home.

OLD MAN: They're not idiots, you know.

MITA: Well . . . idiots. There's nothing in the least idiotic about them. I've heard that they've got carriages that can go even faster than two horses galloping their fastest.

APAL: We killed him.

CLIMANDO: But it was the first time.

MITA [to the old man]: How many times do you have to do it before it's wrong?

OLD MAN: Once is enough.

MITA: And twice?

OLD MAN: That's enough, too.

MITA: And three times?

OLD MAN: I haven't got as far as that, I only know the first two by heart.

CLIMANDO [to APAL]: Apal—but we're good, we don't want to go to war.

APAL: Maybe.

CLIMANDO: We don't walk on the grass, either.

APAL: Pooh!

CLIMANDO: And we don't steal the kids' chocolate, either.

APAL: That doesn't help.

CLIMANDO: And when I had a stomach ache you didn't sleep, so's you could look after me.

APAL: That's not important.

CLIMANDO: What shall we do, Apal?

APAL: Sleep.

    APAL lies down. Long pause.

CLIMANDO: Don't go to sleep, Apal, they're coming to get us.

APAL: They'll wake us up all right.

CLIMANDO [*to the* OLD MAN]: What did they tell you, the cops?

OLD MAN: I've already told you.

CLIMANDO: Yes, but I've forgotten.

MITA [*sing-song voice*]: I thought I was the only one who forgot things.

CLIMANDO: It must be catching.

MITA: Well, tie a knot in your handkerchief, then.

CLIMANDO: Will that stop it being catching?

MITA: I don't remember whether that stops it being catching or whether it helps you to remember.

CLIMANDO: No one's ever taught me anything of that sort.

MITA: Of course not; all anyone ever taught you was to ride a tricycle.

CLIMANDO: It's a profession. Everyone says that a profession is the best thing you can have.

MITA: It's better to have a lot of money.

CLIMANDO: It's even better to be able to swing from branch to branch without ever falling once.

MITA: It's better still to have a thousand aeroplanes.

CLIMANDO: It's better to be able to swim underwater and not come up to the surface for 45 hours.

MITA: It's much better to have a thousand submarines.

CLIMANDO: It's better to sing all day long from the top of a tree.

MITA: It's much better to have a thousand records.

CLIMANDO: You only say all that because you don't like my having learnt to be a professional tricycle driver.

OLD MAN [*tenderly*]: Tricycle driver! Isn't that pretty! It's much prettier than playing the flute.

MITA: There's more to a tricycle than to a flute because you use your feet, too.

OLD MAN: When I have some money I shall buy myself a

tricycle and take the kids for rides in the park and stroke their heads.

CLIMANDO: And pinch their chocolate. I can see it all.

OLD MAN: You're picking on me again. You see?

MITA: Yes, Climando, you really are picking on him. Ask him to forgive you, at once.

OLD MAN [*pleased*]: That's it, that's it, let him ask me to forgive him.

MITA: Come on, Climando, ask him to forgive you.

CLIMANDO: Please forgive me. [*He adds, under his breath.*] With my fingers crossed.

OLD MAN: What did you say?

CLIMANDO: Well—please forgive me . . . [*After a very short pause, he adds.*] With my fingers crossed.

OLD MAN: What d'you say?

CLIMANDO: What d'you think I'm saying? Please forgive me . . . [*Pause.*] My fingers crossed.

OLD MAN [*open-eyed*]: With your fingers crossed?

MITA: Yes, he said he had his fingers crossed.

CLIMANDO: It's two to one, you're bound to win.

MITA: Ah yes, there're two of us.

OLD MAN: But there's one of him, that's only one less.

MITA: He could easily be ten less.

OLD MAN: If he was ten less I'd give him some sand.

MITA: And I'd give him a branch.

CLIMANDO: It's important to be one less, too. For instance, the other day Sato fell in love with a butterfly that I'd put in his pocket and as he didn't know how to declare his love he got up on to a chair and started singing about how love tastes like peaches, until the butterfly understood that as it was going to freeze the river would overflow and that it'd be better to fly over to the hospital pavilion where they keep the potatoes and where the atmosphere is sad. But the potatoes that weren't used to living in sad atmospheres grew blue flags. And in the town they made red sunflowers out of the blue flags. And green poppies out of the red sunflowers. And nightingales out of the green poppies.

He is speaking violently.

And bulbs out of the nightingales, and shoes out of the
bulbs, and feathers out of the shoes, and beadles out of
the feathers, and brooches out of the beadles, and . . .

OLD MAN [*interrupting him*[: Yes, yes, that's fine, but the
cops are over there and any minute now they'll be
coming to put you in prison. They're only waiting for
their chief.

CLIMANDO: Their chief?

OLD MAN: Yes.

CLIMANDO: Aren't I important!

OLD MAN: Not so important as I am.

CLIMANDO: But you're older.

MITA [*pointing to the right*]: Look, one of them's coming
already.

CLIMANDO: Is that the chief?

OLD MAN: No.

CLIMANDO: What's he coming for, then?

OLD MAN: He's the one that's going to deal with you until
the chief arrives.

CLIMANDO: Chiefs give me the creeps.

MITA: Yes, all they can do is sneak.

CLIMANDO: Why?

MITA: Because when they're at home their wives beat them.

CLIMANDO: Oh, how nasty of them.

Enter the POLICEMAN.

POLICEMAN: Caracatchitcho, caracotchotchitchi, tchootcha,
caracatchi.

MITA [*to the* OLD MAN]: What did he say?

OLD MAN: Tcha, tchay, tcho, or something.

MITA: How extraordinary.

OLD MAN: It's incomprehensible.

The POLICEMAN *is furious and says to* MITA *and the* OLD
FLUTE PLAYER:

POLICEMAN: Caracashitcho, caracatchotcha, tch, tchoo, tcha,
caracatchi.

MITA *and the* OLD MAN *are slightly scared and move
away from their friends.*

OLD MAN: He'd like to beat us up.

MITA: He could.

OLD MAN: Oh, he's not very big!

MITA: But he's sure to be very good at spitting.

OLD MAN: Ah!

The indignant POLICEMAN *speaks to them again and finally makes them go out.*

POLICEMAN: Caracashitcho, caracashitcho, tchi, tchoo, tcha, caracatchi.

Then he turns to APAL *and wakes him up. After which he reproaches* CLIMANDO *and* APAL *in cordial tones.*

Lamelee, la meloo, lee, la, lamela salemi, seemee, la melee.

The POLICEMAN *goes out but immediately comes back with a hammock which he lies in. He takes out a book and starts reading.*

CLIMANDO [*to* APAL]: What's going on?

APAL: We've killed.

CLIMANDO: What are you going to do?

APAL: Sleep until they come and get me.

CLIMANDO: Sleep now? And what if the cop starts beating you up just when you least expect it?

APAL: I shan't feel it so much.

CLIMANDO: I don't think you ought to go to sleep now. What for?

APAL: So as not to have to talk . . . so as not to have to hear people talking.

CLIMANDO: Don't I talk properly? D'you want me to recite some poems they taught me when I was little? . . . You never ask me to talk to you about anything in particular. I don't know what you like. Tell me to talk to you about something you like, Apal, I'm very good at talking about hens and staircases, and about grasshoppers, and about tricycles, and about storks, and about fishes and meals. Tell me, Apal, what you'd like me to talk about.

APAL: Nothing.

CLIMANDO: You're cross with me.

APAL: No I'm not.

97

CLIMANDO: Hm! I know you'd rather talk to the old man; he's had more experience and he can play the flute.

APAL: No I wouldn't.

CLIMANDO: Then you must be tired.

APAL: I've no idea.

CLIMANDO: Well, you must know, because it does matter . . . Oh, I know; you're always sleeping because you're sleepy.

APAL: Yes.

CLIMANDO: Why didn't you say so, before?

APAL: I didn't know it.

CLIMANDO [*speaking slowly and at length*]: Well, if you didn't know it before, how come you realise it now? It's incomprehensible. There must be some sort of order. First people think about what they've got to do, and then they try and do what they've thought about. If they can't do it, then they stop trying, and so they don't do it. But if they can try, then they ought to do their best to do it, to put what they've tried to do into practice, or almost, but if they do their best to put what they've tried to do into practice, or almost, and they can't solve the problem, then that's all there is to it, but if they can, then they do what they have to do without any further beating about the bush, without either thinking about the attempts they've made, or the possibility of anything being certain. But with people who don't try to think, what they attempt comes to nothing. In short, what I'm saying is that there must be some sort of order, we must know why we've said what we *have* said, what we're going to do, and what we *will* do. That's the system I use with the old flute player, and that's why I always win. *He* says I cheat. Me, cheat? That can't be true, can it?

APAL: It can't be true. [APAL *falls asleep.*]

CLIMANDO: My motto is: 'To know what you could have done and what you haven't done.' Everything, absolutely everything, in perfect order. It's not for nothing that we are thinking people. That's why I don't understand why you don't remember what you were going to do now or what you did yesterday. It all comes from a lack of order. A hell of a lack of order. We must have some sort of order, a straight, rational path, we must find the best way to behave. Apal, don't go to sleep!

APAL: I'll do my best.

CLIMANDO: I'll go on. It'll help you to understand if I give you an example. A man was carrying a pitcher of wine, and an old woman sitting by the door of a house belonging to another man from the same village said to him . . . —pay attention to this detail, it gives you the key—'why are you carrying a pitcher of wine when you could have bought four elephants?' And the man replied: 'I didn't buy four elephants because they haven't been invented yet' . . . Do you understand? Apal, don't go to sleep. What's the matter with you?

APAL: I'm sleepy.

CLIMANDO: If you go to sleep I'll get bored. And when I get bored it makes me sad.

APAL: Then I'll make an effort not to go to sleep.

CLIMANDO [*dignified*]: Don't make an effort on *my* account.

APAL: Right. [APAL *goes to sleep*].

CLIMANDO: I only said that to see what you'd say.

APAL [*sitting up*]: Ah!

CLIMANDO: Don't you think we'll be bored in prison?

APAL: Haven't thought about it.

CLIMANDO: And what shall we see?

APAL: We'll see that they're soon going to kill us.

CLIMANDO: Are they going to kill us soon?

APAL: Yes.

CLIMANDO: It's because of the man with the banknotes, isn't it?

APAL: Yes.

CLIMANDO: Will they let us ask them to forgive us?

APAL: I don't know.

CLIMANDO: And is it certain that they'll kill us?

APAL: Yes.

CLIMANDO: Well, I'm off, then.

    CLIMANDO *gets on to the tricycle, all set to escape.*

99

POLICEMAN [*reproachfully*]: Caracatchitcho, caracotchotcho, tcha, tche, tchi, caracatchi.

> CLIMANDO *gets off the tricycle and sits down again by* APAL.

CLIMANDO: Then it *is* true that they'll kill us?

APAL: Yes.

CLIMANDO: Both of us?

APAL: Yes.

CLIMANDO: Isn't one enough?

APAL: No.

CLIMANDO: But *we* only killed one person.

APAL: Yes.

> *Pause.*

CLIMANDO: Well you needn't think I'm so pleased at being killed now.

APAL: It doesn't make any difference.

CLIMANDO: Oh go on! Now of all times! When I was least expecting it.

> *Silence.*

And what do you think about it?

APAL: About what?

CLIMANDO: About them killing us.

APAL: Not much.

CLIMANDO: Apal, I'm sorry about this—for you.

APAL: Thanks.

CLIMANDO: Don't think I'm so terribly sorry about myself— what annoys me is that it should be so sudden. I'm sorrier about it for you, Apal.

APAL: Pooh, don't let it worry you.

CLIMANDO: What would you like me to do for you?

APAL: Let me sleep.

CLIMANDO: Won't you be afraid?

APAL: No.

CLIMANDO: Right, goodbye, have a good rest.

> CLIMANDO *walks round the* POLICEMAN *several times, trying to read the title of his book.* APAL *sleeps. Enter* MITA, *on all fours. She is certainly afraid the* POLICEMAN *might see her.*

MITA: Psst!

CLIMANDO: Mita.

MITA *moves towards* CLIMANDO.

Hide, don't let the cop see you.

MITA: He won't see me, he's reading.

CLIMANDO: Yes, but he reads very quickly.

MITA: I read more quickly than he does.

CLIMANDO: All right, but be careful.

MITA: What are they going to do to you?

MITA *moves nearer, her head down and keeping as close to the ground as possible.*

CLIMANDO: They're going to put us in prison and then they'll kill us.

MITA [*terrified*]: Kill you?

CLIMANDO: Are you starting again with your superstitions?

MITA: No, Climando. [*Pause.*] Then you must find some way of saving yourself from going to prison.

CLIMANDO: It's very difficult.

MITA: You *are* in a mess.

CLIMANDO [*joyfully*]: I've got very long legs, I could run.

MITA: And what if they don't know you've got long legs?

CLIMANDO: I'll tell them.

MITA: And what if they catch you?

CLIMANDO: I hadn't thought of that. It'd be better if I told them some stories.

MITA: Yes, do, you know some lovely tales.

CLIMANDO: That's it; if they catch me I'll tell them a story.

MITA [*enthusiastically*]: The one about the little donkey that went to Texas and pricked up his ears and made them V-shaped, you tell it so well.

CLIMANDO: Oh no, not that one, they'll say it's politics.

MITA [*trying to think*]: Right, then the story about the horse that fell in love with a telescope, thinking it was a lamb.

CLIMANDO: They won't like that story either, they'll say they don't understand, and then they'll want to burn me alive.

MITA: Yes, that's the trouble with telling things people don't understand.

CLIMANDO: Which one d'you think I ought to tell?

MITA: Tell them you love me.

CLIMANDO: Oh yes! Isn't that nice! . . . But for that I'd need to have you with me, so that when I say: 'I love her knees, they're so white and smooth and big,' I can lift up your skirts and show them to them. And so that when I say: 'She has a sweet little blond moustache that I like very much,' I can show them. And when I say that your eyes are green, and as pretty as the tricycle was before it got so ugly, and that your hair is as blond as fresh bread, I'll need you to be there, so that we can see each other and they can see us. And when I tell them . . . [*he moves closer to* MITA] that I kiss you . . .

POLICEMAN [*interupting them*]: Caracatchitchipiripipipipi. *The* POLICEMAN *speaks without raising his head from his book.*

CLIMANDO: What did he say?

MITA: Caracatchitcha paripipipi.

CLIMANDO: No no, he said caratchisho piripipipe.

MITA: Don't contradict me.

CLIMANDO: I'm not contradicting you. What I heard was caracatchiche piripipipe.

MITA: How contrary you are, you have a mania for arguing.

POLICEMAN: Caracatchitchi, piripipipi.

    CLIMANDO *goes up to the* POLICEMAN *timidly.*

CLIMANDO: Did you say caracatchishe piripipipe or caracatchitcha parapipipi?

    The POLICEMAN *clicks his tongue four times and doesn't listen to* CLIMANDO. CLIMANDO, *wanting to get into the* POLICEMAN'S *good books, takes various objects out of the box tricycle, and presents them to him humbly; a spanner, a cardboard box, two glass tubes, a chipped chamber pot, some pages from a calendar, and a tin of sardines. The* POLICEMAN *brushes him away with the back of his hand, without stopping reading for a single moment.*

[*To* MITA]: He must have seen you're with me. Try and hide—and specially the bottom of your skirt. I'll walk about a bit, to hide you.

    CLIMANDO *walks up and down.*

CLIMANDO: The duties of a tricycle driver. . . .

> CLIMANDO *is speaking in a sing-song voice like a school-boy.*

are . . . definitions . . . classes . . . relations with bachelors . . . [*to* MITA] I can't go on like that because he'll find out that I don't know it.

MITA: Say 'no news' several times, then.

CLIMANDO [*walking up and down*]: No news, no news, no news.

> CLIMANDO *continues to walk up and down, saying* 'no news' *over and over again.*

MITA [*softly*]: Listen, Climando, say it in different ways, or he'll notice that you keep saying the same thing.

CLIMANDO [*saying it in a different tone of voice each time*]: No news, no news. [CLIMANDO *repeats it several times.*] It's all very well, but it makes me tired.

MITA: You mustn't get tired, though.

CLIMANDO: But I'm going to die soon.

MITA: So you think that entitles you to do whatever comes into your head?

CLIMANDO: That'd be the last straw.

MITA: You can't do it, I tell you. I'm going to die, too, and so's Apal, and the old flute player, but that doesn't mean that *we* do what we like.

CLIMANDO: Well I never.

MITA: Do you think, by any chance, that it gives you any right to know the date?

CLIMANDO [*terrified*]: I don't know.

MITA: It's just that someone's done you a favour.

CLIMANDO: I didn't realise.

MITA: And anyway you'll die painlessly, without any trouble, like almost everyone dies.

CLIMANDO: But if they're going to kill me they'll hurt me.

MITA: Not much. Because it's true they'll hurt you, but by the time you feel it you'll be dead.

CLIMANDO: That's fine.

MITA: Wonderful.

CLIMANDO: And what then?

MITA: Then you'll go to heaven.

CLIMANDO [*tenderly*]: If it exists . . . I'll go to heaven with the lambs and with the buses, and with the little donkeys that prick up their ears and make them V-shaped, and with the men who drive tricycles, and with the kids in the park, and old men who play the flute and the violin, and with the leaves on the trees.

MITA [*interrupting him*]: I shall go, too.

CLIMANDO: Yes, and Apal.

MITA: Apal? Not Apal. He knows too much.

CLIMANDO: But he's good. And he sleeps all day long so that no one should realise that he knows so many things.

MITA: But he won't sleep in heaven. That'd be a fine thing! You must realise that he'll be taking someone else's place.

CLIMANDO: Tell me, Mita—where shall we pee in heaven?

MITA: People don't pee in heaven.

CLIMANDO: Oh I *am* sorry.

MITA: You'll get used to it.

CLIMANDO [*enthusiastically*]: Mita, you're so intelligent, you know everything.

MITA: Of course I do.

CLIMANDO: And what'll I do in heaven without you?

MITA: Don't worry, you won't be so badly off. It'll be worse for me, I shan't see your pretty boots any more.

CLIMANDO: If you like, Mita, I'll let you have my turn and they can kill you instead of me.

MITA: What *do* you think? That the cops are idiots and won't notice?

CLIMANDO: It's quite simple, you dress up in my clothes and when they say: 'Climando, we're going to kill you,' you say 'Present.'

MITA: But I can't tell a lie. Because if you want to go to heaven you mustn't lie.

CLIMANDO: We nearly made a terrible mistake!

MITA: You realise how I have to take care of all the details?

CLIMANDO: Yes.

MITA: If I hadn't realised I'd have been in hell in no time.

CLIMANDO [*horrified*]: Don't say that word: if I were to repeat it I'd get myself into terrible trouble.

MITA: It's not that word, it's crust. Have you forgotten it already?

CLIMANDO: Yes.

MITA: You must remember—I say it several times at the end of every month, to make up for your not wanting to say it.

CLIMANDO: Have you said it this month yet?

MITA: No.

CLIMANDO: Well, you're just saying it.

MITA: Crust, crust, crust: three times are enough.

CLIMANDO: How can we know? I once heard someone say that we ought to wear cups on our head to overcome the force of gravity.

MITA: Yes, that gives us a clue, but I insist on telling you that three times are enough.

CLIMANDO: You're always right.

MITA: Because you never know how to argue.

CLIMANDO: That's true enough. Tell me, what are you going to do when I'm dead?

MITA: Not see you any more.

CLIMANDO: I want you to wear mourning for me. All dressed in black, with a black band as well, on your sleeve.

MITA: No, mourning makes me want to giggle.

CLIMANDO: Aren't you brave! Even braver than the legionnaires who laugh at death. You even laugh at mourning.

MITA: What I *can* do, if you like, is always eat shrimps.

CLIMANDO: You'd rather eat a sardine than shrimps all the time.

MITA: You always criticise me because I eat so little.

CLIMANDO: No, Mita, I want to do what you'd like . . . specially when I think that it won't be long before I'm happy in heaven with the sheep and the little donkeys.

MITA: I want to do a lot for you, too.

CLIMANDO: Then it'd be better not to do anything at all, because that way we won't have to put ourselves out.

105

MITA: Don't we love each other! Don't we understand each other!

CLIMANDO [*amorously*]: Yes.

> *Enter the* OLD FLUTE PLAYER, *hanging his head so as not to be seen.*

OLD MAN: The chief's arrived; he's just over there.

MITA: Tell Apal, then; he ought to know.

CLIMANDO: Apal would rather sleep.

OLD MAN: They say they're going to kill you; I'm so glad.

MITA: So'm I.

CLIMANDO: Me too.

OLD MAN: But you oughtn't to be glad. Just imagine how amusing it's going to be for you!

CLIMANDO: You're the one who oughtn't to be pleased. I don't think it'll be so amusing for you, either.

OLD MAN: I'm pleased because then I shan't argue with you any more and you won't win any more.

MITA: That's an important reason.

CLIMANDO: Is that all?

MITA: Come on, tell the truth, don't be ashamed of it—say that you do love him, really.

OLD MAN [*very much ashamed*]: Well, only a little bit, only a very little bit. That much. [*He points to his nail.*]

MITA [*to* CLIMANDO]: And what about you?

CLIMANDO: That much too.

OLD MAN: I'll leave you the flute, if you like, so you can die to music. [*He gives him his flute.*]

CLIMANDO [*taking it*]: Right.

OLD MAN: It won't disgust you?

CLIMANDO: No, because I wear boots specially for that.

OLD MAN: But what you need is a fur coat for that.

CLIMANDO: But I've got a couple of pairs of pliers for that.

OLD MAN: But you need a couple of cauliflowers for that.

CLIMANDO: But I've got three toothpicks for that.

OLD MAN: But you need three raincoats for that.

CLIMANDO: But I've got four typewriters for that.

OLD MAN: But you need four pairs of cotton pyjamas for that.

CLIMANDO: But I've got five socks for that.

All these last speeches overlap.

OLD MAN: But you need ten ostriches for that.

CLIMANDO [*to* MITA]: Tell him that I can't have five socks because socks come in pairs.

MITA [*talking into the old man's ear*]: Tell him it's not true he can't have five socks because socks come in pairs.

OLD MAN [*very pleased*]: It's not true, it's not true, it's not true. You can't have five socks because socks come in pairs; I've won.

CLIMANDO: You cheated.

OLD MAN: No I didn't.

Enter the POLICE CHIEF.

POLICEMAN [*saluting his superior*]: Cara.

The two policemen talk to each other.

CLIMANDO: Get up, Apal, they've come for us.

APAL: I'm coming.

CLIMANDO: As they're going to kill me, Mita, I'll give you my boots.

CLIMANDO *takes off his boots; his feet are bare. He gives the boots to* MITA.

MITA [*putting them on*]: Pity they've got holes in them.

CLIMANDO [*to the* OLD MAN]: And I leave you the tricycle.

OLD MAN [*enthusiastically*]: The tricycle! Can I stroke the kids?

CLIMANDO: Yes.

OLD MAN: And will you leave me the bells, too?

CLIMANDO: Yes.

OLD MAN: And the pages from the calendar?

CLIMANDO: Yes.

OLD MAN: And the pot?

CLIMANDO: Yes.

OLD MAN: And the pliers?

CLIMANDO: Yes.

OLD MAN: And the wire?

CLIMANDO: Yes. But don't ask me for any more or you'll get to be like a tortoise.

OLD MAN: That's true.

MITA [*to* APAL]: Are they going to kill you, too?

APAL: Looks like it.

MITA: Give me your jacket, then.

APAL: My jacket?

MITA: Yes.

APAL: I'll be cold. It's winter.

MITA: Pooh, you've so little time left to live.

APAL: All right.

He takes off his jacket and gives it to MITA. THE POLICE-
MEN *stop talking. The first* POLICEMAN *goes over to* MITA
and the OLD MAN *and separates them from their friends
by yelling*:

POLICEMAN: Caracatchisho, piripipipi.

The POLICE CHIEF *handcuffs* APAL *and* CLIMANDO. APAL,
without his jacket, is shivering with cold. CLIMANDO
moves his naked toes to try and warm them. The OLD
FLUTE PLAYER *looks at the tricycle.* MITA *looks at the
boots and the jacket.*

Atara!

The POLICEMAN *pushes* APAL *and* CLIMANDO *to get them
started. With the* CHIEF *and the* POLICEMAN *on either side
of them they all four go off.* MITA *and the* OLD MAN *are
left on the stage.* MITA *puts on* APAL'S *jacket. The* OLD
FLUTE PLAYER, *helped by* MITA, *gets into the box part of
the tricycle.* MITA *rides it, the* OLD MAN *rings the bells,
the tricycle crosses the stage and goes off.*

CURTAIN

PICNIC ON THE BATTLEFIELD

translated from the French
by Barbara Wright

CHARACTERS

ZAPO	*A soldier*
MONSIEUR TÉPAN	*The soldier's father*
MADAME TÉPAN	*The soldier's mother*
ZÉPO	*An enemy soldier*
FIRST STRETCHER BEARER	
SECOND STRETCHER BEARER	

Picnic on the Battlefield *premièred on April 25, 1959, in Paris, at the Théâtre de Lutèce, directed by Jean-Marie Serreau.*

PICNIC ON THE BATTLEFIELD

*A battlefield. The stage is covered with barbed wire and
sandbags.*
*The battle is at its height. Rifle shots, exploding bombs
and machine guns can be heard.*
*ZAPO is alone on the stage, flat on his stomach, hidden
among the sandbags. He is very frightened. The sound of
the fighting stops. Silence.*
*ZAPO takes a ball of wool and some needles out of a
canvas workbag and starts knitting a pullover, which is
already quite far advanced. The field telephone, which is
by his side, suddenly starts ringing.*

ZAPO: Hallo, hallo . . . yes, Captain . . . yes, I'm the sentry of
sector 47 . . . Nothing new, Captain . . . Excuse me,
Captain, but when's the fighting going to start again?
And what am I supposed to do with the hand-grenades?
Do I chuck them in front of me or behind me? . . . Don't
get me wrong, I didn't mean to annoy you . . . Captain, I
really feel terribly lonely, couldn't you send me someone
to keep me company? . . . Even if it's only a nanny-goat?
[*The Captain is obviously severely reprimanding him.*]
Whatever you say, Captain, whatever you say.

    ZAPO hangs up. He mutters to himself. Silence. Enter
MONSIEUR *and* MADAME TÉPAN, *carrying baskets as if
they are going to a picnic. They address their son, who
has his back turned and doesn't see them come in.*

MONS. T. [*ceremoniously*]: Stand up, my son, and kiss your
mother on the brow. [ZAPO, *surprised, gets up and kisses
his mother very respectfully on the forehead. He is about
to speak, but his father doesn't give him a chance.*] And
now, kiss *me.*

ZAPO: But, dear Father and dear Mother, how did you dare to come all this way, to such a dangerous place? You must leave at once.

MONS. T.: So you think you've got something to teach your father about war and danger, do you? All this is just a game to me. How many times—to take the first example that comes to mind—have I got off an underground train while it was still moving.

MME. T.: We thought you must be bored, so we came to pay you a little visit. This war must be a bit tedious, after all.

ZAPO: It all depends.

MONS. T.: I know exactly what happens. To start with you're attracted by the novelty of it all. It's fun to kill people, and throw hand-grenades about, and wear uniforms—you feel smart, but in the end you get bored stiff. You'd have found it much more interesting in my day. Wars were much more lively, much more highly coloured. And then, the best thing was that there were horses, plenty of horses. It was a real pleasure; if the Captain ordered us to attack, there we all were immediately, on horseback, in our red uniforms. It was a sight to be seen. And then there were the charges at the gallop, sword in hand, and suddenly you found yourself face to face with the enemy, and he was equal to the occasion too—with his horses—there were always horses, lots of horses, with their well-rounded rumps—in his highly-polished boots, and his green uniform.

MME. T.: No no, the enemy uniform wasn't green. It was blue. I remember distinctly that it was blue.

MONS. T.: I tell you it was green.

MME. T.: When I was little, how many times did I go out on to the balcony to watch the battle and say to the neighbour's little boy: 'I bet you a gum-drop the blues win.' And the blues were our enemies.

MONS. T.: Oh well, you must be right, then.

MME. T.: I've always liked battles. As a child I always said that when I grew up I wanted to be a Colonel of dragoons. But my mother wouldn't hear of it, you know how she will stick to her principles at all costs.

MONS. T.: Your mother's just a half-wit.

ZAPO: I'm sorry, but you really must go. You can't come into a war unless you're a soldier.

MONS. T.: I don't give a damn, we came here to have a picnic with you in the country and to enjoy our Sunday.

MME. T.: And I've prepared an excellent meal, too. Sausage, hard-boiled eggs—you know how you like them!—ham sandwiches, red wine, salad, and cakes.

ZAPO: All right, let's have it your way. But if the Captain comes he'll be absolutely furious. Because he isn't at all keen on us having visits when we're at the front. He never stops telling us: 'Discipline and hand-grenades are what's wanted in a war, not visits.'

MONS. T.: Don't worry, I'll have a few words to say to your Captain.

ZAPO: And what if we have to start fighting again?

MONS. T.: You needn't think that'll frighten me, it won't be the first fighting I've seen. Now if only it was battles on horseback! Times have changed, you can't understand. [*Pause.*] We came by motor bike. No one said a word to us.

ZAPO: They must have thought you were the referees.

MONS. T.: We had enough trouble getting through, though. What with all the tanks and jeeps.

MME. T.: And do you remember the bottle-neck that cannon caused, just when we got here?

MONS. T.: You mustn't be surprised at anything in wartime, everyone knows that.

MME. T.: Good, let's start our meal.

MONS. T.: You're quite right, I feel as hungry as a hunter. It's the smell of gunpowder.

MME. T.: We'll sit on the rug while we're eating.

ZAPO: Can I bring my rifle with me?

MME. T.: You leave your rifle alone. It's not good manners to bring your rifle to table with you. [*Pause.*] But you're

113

absolutely filthy, my boy. How on earth did you get into such a state? Let's have a look at your hands.

ZAPO [*ashamed, holding out his hands*]: I had to crawl about on the ground during the manoeuvres.

MME. T.: And what about your ears?

ZAPO: I washed them this morning.

MME. T.: Well that's all right, then. And your teeth? [*He shows them.*] Very good. Who's going to give her little boy a great big kiss for cleaning his teeth so nicely? [*To her husband*] Well, go on, kiss your son for cleaning his teeth so nicely. [M. TÉPAN *kisses his son.*] Because, you know, there's one thing I *will* not have, and that's making fighting a war an excuse for not washing.

ZAPO: Yes, Mother.

> *They eat.*

MONS. T.: Well, my boy, did you make a good score?

ZAPO: When?

MONS. T.: In the last few days, of course.

ZAPO: Where?

MONS. T.: At the moment, since you're fighting a war.

ZAPO: No, nothing much. I didn't make a good score. Hardly ever scored a bull.

MONS. T.: Which are you best at shooting, enemy horses or soldiers?

ZAPO: No, not horses, there aren't any horses any more.

MONS. T.: Well, soldiers then?

ZAPO: Could be.

MONS. T.: Could be? Aren't you sure?

ZAPO: Well you see . . . I shoot without taking aim, [*pause*] and at the same time I say a Pater Noster for the chap I've shot.

MONS. T.: You must be braver than that. Like your father.

MME. T.: I'm going to put a record on.

> *She puts a record on the gramophone—a pasodoble. All three are sitting on the ground, listening.*

MONS. T.: That really *is* music. Yes indeed, olé!

> *The music continues. Enter an enemy soldier: ZÉPO. He is dressed like ZAPO. The only difference is the colour of*

their uniforms. ZÉPO *is in green and* ZAPO *is in grey.*
ZÉPO *listens to the music openmouthed. He is behind the*
family so they can't see him. The record ends. As he
gets up ZAPO *discoveres* ZÉPO. *Both put their hands up.*
M. *and* MME. TÉPAN *look at them in surprise.*

What's going on?

> ZAPO *reacts—he hesitates. Finally, looking as if he's*
> *made up his mind, he points his rifle at* ZÉPO.

ZAPO: Hands up!

> ZÉPO *puts his hands up even higher, looking even more*
> *terrified.* ZAPO *doesn't know what to do. Suddenly he*
> *goes quickly over to* ZÉPO *and touches him gently on the*
> *shoulder, like a child playing a game of 'tag'.*

Got you! [*To his father, very pleased.*] There we are! A
prisoner!

MONS. T.: Fine. And now what're you going to do with him?

ZAPO: I don't know, but, well, could be—they might make
me a corporal.

MONS. T.: In the meantime you'd better tie him up.

ZAPO: Tie him up? Why?

MONS. T.: Prisoners always get tied up!

ZAPO: How?

MONS. T.: Tie up his hands.

MME. T.: Yes, there's no doubt about that, you must tie up
his hands, I've always seen them do that.

ZAPO: Right. [*To the prisoner.*] Put your hands together, if
you please.

ZÉPO: Don't hurt me too much.

ZAPO: I won't.

ZÉPO: Ow! You're hurting me.

MONS. T.: Now now, don't maltreat your prisoner.

MME. T.: Is that the way I brought you up? How many times
have I told you that we must be considerate to our fellow-
men?

ZAPO: I didn't do it on purpose. [*To* ZÉPO.] And like that,
does it hurt?

ZÉPO: No, it's all right like that.

115

MONS. T.: Tell him straight out, say what you mean, don't mind us.

ZÉPO: It's all right like that.

MONS. T.: Now his feet.

ZAPO: His feet as well, whatever next?

MONS. T.: Didn't they teach you the rules?

ZAPO: Yes.

MONS. T.: Well then!

ZAPO [*very politely, to* ZÉPO]: Would you be good enough to sit on the ground, please?

ZÉPO: Yes, but don't hurt me.

MME. T.: You'll see, he'll take a dislike to you.

ZAPO: No he won't, no he won't. I'm not hurting you, am I?

ZÉPO: No, that's perfect.

ZAPO: Papa, why don't you take a photo of the prisoner on the ground and me with my foot on his stomach?

MONS. T.: Oh yes, that'd look good.

ZÉPO: Oh no, not that!

MME. T.: Say yes, don't be obstinate.

ZÉPO: No. I said no, and no it is.

MME. T.: But just a little teeny weeny photo, what harm could that do you? And we could put it in the dining room, next to the life-saving certificate my husband won thirteen years ago.

ZÉPO: No—you won't shift me.

ZAPO: But why won't you let us?

ZÉPO: I'm engaged. And if she sees the photo one day, she'll say I don't know how to fight a war properly.

ZAPO: No she won't, all you'll need to say is that it isn't you, it's a panther.

MME. T.: Come on, do say yes.

ZÉPO: All right then. But only to please you.

ZAPO: Lie down flat.

    ZÉPO *lies down.* ZAPO *puts a foot on his stomach and grabs his rifle with a martial air.*

MME. T.: Stick your chest out a bit further.

ZAPO: Like this?

MME. T.: Yes, like that, and don't breathe.

116

MONS. T.: Try and look like a hero.

ZAPO: What d'you mean, like a hero?

MONS. T.: It's quite simple; try and look like the butcher does when he's boasting about his successes with the girls.

ZAPO: Like this?

MONS. T.: Yes, like that.

MME. T.: The most important thing is to puff your chest out and not breathe.

ZÉPO: Have you nearly finished?

MONS. T.: Just be patient a moment. One . . . two . . . three.

ZAPO: I hope I'll come out well.

MME. T.: Yes, you looked very martial.

MONS. T.: You were fine.

MME. T.: It makes me want to have my photo taken with you.

MONS. T.: Now there's a good idea.

ZAPO: Right. I'll take it if you like.

MME. T.: Give me your helmet to make me look like a soldier.

ZÉPO: I don't want any more photos. Even one's far too many.

ZAPO: Don't take it like that. After all, what harm can it do you?

ZÉPO: It's my last word.

MONS. T. [to his wife]: Don't press the point, prisoners are always very sensitive. If we go on he'll get cross and spoil our fun.

ZAPO: Right, what're we going to do with him, then?

MME. T.: We could invite him to lunch. What do you say?

MONS. T.: I don't see why not.

ZAPO [to ZÉPO]: Well, will you have lunch with us, then?

ZÉPO: Er . . .

MONS. T.: We brought a good bottle with us.

ZÉPO: Oh well, all right then.

MME. T.: Make yourself at home, don't be afraid to ask for anything you want.

ZÉPO: All right.

MONS. T.: And what about you, did you make a good score?

ZÉPO: When?

MONS. T.: In the last few days, of course.

ZÉPO: Where?

MONS. T.: At the moment, since you're fighting a war.

ZÉPO: No, nothing much. I didn't make a good score, hardly ever scored a bull.

MONS. T.: Which are you best at shooting? Enemy horses or soldiers?

ZÉPO: No, not horses, there aren't any horses any more.

MONS. T.: Well, soldiers then?

ZÉPO: Could be.

MONS. T.: Could be? Aren't you sure?

ZÉPO: Well you see . . . I shoot without taking aim [*pause*], and at the same time I say an Ave Maria for the chap I've shot.

ZAPO: An Ave Maria? I'd have thought you'd have said a Pater Noster.

ZÉPO: No, always an Ave Maria. [*Pause.*] It's shorter.

MONS. T.: Come come, my dear fellow, you must be brave.

MME. T. [*to* ZÉPO]: We can untie you if you like.

ZÉPO: No, don't bother, it doesn't matter.

MONS. T.: Don't start getting stand-offish with us now. If you'd like us to untie you, say so.

MME. T.: Make yourself comfortable.

ZÉPO: Well, if that's how you feel, you can untie my feet, but it's only to please you.

MONS. T.: Zapo, untie him.

ZAPO *unties him.*

MME. T.: Well, do you feel better?

ZÉPO: Yes, of course. I really am putting you to a lot of inconvenience.

MONS. T.: Not at all, just make yourself at home. And if you'd like us to untie your hands you only have to say so.

ZÉPO: No, not my hands, I don't want to impose upon you.

MONS. T: No no, my dear chap, no no. I tell you, it's no trouble at all.

ZÉPO: Right . . . Well then, untie my hands too. But only for lunch, eh? I don't want you to think that you give me an inch and I take an ell.

MONS. T.: Untie his hands, son.

MME. T.: Well, since our distinguished prisoner is so charming, we're going to have a marvellous day in the country.

ZÉPO: Don't call me your distinguished prisoner, just call me your prisoner.

MME. T.: Won't that embarrass you?

ZÉPO: No no, not at all.

MONS. T.: Well, I must say you're modest.

Noise of aeroplanes.

ZAPO: Aeroplanes. They're sure to be coming to bomb us.

ZAPO *and* ZÉPO *throw themselves on the sandbags and hide.*

[*To his parents*]:Take cover. The bombs will fall on you.

The noise of the aeroplanes overpowers all the other noises. Bombs immediately start to fall. Shells explode very near the stage but not on it. A deafening noise.

ZAPO *and* ZÉPO *are cowering down between the sandbags.*

M. TÉPAN *goes on talking calmly to his wife, and she answers in the same unruffled way. We can't hear what they are saying because of the bombing.* MME. TÉPAN *goes over to one of the baskets and takes an umbrella out of it. She opens it.* M. *and* MME. TÉPAN *shelter under it as if it were raining. They are standing up. They shift rhythmically from one foot to the other and talk about their personal affairs.*

The bombing continues.

Finally the aeroplanes go away. Silence.

M. TÉPAN *stretches an arm outside the umbrella to make sure that nothing more is falling from the heavens.*

MONS. T. [*to his wife*]: You can shut your umbrella.

MME. TÉPAN *does so. They both go over to their son and tap him lightly on the behind with the umbrella.*

Come on, out you come. The bombing's over.

ZAPO *and* ZÉPO *come out of their hiding place.*

ZAPO: Didn't you get hit?

MONS. T.: What d'you think could happen to your father? [*Proudly.*] Little bombs like that! Don't make me laugh!

119

Enter, left, two RED CROSS SOLDIERS. *They are carrying a stretcher.*

1st STRETCHER BEARER: Any dead here?

ZAPO: No, no one around these parts.

1st STRETCHER BEARER: Are you sure you've looked properly?

ZAPO: Sure.

1st STRETCHER BEARER: And there isn't a single person dead?

ZAPO: I've already told you there isn't.

1st STRETCHER BEARER: No one wounded, even?

ZAPO: Not even that.

2nd STRETCHER BEARER [*to the* 1st S. B.]: Well, now we're in a mess! [*To* ZAPO *persuasively.*] Just look again, search everywhere, and see if you can't find us a stiff.

1st STRETCHER BEARER: Don't keep on about it, they've told you quite clearly there aren't any.

2nd STRETCHER BEARER: What a lousy trick!

ZAPO: I'm terribly sorry. I promise you I didn't do it on purpose.

2nd STRETCHER BEARER: That's what they all say. That no one's dead and that they didn't do it on purpose.

1st STRETCHER BEARER: Oh, let the chap alone!

MONS. T. [*obligingly*]: We should be only too pleased to help you. At your service.

2nd STRETCHER BEARER: Well, really, if things go on like this I don't know what the Captain will say to us.

MONS. T.: But what's it all about?

2nd STRETCHER BEARER: Quite simply that the others' wrists are aching with carting so many corpses and wounded men about, and that we haven't found any yet. And it's not because we haven't looked!

MONS. T.: Well yes, that really is annoying. [*To* ZAPO.] Are you quite sure no one's dead?

ZAPO: Obviously, Papa.

MONS. T.: Have you looked under all the sandbags?

ZAPO: Yes, Papa.

MONS. T. [*angrily*]: Well then, you might as well say straight out that you don't want to lift a finger to help these gentlemen, when they're so nice, too!

1st STRETCHER BEARER: Don't be angry with him. Let him be. We must just hope we'll have more luck in another trench and that all the lot'll be dead.

MONS. T.: I should be delighted.

MME. T.: Me too. There's nothing I like more than people who put their hearts into their work.

MONS. T. [*indignantly, addressing his remarks to the wings*]: Then is no one going to do anything for these gentlemen?

ZAPO: If it only rested with me, it'd already be done.

ZÉPO: I can say the same.

MONS. T.: But look here, is neither of you even wounded?

ZAPO [*ashamed*]: No, not me.

MONS. T. [*to* ZÉPO]: What about you?

ZÉPO [*ashamed*]: Me neither. I never have any luck.

MME. T. [*pleased*]: Now I remember! This morning, when I was peeling the onions, I cut my finger. Will that do you?

MONS. T.: Of course it will! [*Enthusiastically.*] They'll take you off at once!

1st STRETCHER BEARER: No, that won't work. With ladies it doesn't work.

MONS. T.: We're no further advanced, then.

1st STRETCHER BEARER: Never mind.

2nd STRETCHER BEARER: We may be able to make up for it in the other trenches.

They start to go off.

MONS. T.: Don't worry! If we find a dead man we'll keep him for you! No fear of us giving him to anyone else!

2nd STRETCHER BEARER: Thank you very much, sir.

MONS. T.: Quite all right, old chap, think nothing of it.

The two STRETCHER BEARERS *say goodbye. All four answer them. The* STRETCHER BEARERS *go out.*

MMT. T.: That's what's so pleasant about spending a Sunday in the country. You always meet such nice people. [*Pause.*] But why are you enemies?

ZÉPO: I don't know, I'm not very well educated.

MME. T.: Was it by birth, or did you become enemies afterwards?

ZÉPO: I don't know, I don't know anything about it.

MONS. T. Well then, how did you come to be in the war?

ZÉPO: One day, at home, I was just mending my mother's iron, a man came and asked me: 'Are you Zépo?' 'Yes.' 'Right, you must come to the war.' And so I asked him: 'But what war?' and he said: 'Don't you read the papers then? You're just a peasant!' I told him I did read the papers but not the war bits. . . .

ZAPO: Just how it was with me—exactly how it was with me.

MONS. T.: Yes, they came to fetch you too.

MME. T.: No, it wasn't quite the same; that day you weren't mending an iron, you were mending the car.

MONS. T.: I was talking about the rest of it. [*To* ZÉPO.] Go on, what happened then?

ZÉPO: Then I told him I had a fiancée and that if I didn't take her to the pictures on Sundays she wouldn't like it. He said that that wasn't the least bit important.

ZAPO: Just how it was with me—exactly how it was with me.

ZÉPO: And then my father came down and he said I couldn't go to the war because I didn't have a horse.

ZAPO: Just what my father said.

ZÉPO: The man said you didn't need a horse any more, and I asked him if I could take my fiancée with me. He said no. Then I asked whether I could take my aunt with me so that she could make me one of her custards on Thursdays; I'm very fond of them.

MME. T. [*realising that she'd forgotten it*]: Oh! The custard!

ZÉPO: He said no again.

ZAPO: Same as with me.

ZÉPO: And ever since then I've been alone in the trench nearly all the time.

MME. T.: I think you and your distinguished prisoner might play together this afternoon, as you're so close to each other and so bored.

ZAPO: Oh no, Mother, I'm too afraid, he's an enemy.

MONS. T.: Now now, you mustn't be afraid.

ZAPO: If you only knew what the General was saying about the enemy!

MME. T.: What did he say?

ZAPO: He said the enemy are very nasty people. When they take prisoners they put little stones in their shoes so that it hurts them to walk.

MME. T.: How awful! What barbarians!

MONS. T. [*indignantly*, *to* ZÉPO]: And aren't you ashamed to belong to an army of criminals?

ZÉPO: I haven't done anything. I don't do anybody any harm.

MME. T.: He was trying to take us in, pretending to be such a little saint!

MONS. T.: We oughtn't to have untied him. You never know, we only need to turn our backs and he'll be putting a stone in our shoes.

ZÉPO: Don't be so nasty to me.

MONS. T.: What d'you think we *should* be, then? I'm indignant. I know what I'll do. I'll go and find the Captain and ask him to let me fight in the war.

ZAPO: He won't let you, you're too old.

MONS. T.: Then I'll buy myself a horse and a sword and come and fight on my own account.

MME. T.: Bravo! If I were a man I'd do the same.

ZÉPO: Don't be like that with me, Madame. Anyway I'll tell you something—our General told us the same thing about you.

MME. T.: How could he dare tell such a lie!

ZAPO: No—but the same thing really?

ZÉPO: Yes, the same thing.

MONS. T.: Perhaps it was the same man who talked to you both?

MME. T.: Well if it was the same man he might at least have said something different. That's a fine thing—saying the same thing to everyone!

MONS. T. [*to* ZÉPO, *in a different tone of voice*]: Another little drink?

MME. T.: I hope you liked our lunch?

MONS. T.: In any case, it was better than last Sunday.

ZÉPO: What happened?

MONS. T.: Well, we went to the country and we put the food on the rug. While we'd got our backs turned a cow ate up all our lunch, and the napkins as well.

ZÉPO: What a greedy cow!

MONS. T.: Yes, but afterwards, to get our own back, we ate the cow.

    They laugh.

ZAPO [*to* ZÉPO]: They couldn't have been very hungry after that!

MONS. T.: Cheers! [*They all drink.*]

MME. T. [*to* ZÉPO]: And what do you do to amuse yourself in the trench?

ZÉPO: I spend my time making flowers out of rags, to amuse myself. I get terribly bored.

MME. T.: And what do you do with the flowers?

ZÉPO: At the beginning I used to send them to my fiancée, but one day she told me that the greenhouse and the cellar were already full of them and that she didn't know what to do with them any more, and she asked me, if I didn't mind, to send her something else.

MME. T.: And what did you do?

ZÉPO: I tried to learn to make something else, but I couldn't. So I go on making rag flowers to pass the time.

MME. T.: Do you throw them away afterwards, then?

ZÉPO: No, I've found a way to use them now. I give one flower for each pal who dies. That way I know that even if I make an awful lot there'll never be enough.

MONS. T.: That's a good solution you've hit on.

ZÉPO [*shyly*]: Yes.

ZAPO: Well, what I do is knit, so as not to get bored.

MME. T.: But tell me, are all the soldiers as bored as you?

ZÉPO: It all depends on what they do to amuse themselves.

ZAPO: It's the same on our side.

MONS. T.: Then let's stop the war.

ZÉPO: How?

MONS. T.: It's very simple.[*To* ZAPO.]You just tell your pals that the enemy soldiers don't want to fight a war, and you [*to* ZÉPO] say the same to your comrades. And then everyone goes home.

ZAPO: Marvellous!

MME. T.: And then you'll be able to finish mending the iron.

ZAPO: How is it that no one thought of such a good idea before?

MME. T.: Your father is the only one who's capable of thinking up such ideas; don't forget he's a former student of the Ecole Normale, *and* a philatelist.

ZÉPO: But what will the sergeant-majors and corporals do?

MONS. T.: We'll give them some guitars and castanets to keep them quiet!

ZÉPO: Very good idea.

MONS. T.: You see how easy it is. Everything's fixed.

ZÉPO: We shall have a tremendous success.

ZAPO: My pals will be terribly pleased.

MME. T.: What d'you say to putting on the pasodoble we were playing just now, to celebrate?

ZÉPO: Perfect.

ZAPO: Yes, put the record on, Mother.

MME. TÉPAN *puts a record on. She turns the handle. She waits. Nothing can be heard.*

MONS. T.: I can't hear a thing.

MME. T.: Oh, how silly of me! Instead of putting a record on I put on a beret.

She puts the record on. A gay pasodoble is heard. ZAPO *dances with* ZÉPO, *and* MME. TÉPAN *with her husband. They are all very gay. The field telephone rings. None of the four hears it. They go on dancing busily. The telephone rings again. The dance continues.*

The battle starts up again with a terrific din of bombs, shots and bursts of machine-gun fire. None of the four has seen anything and they go on dancing merrily. A burst of machine-gun fire mows them all down. They fall to the ground, stone dead. A shot must have grazed the gramo-

*phone; the record keeps repeating the same thing, like a
scratched record. The music of the scratched record can
be heard till the end of the play.
The two* STRETCHER BEARERS *enter left. They are carrying
the empty stretcher.*

SUDDEN CURTAIN

**AND THEY PUT HANDCUFFS
ON THE FLOWERS**

translated from the French
by Charles Marowitz

Production Information

The performing edition contained in this book was revised by Lois Messerman from the translation by Charles Marowitz especially for the first Off-Broadway production of this play. With Arrabal's guidance it has been further revised for publication by James Denton. The play opened on April 21, 1972 at the Mercer O'Casey Theater in New York. The production was directed by the playwright. Duane Mazey designed the setting; James Denton was the production director and assistant to Arrabal; Lawrence Sellars was the stage manager.

The cast included George Shannon (AMIEL), Peter Maloney (KATAR), Ron Faber (PRONOS), Baruk Levi (TOSAN), Muriel Miguel (DRIMA), Patricia Gaul (LELIA), Ellen Schindler (FALIDIA), and Riley Kellogg (THE APPARITION).

The photographs by James Denton included in this book are of this production.

Cast
of Characters

FOUR WOMEN: DRIMA (also plays the roles of A WIFE
and ROUPA)

FALIDIA

IMIS

LELIA (also plays the role of DESDEMONA)

FOUR MEN: TOSAN (also plays the roles of A PICKER
and CHRIST)

PRONOS (also plays the roles of A REVOLU-
TIONARY LEADER, A PRIEST, A JUDGE, A WAR-
DEN, A LAWYER, and A BANKER)

AMIEL (also plays the roles of DURERO, [PE-
TER PAUL] RUBENS, A CONFESSOR, and AN
EXECUTIONER)

KATAR (also plays the roles of ARISTODOME,
A PRIEST, A JAILER, [THE PROPHET] ELIJAH,
and A GENERAL)

THE APPARITION (played by a boy)

THE LOUDSPEAKER (an actor speaking through
a megaphone, offstage)

A NUN'S VOICE (an actress speaking through
a megaphone, offstage)

THE PRESIDENT'S VOICE (an actor speaking
through a megaphone, offstage)

STAGE MANAGER (in the Prologue)

The play is performed without any breaks or intermissions.

Prologue

The play begins before the start of the action, before the spectator takes his seat.

The theater foyer will lead into a "dark room" which will in turn be connected by a door to the actual theater where the action takes place.

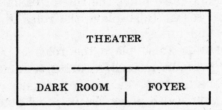

At the beginning of the performance the theater is plunged in absolute darkness. The adjoining room will be in half darkness; only a little light will come through via the door to the foyer. This is lit in normal fashion. The air is heavy with oriental perfumes, incense, and myrrh.

The audience will pass one by one from the foyer to the dark room. At this point it will be necessary to separate couples and groups of people.

The STAGE MANAGER *will grip people by the wrist and whisper something in their ear. For example:*

"A man is going to be murdered tonight."
"You are entering the penitentiary alone."
"You are dust and to dust you will return."
"Slip into the night of your birth."
"Tosan enters the penitentiary today."
"Relive as in a dream the experience of being born."

Strange cries can be heard coming from the theater, a melancholy flute, pygmy music, a woman crying. With extreme care the STAGE MANAGER hands the new arrival from the dark room over to one of the actors at the door which leads into the theater.

Once inside the spectator has the impression of being blind and in total darkness. The actor guides the spectator to a place which he considers suitable for him. (Don't forget: Couples should be separated and groups dispersed throughout the theater.) Each actor may guide his spectator, either by holding his hand, pushing him with one hand on his bottom and the other on the back of his neck, or else carrying him on his back like a donkey.

The actresses will guide the male spectators, gently murmuring to them and expressing their joy and fear at starting the play. The actors will guide the female spectators, gripping them as forcefully as possible. They will murmur to them, perhaps something incomprehensible.

The audience will feel that they have been plunged into darkness. If any of the spectators fearfully grasps the actors during the proceedings, the latter must caress and reassure them.

The spectators—one by one—are in their seats; they are sitting on the ground, on different levels which divide up the theater space (no chairs or cushions should be provided). From that moment on one of the fundamental principles of this performance is established: there is no actor/audience opposition. The actors invent a game, and invite the audience to join them. It is impossible to predict or envisage the audience's reactions. The actors must be able to tell each evening how to accommodate themselves in order to choose the most effective way of carrying out the proceedings. They will try to adapt themselves individually to the spectators they are in charge of. The environment—the theater—is made up of planks or scaffolding placed at different levels. There will be seven or eight little scenic platforms scattered amongst the audience. In the center (at ground level) the prison scenes will take place in an irregularly-shaped space. The audience will sit on the ground, on the planks and scaffolding. As a result of the varied levels, they will easily be able to see the action. The incantations become more prolonged. Flute.

When the audience is in (there should never be more than 100 or 120 people), a VOICE *is heard:*

VOICE   Open the grill. The prisoner Tosan is entering the penitentiary.

In the dark a noise of chains mingled with a woman's cries can be heard. Little by little the lights come up. The STAGE MANAGER *who welcomed the audience into the dark room will look after the lighting. Everyone, actors and actresses, is dressed the same: tight jeans and black T-shirts. The T-shirts may have a pattern on them. They all wear grey skull caps on their heads.*

When the actors play the part of oppressors they are to wear hoods. When it is neither a prisoner nor an oppressor they are to wear a hat— for example, a top hat. When they adopt a role different from their own but of the same kind they will put on a plastic mask to disguise themselves. The actors, when they are not "acting," are to sit in the audience: the actresses could perhaps lay their heads on the spectators' knees.

At last the lights are full up. Center stage, AMIEL, KATAR, *and* PRONOS.

The Play

AMIEL   Where are we? On a mountain?

KATAR   No, inside four walls.

AMIEL   More like a womb—with infinity out there waiting for us. (*Siren.*) He's just arrived.

KATAR   Tosan. Tosan himself!

AMIEL   They're taking him to solitary.

AMIEL AND KATAR   Tosan, Tosan.

Siren.

THE LOUDSPEAKER   Quiet in the cellblock. Everyone go to sleep.

Pause.

KATAR   Go on, tell us. Did you find out what's happening? Did you get the full story? What did they say when they got there?

AMIEL   Bzzz, bzzz, this is Tranquility Base. The Eagle has landed.

KATAR   And then they got out?

AMIEL   First one came down. He reached out his foot to touch the moon's surface. He appeared to be trembling—that's what I read in the paper—and then at last he took the first step.

PRONOS, *who is dumb, is following the conversation with the greatest of interest.*

KATAR   What have you done with the clippings?

AMIEL   I ate them.

KATAR   You ate them?

AMIEL   Suppose there was a search and they found them on me—I'd have been a goner.

KATAR   So what did he say?

AMIEL   When?

KATAR   When he landed on the moon.

AMIEL   Numbers, I think.

KATAR   What about the other one?

AMIEL   He came out later. According to the paper, the whole world was watching on television.

KATAR   Except us.

AMIEL   It wasn't till later that they spoke. One of them said . . .

THE LOUDSPEAKER   I would like to take this opportunity of asking all our listeners, wherever they may be, to pause for a moment, to meditate on the events of these last few hours, and to give thanks each in his own way.

PRONOS *starts to fidget excitedly.*

AMIEL   Look, he's trying to tell us something.

KATAR   They didn't mention us.

AMIEL   What do you mean, us?

KATAR   Us here.

AMIEL   Nobody ever mentions us.

KATAR   Even the first men on the moon have forgotten us . . .

Pause.

AMIEL   I've been dreaming.

KATAR   As usual.

AMIEL   As soon as the lights go out I dream. Do you know what about?

136

KATAR   All I dream about is this fucking jail.

AMIEL   I dream I'm with this girl, a beautiful girl, and I'm drawing circles on her with a compass. I put one end of it on her navel and with the other I stroke her breasts and lips and cunt. I dream we kiss and offer each other little electric engines full of dew. We teeter on satisfaction and splash each other in the sea while thousands of salmon swim between our buttocks . . . and then I come.

A loud drum roll.

THE APPARITION   Melquesidez wrote: "The penitentiary is a legend. Atrocious crimes have been committed there. You can still see the repairs in the walls of the acacia garden where they were used as targets during mass executions. It has been the mute witness of innumerable beatings and torture sessions."

KATAR   You remember what happened to Durero?

AMIEL   How could I forget? You know, often I think of what happened to him as if it had been me that got out of here.

KATAR   Maybe a lot of people saw themselves on television walking on the moon like the first astronauts.

AMIEL   It's not the same. I feel as if I *am* Durero. I close my eyes and I see myself in the city, running

137

all over the place, the happiest I've been for twenty years, admiring all those free people, living my first adventure.

> AMIEL's *dream: Flash of light. Eventually the theater is suffused with a strange light which prevents one from knowing whether one is there in reality or part of* AMIEL's *delirious imaginings.* AMIEL *puts on a plastic mask to "transform himself" into* DURERO. *He takes off his prisoner's cap and puts on a top hat. He walks around happily.* KATAR *follows him, his face hidden under another mask. He is also wearing a hat.*

KATAR (*Aristodome*)   Durero! Durero!

AMIEL (*Durero*)   Yes?

KATAR (*Aristodome*)   Remember me? I'm Aristodome. So long since we met.

AMIEL (*Durero*)   Aristodome! I didn't recognize you. I only came out yesterday . . . it's as if I'm a blind man.

KATAR (*Aristodome*)   Came out? Where from?

AMIEL (*Durero*)   The penitentiary.

KATAR (*Aristodome*)   I didn't realize you had been in prison.

AMIEL (*Durero*)   The press wasn't allowed to print anything.

KATAR (*Aristodome*)   I've got a terrific idea. I've got a girlfriend . . . she's a whore. She's fantastic. I'll tell you what, I'll pay her and you'll have a great night with her . . . I'll call her right now. Roupa! Roupa!

Enter DRIMA *as Roupa.*

KATAR (*Aristodome*)   Let me introduce you to Roupa, the queen of the tango. (*He exits.*)

DRIMA (*Roupa*)   You a friend of Aristodome's?

AMIEL (*Durero*)   My name's Durero.

DRIMA (*Roupa*)   Let's go, then.

AMIEL (*Durero*)   Where to?

DRIMA (*Roupa*)   To the hotel. Where do you think?

AMIEL (*Durero*)   Couldn't we wait a minute?

DRIMA (*Roupa*)   The sooner we finish the sooner I can start with someone else.

AMIEL (*Durero*)   I'd like to look around the town— paddle in the lakes, stare at the moon from high up on a toboggan, multiply the stars in the sky.

DRIMA (*Roupa*)   It's no good trying to impress me. I can tell from your accent you come from around here.

AMIEL (*Durero*)   Yes, I was born here.

DRIMA (*Roupa*)   Well, then?

AMIEL (*Durero*)   I was seventeen. I was very young when they took me away.

DRIMA (*Roupa*)   Yes. Well, make up your mind. I can't stand around here talking.

AMIEL (*Durero*)   Do you mind if we go for a walk?

DRIMA (*Roupa*)   Not at all. Then we could look at the moon with its rockets, its LEM, its astronauts, and its consecrated bread.

AMIEL (*Durero*)   From the aqueduct we can look out over the roofs of the town.

DRIMA (*Roupa*)   Are you coming to the hotel or not?

AMIEL (*Durero*)   You know . . . I've never been with a woman before.

DRIMA (*Roupa*)   Impotent are you? Well, you're in luck. If *I* can't get it up for you, I'll turn in my union card.

AMIEL (*Durero*)   As a matter of fact, it's twenty-three years since I last saw a woman.

DRIMA (*Roupa*)   What are you, a monk? One of those Trappists? You're not from a sanatorium? I don't want to catch anything.

AMIEL (*Durero*)   I was in the penitentiary.

DRIMA (*Roupa*)   Oh, you're somebody important like they have on television.

AMIEL (*Durero*)   I was still young when they arrested me. It was at the end of the war.

Long pause.

DRIMA (*Roupa*)   Why didn't you say so earlier?

AMIEL (*Durero*)   It's all right. Just now I was thinking about the astronauts going to the moon.

DRIMA (*Roupa*)   Go on, tell me all about it. (*She doesn't give him time to speak.*) Lean against me if you want and I'll rub your back and bottom. I'm really good. Everybody knows me. I started in a really rough area. Now things are working out for me. I charge more now, but my old friends keep coming back. We'll tell the zoo-keeper to give us a private show, and we'll feed caviar to the giraffe and give the hippopotamus champagne. I've got a sugar pink dress with a cleavage down to here, and specially for you I've got one with panties embroidered in nylon and fuse wire. I'll take you to night clubs and we'll dance the green tango on a porcelain sink covered with mosaics dating from the Peloponnesian War. Oh, we'll have the time of our lives!

AMIEL (*Durero*)   Fine! What are we waiting for?

DRIMA (*Roupa*)   Weren't you saying something about the moon and the astronauts?

AMIEL (*Durero*)   I was saying . . . it reminds me of a country wedding. When I was little the children used to gather around the married couple and throw handfuls of rice over the bride. It was as if they wanted to cover her with sperm, their sperm.

DRIMA (*Roupa*)   What's that got to do with the moon?

AMIEL (*Durero*)   Well, the astronauts are getting married on the moon. They were wearing white.

DRIMA (*Roupa*)   Two men, married?

AMIEL (*Durero*)   Shape of things to come. In the future you'll be able to marry several people at a time—a woman, the moon, and two men. Or even homosexual marriages.

DRIMA (*Roupa*)   Homosexuals *married?*

AMIEL (*Durero*)   Those two men on the moon are the

first. It's a sign of what to expect. That's why those two gay forerunners got married in the Sea of Tranquility. We're leaving the age of Pisces for that of Aquarius.

DRIMA (*Roupa*) You do speak well. But what about the rice?

AMIEL (*Durero*) The astronauts took some earth and one after another they put it in a plastic cup. They made themselves a vagina and shot their sperm— that is, the moon dust—up inside themselves till their prostates quivered.

DRIMA (*Roupa*) Poor baby, how you must have suffered to have such weird thoughts.

AMIEL *gets up as if illuminated. Organ music.*

AMIEL (*Durero*) We're leaving the age of fanaticism, dogma, and the inquisition and entering an age of tolerance—a time when penitentiaries and prisons will remain only as outdated relics of the past.

DRIMA (*Roupa*) Come here. You remind me of the angel Gabriel. Come on, let me show you the way. I'll be your seeing-eye dog. I'll look after you and you'll be happy. I'm the woman to pleasure you.

Blackout. End of AMIEL's *dream. Back in prison —lying on the ground:* AMIEL, PRONOS, *and* KATAR.

KATAR   There you go, dreaming again. You get so worked up. All you get is wet dreams.

AMIEL   Yes, I was dreaming.

KATAR   What about?

AMIEL   I was dreaming I was Durero when he got out of here.

KATAR   When Durero got home he found a small package in his jacket pocket containing money from his friend and a note from the girl asking him to come back the next night . . . now that she knew he had money.

AMIEL   She wanted him to come back every night, didn't she?

KATAR   That's what Durero must have thought. But then he decided the girl was just another victim of the society that had imprisoned him. So he spent all the money on an enormous bouquet of flowers, which he left for her at the night club where she worked with an affectionate little note attached.

   Pause.

AMIEL   How many years did we spend here with him?

KATAR   Right from the beginning. Do you remember those early years?

Blackout.

THE APPARITION   The penitentiary was built to house four hundred prisoners, but as many as six thousand have been incarcerated there. The prisoners sleep piled on top of each other with hardly any covering. Everyone is on the lookout for a piece of paper thick enough to offer some protection. In the cells, looking through the judas was forbidden. (*The scene conjured by* THE APPARITION *is mimed by* PRONOS *and* TOSAN.) A prison guard nicknamed Coyote noticed one of the prisoners looking through the spy hole. Sticking close to the wall, he approached the cell door on tiptoe and jabbed the point of his knife into the prisoner's eye. (*When the actors have finished miming this scene, the one who took the part of the prison guard eats the eye* [*simulated by a big black olive*].)

KATAR   Do you think people know there are men who have been shut away for years and years?

PRONOS *shakes his head.*

AMIEL   Do people know we have to crap into a common earthenware bowl?

PRONOS—*as before.*

KATAR   Do people know that the nurses inject turpentine into our veins?

145

PRONOS—*as before.*

AMIEL   Why does nobody say anything?

KATAR   I don't know. I suppose they think it isn't good to protest or complain.

AMIEL   Before coming to prison . . . just a few days before . . .

KATAR   Your sweetheart—go on, tell us again.

AMIEL   She was at the window, looking so beautiful, and I told her we're made for each other like fire and water and we'll love each other always.

   AMIEL's *memory. Very artificial light.* AMIEL *and* LELIA.

AMIEL   One day the war will be over. We'll have peace and freedom and men will be brothers and all equal. We'll be happy, and we'll go to the moon in a yacht with bicycle wheels.

LELIA   You're not a soldier, stay here.

AMIEL   I may not be a soldier, but I have to go.

LELIA   Stay and we'll play the trumpet together. Look, I've got a live frog in my pants. (*She shows him.*)

AMIEL   Poor thing—it'll suffocate.

LELIA   No it won't. Sometimes I piss on it and it jumps for joy. Tree frog, tree frog, do a somersault and you'll be as big as God.

AMIEL   There is no God any more. This war's frightened Him away for good.

LELIA   God does too exist, though I don't imagine he spends much time with those vultures in cassocks, the black sheep of Christ's flock. God is very tender. Sometimes he slips into me and sings to me . . . Ain't She Sweet . . .

AMIEL   We don't need God any more. Now when I dream all I see is a happy world where we spend years just walking hand in hand and you play the harpsichord while doves in corsets flutter round about us. I'll dance for you. Watch. (*He does a grotesque dance.*)

LELIA   Hit me.

AMIEL   Hit you?

LELIA   I'll close my eyes and you punch me in the face. But don't hurt me too much. (*She closes her eyes and waits for the blow.*)

AMIEL   I'm not going to hit you. I'll go for a ride in a zeppelin and throw you coils of rainbow milk.

LELIA For you I'm like a little goldfinch you hold in your hand. If you squeeze me, I'll suffocate, and if you stroke me my breasts will swell out like the sails of a frail boat.

AMIEL Are you honest?

LELIA My Lord?

AMIEL Are you fair?

LELIA What means your lordship?

AMIEL That if you be honest and fair, your honesty should admit no discourse to your beauty.

LELIA Could beauty, my Lord, have better commerce than with honesty?

AMIEL Get thee to a nunnery.

LELIA Don't go to the war.

AMIEL I'll go like a rogue stallion, but I'll be thinking of you all the time.

LELIA Yesterday the troops went through on their way to the front. The leader was stirring up the crowd. I felt so happy listening to him I forgot all about you and I went up and touched his khaki shirt.

Flashes of light. PRONOS *addressing the crowd from a balcony.*

PRONOS (*a leader*) Young barbarians of today, we must sweep down and sack the decadent civilization of this miserable country. We must destroy its temples and abolish its gods. We shall strip the veils from the novices, raise them to the dignity of motherhood, begetting on them a new generation of sturdy children. We shall tear up deeds of ownership, make bonfires with them—and in those flames purge our ailing state. We must win the humble to our cause, enlist the legions of the proletariat and make the world tremble before its new judges. There must be no holding back. Fight to the death. Kill and be killed.

A burst of enthusiastic cheering.

LELIA Oh, fortunate young man, Homer was the herald of your virtues. May I touch your shirt?

PRONOS (*a leader*) Comrade, I am a man like any other.

LELIA Oh, wonderful—everyone who hears him is converted. Do you know *The Iliad* by heart?.

PRONOS (*a leader; taking the microphone*) We are not in the least afraid of ruins . . . we shall inherit the earth . . . we are carrying a new world here in our

149

hearts and even as I talk this world is becoming stronger.

LELIA Did you burn down a lot of churches in the capital?

PRONOS (*a leader*) A lot? We burned them all.

LELIA Look. Here comes one of the pickers.

Enter TOSAN.

PRONOS (*a leader*) Comrade, you're poor like us and we'll help you win back your dignity.

TOSAN (*a picker*) Thank you, sir.

PRONOS (*a leader*) Comrade.

TOSAN (*a picker*) Sir, what good can we do? Leave us to our trucks and our own ways.

PRONOS (*a leader*) You are going to do something much more uplifting. You're going to arm yourselves and leave for the front to fight our oppressors.

TOSAN (*a picker*) Comrade Sir, how could we kill our brothers . . . our brothers . . . never.

Flash of light. End of AMIEL'*s memory.* PRONOS, AMIEL, *and* KATAR *in prison.*

150

AMIEL   I can remember the war as if it were yesterday.

KATAR   Me too . . . but a lot of time's gone by since then.

AMIEL   You know, before I used to think only of my girl . . . now I think about God.

KATAR   Oh yeah, what's He like?

AMIEL   Sometimes like a little bubble of air that goes from my brain to my heart and back to my brain. When I'm sad, the bubble becomes heavy and sometimes, when I cry, it feels like quicksilver.

KATAR   They're always talking about God.

AMIEL   But they speak with whips.

Lighting change. Corrida *music.* PRONOS *as a priest with a bell is singing church music.*

PRONOS (*a priest*)   I don't want any complaints. The first one of you to open his mouth—I'll whip him till his soul melts. Let us pray. Who was that whispering? (*Pause.*) The first one to speak or make the slightest remark, I'll split his skull—understand? Twice a day you must kneel down and pray to God: Mass in the morning and vespers in the evening. Where's Abrameline? You, Katar, answer me.

KATAR   He's in the hole.

PRONOS (*a priest*)   You mean "He's in the hole, *sir*."
And why is he in the hole?

KATAR   Because he refused to kiss Baby Jesus' foot
after Mass.

PRONOS (*a priest*) Infidel! How dare you short change
me! Abrameline committed the worst blasphemy
there is—he didn't bow down at our Redeemer's
feet. Now, you say it.

KATAR   Abrameline committed the worst blasphemy
there is: he didn't bow down at our Redeemer's feet.

PRONOS (*a priest*)   Tell me, where is he now?

KATAR   He's in the adjustment center.

PRONOS (*a priest*)   You hear that, all of you?

   Pause. KATAR *is obviously on the verge of some
   outburst.* PRONOS (*a priest*) *is delighted and gets
   ready to bring him to heel.*

PRONOS (*a priest*)   How big is the cell?

KATAR   Six feet by three.

PRONOS (*a priest*)   How long will he stay locked up
there?

KATAR   Six months.

PRONOS (*a priest*)   Six months, that's right. It's better for him to atone for his sins on earth than in hell. What are the conditions like?

KATAR   Abrameline is kept locked up day and night and has no contact with the outside world. All he gets is a bowl of watery soup.

PRONOS (*a priest*)   Not so fast. You lack conviction. Now, go on. He is forbidden . . .

KATAR   Everything: reading, writing, sleeping during the day.

PRONOS (*a priest*)   And allowed—?

KATAR   To st-stink like a rat.

PRONOS (*a priest*)   You missed a word.

KATAR   To stink like a *mangy* rat.

PRONOS (*a priest*)   Did you hear that, the rest of you? And now let us offer up a prayer. Let us pray. Wait a minute. There's something you ought to hear. Some years ago a prisoner thought he could get the better of me. Don't anybody laugh. He came to me as humble and meek as a lamb—even though he was a great revolutionary before his arrest—and I allowed him the signal honor of helping me say Mass.

He seemed altogether a different man. One morning, when I was preparing to say Mass, I saw what he'd done in the chalice; he'd put a slice of sausage in place of the holy wafer and he was chewing the sacred Host before my very eyes. The most appalling transgression—eating the flesh of our Lord Jesus Christ. We threw him in the adjustment center and we forgot all about him. No bread or water, nothing. Four months later when we opened the door we found his body half-rotted, half-mummified, and where his arms had been there was just bare bone— all the flesh had been stripped away. Shut up in that hole of a cell, he'd eaten his arms before he died. (*Pause.*) May that serve as an example to you . . . Silence! I don't want any comments. Let us pray.

Flashes of light. The prisoners shout.

VOICES   Down with the priest! Down with the priest! Beat him up! Chop him to pieces!

KATAR   Leave him to me! Leave him to me!

They all shout, moving together around the priest.

TOSAN   Crucify him!

VOICES   Crucify him!

KATAR   First, I'm going to gouge his eyes out. (*He puts his eyes out.*)

KATAR   These are the eyes that watched us being tortured.

AMIEL   They've seen us on our knees, locked up, torn, humiliated.

They trample on his eyes.

KATAR   Step on them. Now, I'm going to tear his balls off. (*Slowly he tears off the priest's testicles, which can be seen bleeding in his hand.*)

AMIEL   Put them in his mouth!

KATAR   Now, leave him alone. Let him bleed to death slowly.

They draw back. The priest lifts up his empty eye sockets. He puts on welder's goggles. And slowly munches his own testicles.

PRONOS (*a priest*)   Oh, my balls, oh they do taste good. For what we are about to receive . . . (*Organ music. He continues to chew unctuously. He takes them out with his fingers—they look like chewing gum; all stretchy.*) Oh, God, I can no longer see, but my pleasure is all the greater. Oh, what joy to eat my own balls. And not be able to see. All my enjoyment is concentrated in my mouth, my tongue—the mouth you gave me, Lord. The Lord giveth balls and the Lord taketh them away. Blessed be the name of the Lord. (*He chews joyfully. He moves with difficulty.*)

O Lord, let me savor my balls. Grant that this pleasure which my body gives itself, this auto-satisfaction afforded by my tongue and which is so sweet to me, shall not kindle in me luxurious appetites.

AMIEL   Listen to him. He's enjoying it too much.

KATAR   Yes, kill him. He's going mad, his brain's rattling around like an empty bell.

AMIEL   Kill him. He's enjoying it too much.

The priest falls to his knees, his arms in the shape of a cross.

PRONOS (*a priest*)   O Lord, now that my sight is gone I see you with the eyes of faith and I love you madly. I hope for a life so long that I die from not dying. The thought of it, O Lord, fills me with love for you. It is not the promise of heaven nor the fear of hell which keep me from sinning against you. (*He prays on his knees.*) Look down on me, O Lord. My testicles are gone, I've been castrated in your service, that no one may distract me from my song of praise. I have already swallowed them. God grant they do not grow again before my sacrifice is complete. (*He shuffles across the stage on his knees.*) O Lord, forgive me my sins, I beseech you. O Christ our Saviour, forgive me all the suffering I've caused the prisoners in the years gone by—for the hellish tortures I've inflicted upon them. Forgive my infinite trespass. Show yourself, Saviour.

Suddenly Christ appears. Divine light. Harmonium. KATAR *plays bongos.*

TOSAN (*Christ; singing*) I have two loves: my daddy and the cross. Two loves have I: God, the Father, and Judas. (*He is seated, his privates covered with a sheet.*)

PRONOS (*a priest*) It's you, Master.

TOSAN (*Christ*) I am Christ the Saviour.

PRONOS (*a priest*) May I be with you this day in paradise?

TOSAN (*Christ*) No, first I shall do a miracle. Come here, man of little faith. With some saliva, I shall restore your sight. (*He puts some spit on the priest's eyelids. His sight is restored.*)

PRONOS (*a priest*) O Lord Jesus Christ, thank you for your miracle. I am not worthy to kiss the soles of your shoes.

TOSAN (*Christ*) There's more to come. Feel!

PRONOS (*a priest; touches his own crotch*) I don't believe it!

TOSAN (*Christ*) Yes, my son, your faith has saved you.

PRONOS (*a priest*)   But are such miracles possible?

TOSAN (*Christ*)   You mean you didn't think it would work?

PRONOS (*a priest*)   Of course I did . . . how foolish of me to doubt your miraculous gifts.

TOSAN (*Christ*)   As soon as Cleopatra's done, she'll get on to you. *Then* you'll see.

> *Christ pulls away the sheet, revealing a woman—* DRIMA—*in the act of sucking his enormous cock.* DRIMA *winks saucily. Flashes of light. Organ music. Lighting change.* AMIEL *is very excited.*

AMIEL   Revenge! Revenge!

KATAR   Stop dreaming.

> *Pause.*

AMIEL   One day man left his home in paradise for a life of meanness and deceit. Today he leaves the earth and jumps to the moon like a horse's neigh.

KATAR   But we're still in prison.

AMIEL   I think of them arriving on the moon. With their neat little suits and rounded shapes, they must have looked like the three little pigs.

KATAR And who's the big bad wolf?

AMIEL The wolf was the serpent in paradise, but in our brave new world there'll be no devil.

KATAR Still dreaming, I see.

AMIEL I dream . . . and I dream that I'm dreaming and I think that I'm dreaming. I even dream that I'm thinking. The other day I dreamt a whole sentence: Moses, you're talking through your hat. I'd never given him a thought.

KATAR You know what's wrong with you? You read the Bible too much.

AMIEL What?

KATAR Yes, and that's the weapon of those who keep us here.

AMIEL Everything is their weapon—the Bible, love, everything. They do dirt on it and cover it in their slime.

KATAR That's why the book flew into space the other day.

AMIEL Don't tease me. (*He lights up.*) I was just playing around with the book and all of a sudden I put it on a shelf at chest height . . . only there was no shelf—the book was suspended in mid-air, defying the laws of gravity.

KATAR   You're imagining things.

AMIEL   Everyone saw it.

    PRONOS *nods his head with conviction.*

KATAR   And how the fuck do you explain that?

AMIEL   Perhaps the prophet Elijah came to the prison to carry the book to heaven in his chariot of fire.

KATAR   Chariot of fire? You mean the Saturn rocket. (*Annoyed.*) Let's take a shit.

AMIEL   You were saying we should set an example to the ordinary prisoners.

KATAR   I said let's take a shit. (*He installs the receptacle.*)

AMIEL   Shall we ask Pronos to join us?

KATAR   Yes. Tosan, too, when he arrives.

AMIEL   The four of us together.

KATAR   Hey, Pronos, come on, join us. But first tell us the story about the day you lost your voice.

PRONOS *buries his face in the ground and weeps.*

AMIEL   Poor man. Leave him alone, nobody will ever know.

They pull down their trousers and share the same pot. They sit back to back.

KATAR   Yours is so soft, isn't it?

AMIEL   I like touching it and eating little bits. My mouth fills with earth, life, infinity. I can feel myself being born and dying. I'm a golden insect and an angel of mud.

Flashes of light. AMIEL's dream. Lighting change. Two very beautiful women dancing: IMIS and LELIA.

KATAR   Girls! Girls!

IMIS   What do you want?

KATAR   Please allow me to introduce to you my friend, the painter Rubens.

IMIS   Is that right?

AMIEL (*Rubens*)   You've heard of me?

IMIS   Of course I have. You're the one who paints all those beautiful, voluptuous women and little cherubs.

When I was young, when I had a free moment, I used to look at your paintings and imagine myself surrounded by jasmine and cats while you painted me in the nude perched on a ladder of navy blue ivory.

AMIEL (*Rubens*)   Do you like my paintings?

LELIA   I love them—crazy about them.

AMIEL (*Rubens*)   Would you mind brushing off this stain? (*He points to a stain on the fly of his trousers.*)

LELIA   But of course. (*She kneels down to brush it off.*)

AMIEL (*Rubens*)   Just a minute. Let me introduce you to a friend.

IMIS   Who is it?

AMIEL (*Rubens*)   The prophet Elijah.

KATAR (*Elijah*)   Hallelujah!

IMIS   The same one that's in the Bible?

AMIEL (*Rubens*)   That's right.

IMIS   The one born at Thesbe?

AMIEL (*Rubens*)   You know all about him.

IMIS I should say so. I've read everything written on him several times. What adventures!

LELIA What's he done with his chariot of fire?

IMIS Don't be so forward. If he wants to show us his chariot of fire, he will.

KATAR (*Elijah*) No trouble at all. Of course I'll show it to you and if you like I'll take you up to heaven—or we'll go for a ride down underground passages of hot blood.

AMIEL (*Rubens*) He's very accommodating.

KATAR (*Elijah*) But first of all, rub me here. (*He indicates his fly.*)

IMIS *and* LELIA *kneel down to rub him. He stops them.*

KATAR (*Elijah*) Do you know that I'm being fed by angels right now?

AMIEL (*Rubens*) Yes, I'm a witness to it. I've painted a really toothsome little picture. Every day the angels come down and give him chocolate and biscuits and sardine sandwiches. They come down from heaven with a flotilla of blind doves.

KATAR (*Elijah*) And who are you?

LELIA I'm Desdemona.

AMIEL (*Rubens*) We'll get married, all four of us.

KATAR (*Elijah*) Terrific. (*Indicating his fly.*) But first, give this a lick.

They kneel to caress him with their tongues.

KATAR (*Elijah*) Just a minute. Let Rubens tell Desdemona his life story.

AMIEL (*Rubens*) If I must tell the story of my life
I'll speak of most disastrous chances,
Of moving accidents by flood and field
Of hairbreadth scapes in the imminent deadly breach
Of being taken by the insolent foe
And sold to slavery; of my redemption thence
And portance in my travel's history.
Wherein of anters vast and deserts idle,
Rough quarries, rocks and hills whose heads touch heaven
It is my wont to speak.
And of the cannibals that each other eat,
The anthropophagi, and men whose heads
Do grow beneath their shoulders—
And of my suffering . . .

LELIA (*Desdemona*) I swear i' faith 'tis strange, 'tis
passing strange,
'Tis pitiful, 'tis wondrous pitiful,
I wish I had not heard it, yet I
wish
That heaven had made me such a
man. I thank you.

They kiss.

AMIEL (*Rubens*) Let's get married, Desdemona.

LELIA (*Desdemona*) Yes, my Rubens.

AMIEL (*Rubens*) We'll get married with a broom up
our ass and go on our honeymoon in a chariot of fire.

LELIA (*Desdemona*) Yes, my love.

Grotesque marriage.

PRONOS (*a priest*) Wilt thou have this woman to be
thy lawful wedded wife? Do you promise to cherish
her, to have her and hold her, in the depths of misfortune and the dizzy froth of happiness till death
do you part?

Whistles. Blackout.

THE LOUDSPEAKER What's going on in the cellblock,
swine? No dreaming out loud!

KATAR   Wake up, Amiel, or you're going to get it.

AMIEL   You woke me in the middle of a marvellous dream.

KATAR   You were crying and shouting. The guard heard you.

AMIEL   You sure?

KATAR   Don't thrash around like that, you'll knock the crapper over.

THE APPARITION   In the middle of each cell there was a clay receptacle shaped like a cocked hat upside down—into which the prisoners relieved themselves at night. There were so many prisoners in a cell that it was only too easy to upset this receptacle if you so much as stretched your legs, and so the prisoners slept in a constant state of watchfulness. If one of them needed to ease his bowels, a likely occurrence, the others had to put up with the stench since they were shut up from six every evening till seven the next morning. The peasants wasted no time in showing the others how after easing yourself you lit a piece of paper and threw it in the bowl to get rid of the stench. And this is what they used to do.

TOSAN *makes a spectacular entrance.*

AMIEL AND KATAR   Tosan! Tosan!

KATAR   What did you say when they got you?

TOSAN   I told them it's a waste of time torturing me. I won't tell you anything. All I'll tell you is that I'm the head of the movement in this area.

KATAR   I'll bet they were impressed.

TOSAN   It's all I could say without compromising the others.

AMIEL   And what did they say to that?

TOSAN   Go on, they said, talk big. Considering the amount of time you have left to live, you can well afford to brag.

AMIEL   I don't believe it . . . even under their laws.

TOSAN   That's what I said: Twenty-five years after the war.

AMIEL   Who was in charge?

TOSAN   He was short and fat.

AMIEL   They're all different now.

KATAR   Tosan is here! Tosan is here! Tosan is with us!

TOSAN   How long have you been in?

AMIEL   Twenty-three years! And I just escaped hanging.

Flashes of light. Courtroom. Judge.

PRONOS (*a judge*)   The defense having been read by our illustrious army lieutenant . . .

AMIEL   Defense! More like a prosecution.

PRONOS (*a judge*)   Scum! Don't you know it's forbidden for the defendant at a court-martial to speak? He may only address the bench through the intermediary of his counsel—and since your counsel sent a letter saying that he can't be with us today, you'd better be quiet. Keep your mouth shut or I'll blow your brains out with this pistol.

Enter a priest.

KATAR (*a priest*)   General, could I have a word with you please?

PRONOS (*a judge*)   Reverend Father, how dare you interrupt the course of justice! Despite the profound respect we in the service have for men of the cloth . . .

KATAR (*a priest*)   It's something very serious. And you know what an excellent record our clergy has.

PRONOS (*a judge*)   Yes, I am aware that many of them
—the pick of the bunch, in fact—refused Communion to the Red Catholics who were about to be shot.
So that after their death they'd go straight to hell.

KATAR (*a priest*)   It's certainly something to be proud
of. I myself have suffered bodily harm at their hands.

PRONOS (*a judge*)   Well, now, what warrants your
presence at this trial?

KATAR (*a priest*)   I have something very important to
say.

PRONOS (*a judge*)   It's an open and shut case. There's
nothing *to* say. This man stands accused of murder-
ing his village priest. His defense counsel pleaded
guilty and asked that justice be done. That is precisely what this court is about to do. May I point
out that this trial has already taken six minutes—
we've already spent more time on this verdict than
on any other this morning, thanks to your butting
in. This court has already passed sentence of death
on sixteen offenders.

KATAR (*a priest*)   But he can't have killed his village
priest.

PRONOS (*a judge*)   Don't be naive. These people know
only too well how to play on the sympathies of well-
meaning people like yourself, Father.

KATAR (*a priest*)   No, I'm nobody's dupe.

PRONOS (*a judge*)   What do you mean?

KATAR (*a priest*)   I have irrefutable evidence.

PRONOS (*a judge*)   It's no longer a question of evidence. The prosecution has put its case, the defense has pleaded guilty. All that remains for us is to pass sentence of death.

KATAR (*a priest*)   But he couldn't have killed his village priest, for the simple reason that *I* am his village priest.

PRONOS (*a judge*)   What?

KATAR (*a priest*)   I said I'm his village priest.

PRONOS (*a judge*)   But . . .

> *The judge appears defeated.*

KATAR (*a priest*)   I should also add that he saved my life. A mob of peasants was getting ready to lynch me. He stopped them from laying a finger on me.

> *This piece of information seems to defeat the judge. He thinks for a moment.*

PRONOS (*a judge*)   But . . . (*Pause.*) Very well. (*Recovering his martial bearing.*) In the name of the defense and the prosecution, I withdraw the murder charge . . . But, in view of the fact that during the Civil War the prisoner wielded such influence in the Red Zone that he succeeded in saving a priest's life, I sentence him herewith to life imprisonment.

Light flashes. Lighting change. A very strange creature (PRONOS) *in a ballerina's tutu does an effeminate dance to* The Swan *by Saint-Saëns. The executioner* (AMIEL) *holds down* KATAR *and is tying him up.*

KATAR   Help! Help!

DRIMA (*a wife*)   Quiet. You're a fine father to the children.

PRONOS, *The Swan, continues the ridiculous dance in tutu and on skates.*

KATAR   I'm in prison alone, not a friend in the world.

DRIMA (*a wife*)   Quiet. Suffer. You must pay for your sins.

The Swan continues as PRONOS *performs a series of fantastic, ridiculous little leaps.*

KATAR   What made you denounce me?

DRIMA (*a wife*)   Because you are guilty and must pay

171

the penalty. Say thank you to these gentlemen for all the interest they're taking in you.

At this point THE EXECUTIONER *strikes* KATAR. PRONOS *goes on dancing and leaping around like a grasshopper.*

KATAR   Twenty years I've spent by myself in prison. Bring me a box of crayons, I want to draw some color pictures.

DRIMA (*a wife*)   You must pay for your sins.

AMIEL (*an executioner*) *violently seizes* KATAR *and whips him. Then he holds him in a vice-like grip while* DRIMA *stabs him in the back.* PRONOS *is now dancing like Frank Sinatra.*

AMIEL (*an executioner*)   Shit on him, madam. Shit on him.

The wife brings out a pot, puts it on her husband, and starts defecating. Farting noises. PRONOS *dances frantically.*

KATAR   Are you shitting on me?

DRIMA (*a wife*)   Yes, it'll be balm on your wounds. Ge-e-e-e-ently does it, it'll do you good.

Farting noises. The dancer kisses DRIMA. *Flashes of light. Lighting change.*

172

THE LOUDSPEAKER   Prisoner Tosan, a visitor for you.

TOSAN   Falidia!

FALIDIA   Tosan, are you hurt?

TOSAN   It's bugged. They're listening to us.

FALIDIA   But your head. Are you hurt?

TOSAN   They threw me out of a window.

THE LOUDSPEAKER   For the first and last time, Prisoner Tosan, you may talk of family matters and nothing else.

FALIDIA   Tosan, can I bring you anything? Is there anything you need, anything you want?

TOSAN   To get out of here.

FALIDIA   Tosan, I miss you so much when you're not with me sometimes I just sit and cry.

TOSAN   Take care of the children.

FALIDIA   When's the trial?

TOSAN   I don't know.

FALIDIA   They've appointed a captain to defend you, but we haven't been able to see him.

TOSAN   I meet him on the day of the trial.

FALIDIA   Oh, Tosan, I want to be with you, have your arms around me, be cradled by your body. I want to feel your heart beating against mine.

TOSAN   Take care of the children.

FALIDIA   We'll see you at the trial.

TOSAN   No, it'll be a closed hearing and they fix the time an hour beforehand.

FALIDIA   I'll be at the Central Court every morning.

TOSAN   They don't know which court will try me. It's no good. They won't let you.

FALIDIA   It's so awful. I want to see you every day, and they only let me visit ten minutes once a week.

TOSAN   I think about you all the time.

FALIDIA   Me too. How I want to touch you, kiss you, be touched by you and bathe you all over in tears of joy . . .

TOSAN   I want to see you too.

FALIDIA   One yard apart—and two metal screens in the way. But it's better than those four months when I didn't hear from you at all.

TOSAN   Your life is in danger. Go abroad, you'll be more use to me there.

Whistles blow.

TOSAN   Bye, my love.

FALIDIA   Bye, my love. Soon.

Lighting change.

THE APPARITION   The prison was full to bursting. Each prisoner was allowed the space of two flag-stones to stretch out in, which meant that they all had to sleep lying on the same side; and when anyone turned over in the night the whole row had to turn with him, with cries of "Eastward-Ho" if they were turning to the right, and "Westward-Ho" if they were turning to the left.

AMIEL   Where are we? On a mountain?

KATAR   No. Inside four walls.

AMIEL   More like a womb—with infinity out there waiting for us.

Pause.

TOSAN   What's it like in winter?

AMIEL   Very cold.

PRONOS *mimes cold.*

TOSAN   Isn't there any heating?

KATAR   No. There is no heating in prisons in this country. In winter the convicts die like flies.

AMIEL   You'll get used to it. Like everyone else, you'll start dreaming. You'll even have love dreams.

KATAR   Pronos here got the worst of it. When he first came in he could talk all right, then they put him in the condemned cell and when they reprieved him he lost his voice.

AMIEL   Do you dream too? (PRONOS *nods.*) What sort of dreams? Happy? (PRONOS *nods.*) Fantastic? (*Nods.*) Sad? (*Nods vehemently.*) Don't upset yourself. Those who suffer are the more loved. Our sorrows are the spiritual food of a being from another world whom we carry on our backs. (PRONOS *gesticulates.*) And yours is very heavy—is that right? (PRONOS *nods enthusiastically.*)

Flashes of light. The light concentrates on PRONOS. *He is now wearing a sort of muzzle.*

IMIS   Do you remember me? (*He nods.*) That muzzle really suits you. It's marvellous. That way you can't say anything. You used to be so talkative before the war. (*He nods.*) Shall we live together, happily ever after, beneath a sky of multicolored airships? (*He

nods, Yes, yes.) Did you know I can understand what
people are saying with their hands? (*He seems surprised.*) Go on, talk to me. (*He strokes her breasts.*)
You said, "Solomon used to take his pleasure with
four spirits of the night who lived on Mount Naspa.
One for each season of the year. These four female
genies had girl babies by him." (*He moves away
from her.*) You know such a lot of things. (*He
touches her again.*) "They even say Solomon was a
pervert as well." Amazing! Touch my slim belly and
I'll understand you even better. (*He touches her
belly.*) Aah. That's nice. Lower. (*He scratches
lower.*) It's really lovely. Do you want me to do it
for you? (*She listens for his reply.*) Oh, you mean
your stomach's not as nice as mine. It doesn't matter.
(*She puts her hand down* PRONOS' *pants.*) What's
this? A snake? Oh, how funny. Look, it's throbbing.
And it doesn't bite. Oh, and the smell. (*She sniffs
her fingers.*) You're my lonely little kangaroo. It's
good, your being dumb. I'll shut you in a cage like a
palm-tree alarm clock and carry you close to my
heart. Would you like that? (*He nods.*) What a fool
I am. You're too old to be put in a cage. And then
there's your muzzle. (*He talks to her with his fingers. She interrupts his sign language.*) "I'm wearing
a muzzle so I don't have to speak, and to keep my
senses alert for the day when they'll make me a real
live king." Yes, yes. You'll be king of the moon. In
the beginning man left paradise. He was driven out
and came down to earth. Today he's leaving earth for
the moon, for the universe. A new era is dawning,
and we'll be happy, you and I. They'll call you king

of the moon, and crown you with a steel crown. It'll weigh a ton but you'll carry it as if it was a feather. Let me clean your teeth. (*She cleans his teeth by rubbing his knee.*) You used to be so talkative before the war—and the stories you used to tell. It's a change for the better, I must say. I remember the day you left the village on that wagon to be a strolling player. (*He scratches her.*) "What have I been doing all these years?" Waiting for you. (*He scratches her.*) "And why didn't I visit you in the twenty years you've been in prison?" . . . It slips my memory. (*Annoyed.*) Don't keep on about the past. Let's think about the future. We'll roam the world together till we find a road leading skyward to happiness. We'll travel in a chariot of rain and when we get there, we'll crown each other. (*He scratches her.*) Are you out of your mind? No, *no!* Supposing people saw! (*He scratches her.*) The place is full of people . . . I don't want to . . . think of what they'll say. All right then, if you insist. You can go so far and no further. (PRONOS *nods his head insistently. He sulks. He is becoming visibly more stubborn.*) Don't be angry. I'll catch cold . . . Oh, all right. But only because I don't want you to think I don't love you.

She takes her clothes off, gets down on all fours and starts to bray. PRONOS, *very happy now, skips around her. Occasionally he adjusts her position so that she is on all fours with her face to the ground and her bottom in the air.* IMIS *carries on braying in this position.* PRONOS *continues to skip about and from time to time gives her a smack on the ass. Then he resumes his dancing. Finally, he utters a Tarzan-like cry, strips off his clothes and throws himself on her. They both bray. Lighting change.*

THE APPARITION   In the prisons people used to die in droves. The nuns who cooked for them were partly responsible. When the prisoners asked for an extra ration for their sick comrades they were told:

A NUN'S VOICE   Sick people don't need extra because they're going to die anyway. We'd rather give improved rations to the healthy—the guards and the prisoners who collaborate—to prevent them from falling ill.

Lighting change.

PRONOS (*a warden*)   In this prison we do things by the book. If I've said it once I've said it a hundred times. You all know the penalties. No one has the excuse of ignorance . . . What's this? Open this door at once. Open the latrine door.

KATAR *and* TOSAN, *naked, are busy fucking each other.*

PRONOS (*a warden*)   I can hardly believe my eyes . . . two prisoners . . . Throw 'em in the hole. They'll get six months on bread and water for this.

179

TOSAN   Yes sir, but let me finish here first.

Flashes of light.

PRONOS (*a warden*)   There is one particularly serious offense which demands the maximum penalty and that is assaulting a prison officer, and you all know the penalty for *that*. It is now twenty degrees. Tonight this will go down to, let's say, ten or fifteen degrees. Those of you who had the effrontery to talk back to the guard in charge of your block will be hung in the middle of the courtyard by your feet and left there overnight. Take 'em away. (*He taps his gloves against his hand.*) You'll be stiff as icicles. You won't last an hour. I hope your death serves as an example. Oh, I almost forgot. Tomorrow morning we'll bring each of you your breakfast—hot coffee and milk and biscuits—just like the guards.

Flashes of light. Blackout.

AMIEL (*in the dark*)   I will not die . . . I will not die . . . (*Stronger.*) I will not die.

Lighting change. AMIEL *is hanging by his feet.*

PRONOS (*a warden, holding a mug of coffee*)   What? Still alive? This prisoner's got balls. I've never seen anything like it.

PRONOS (*warden*) *cuts the rope and lets him down.* AMIEL *is on the verge of collapse. His voice comes in jerks.*

AMIEL   Your promise.

PRONOS (*a warden*)   You still have the strength to talk?

AMIEL   Your promise.

PRONOS (*a warden*)   Here you are. Coffee and biscuits.

He drops the dish at AMIEL's *side.*

AMIEL   No, that's not what you promised.

PRONOS (*a warden*)   What do you mean?

AMIEL   You promised two breakfasts.

PRONOS (*a warden*)   Two?

AMIEL   Yes, two. One for me and one for the dead man. I'll take them both.

PRONOS (*a warden*)   As you wish.

He pulls a canteen from his uniform, drinks from it, and spits the liquid into the dish and onto AMIEL. *He leaves.* AMIEL *makes a pig of himself. He continues to eat ravenously from the bowl, but little by little he is transformed. Lifting himself up, he kneels, clutching the bowl. Gregorian chant.*

AMIEL   O Lord, permit me to eat of thy body and drink of thy blood.

Lighting change. Organ music. Three shepherdesses appear: FALIDIA, IMIS, *and* LELIA.

AMIEL Shepherdesses, I am the Virgin of Fatima made flesh.

The three shepherdesses kneel. Sound of bells.

IMIS Listen to the bells, Master. They are calling us. We are getting married today.

FALIDIA Yes, yes, today you will be our heavenly bridegroom.

LELIA Listen to the bells. From today the three of us will be your lawful wedded wives.

AMIEL No. I shall be your Lady of Fatima made man. Your Redeemer in his garment of flesh.

IMIS Master, we are your shepherdesses. Why are you deceiving us?

AMIEL O ye of little faith.

IMIS If you're the Virgin, prove it!

AMIEL Come. I'll urinate in your mouth—but instead of urine there will be hot chocolate. And your eyes will be opened.

IMIS Oh Master! Is it possible?

FALIDIA   Let's see.

IMIS   Me first.

> AMIEL *lies down and spreads his knees.* IMIS *puts his penis in her mouth and cries, "A miracle, a miracle!" All three of them drink, commenting enthusiastically, and shouting, "A miracle, a miracle!"*

IMIS   Oh, it's so good! So hot! So sweet! Milk chocolate!

> *They sing hymns and dance grotesquely. They put lavatory seats on their heads. They sing and dance. Flashes of light. Lighting change. Prison.*

KATAR   Who invented prison?

AMIEL   Animals don't have them.

KATAR   Do people know that a lot of guys in here would rather give up one of their eyes instead of staying shut up in here for another ten years?

AMIEL   People today find prison an acceptable punishment . . . but they'd be horrified if someone started putting criminals' eyes out . . . even though there'd be less suffering.

KATAR   I've read of countries that people call savage where a man who commits a crime gets one of his hands cut off. (*He laughs.*) How many of us wouldn't give a hand to get the fuck out of here?

AMIEL   Is it more barbaric to cut off a hand and let the man go free? Is putting people in prison more civilized?

KATAR   Not much to choose between them. They're both the same.

AMIEL   It's the Penal Code that always amazes me.

KATAR   Why?

AMIEL   How do you suppose they worked it out? Think of it. A group of lawyers compiling the code and saying, "Let's see—insult to the Fatherland, how much is that worth?" And one says he thinks it's worth ten years in prison. And another says, "Eight—or six would be fairer."

KATAR   Between a couple of drinks they decide the total pain. . . .

TOSAN   The country's anesthetized. One thing tyranny does is force talent to degrade itself. People have grown used to oppression. As time goes by a lot of people, rather than spend the rest of their lives behind bars, compromise, then collaborate, and end by losing all self-respect.

KATAR   So what's the answer?

AMIEL   We're put in prison, our ideas are banned, our people divided, vengeance stalking the land—it's got to stop.

KATAR   But how?

AMIEL   The man in the moon.

KATAR   Man in the moon, yourself. You're the looney one.

AMIEL   Do you remember what he said when he first set foot on the moon?

THE LOUDSPEAKER   One small step for man . . . a giant leap for mankind.

AMIEL   It was a peaceful conquest—the first in history. The first victory in which other men weren't the losers.

KATAR   But we're still in prison, right?

AMIEL   This success will force people to come together and forget the witch hunts and intolerance that put us away.

KATAR   Tell that to the tyrants, to the dictators.

AMIEL   It's over—or nearly over—the time when they put handcuffs on the flowers.

KATAR   Why don't you shut up about the flowers.

AMIEL   No. It's time for a little sentiment. Once upon a time there was a demonstration. Among the crowd was a little man with a slight limp who wanted to protest along with the others. When the armies of the night—the police, that is—attacked, the little man was left by himself—he couldn't run because of his bad leg. And this small frail man said, "The hour has come when they put handcuffs on the flowers." He wasn't trying to be a poet. He just wanted to innocently express what he felt. A few weeks later he was shot in front of a fascist firing squad . . . (PRONOS *and* TOSAN *mime the scene.*) And because when he was alive he had the reputation of being a homosexual, as a little joke the commanding officer finished him off with a bullet up the ass. And this frail little man who foretold the tyranny we live under today, foretold freedom and justice for tomorrow.

KATAR   Who was he, the man with the limp? The poet?

AMIEL   Federico García Lorca.

Cannon shot. Flashes of light.

KATAR   Darling, it's me, Katar. I'm being held prisoner.

DRIMA   Don't cry. Bear it like a man.

KATAR Bring me my children. Let me say goodbye. Let me see them.

DRIMA You don't deserve to see them. They'll never kiss you again. You'll never see them again.

KATAR You can't do this to me, darling.

DRIMA Why not? Now you're out of the way. You can't boss me around the way you did before.

KATAR Have pity on me.

DRIMA I'd rather save it for the children.

> *Enter two girls,* FALIDIA *and* LELIA. *They take* KATAR *by the arms and hold him spread-eagled.* AMIEL *picks up a thick chain to beat him with.*

DRIMA You may begin. (AMIEL *beats* KATAR. DRIMA *continues, slowly, with relish, her eyes shut.*) I'll tell the children you're dead. I'll explain to them who you were. How you risked your future and theirs for the sake of your criminal ideas. (*Lashes.* KATAR *groans.*) Now you'll find out what it's like—how I suffered all those years I lived with you. (*Lashes. Groans.*) Suffer with dignity. (AMIEL, FALIDIA, *and* LELIA *leave him half-dead from beating.*) Don't you feel like playing horsie with me any more? (*She laughs. She rides him like a horse.*) Your back's all bloody. I'll stain my dress. (*She rides him.*) Giddyup

187

—go on! (*She takes the chain and beats him herself.*) We'll be very happy, me and the children. They'll forget they ever had a father who didn't deserve them. They'll forget in no time at all. Giddyup! We're on our way to Bethlehem to see the Christ child and bring him gold, frankincense, and myrrh.

Flashes of light. Lighting change.

AMIEL What's the matter? You're trembling. (KATAR *gesticulates.*) Your wife? Forget her. Don't upset yourself like that. You see how it is—when I dream, I dream fantastic things, strange adventures, but you return time and again to that business with your wife and kids. Your children . . . when they grow up, then you'll see. You'll be their idol. And the more hatefully she treated you—she and her friends and her family—the more devoted they'll be to you. (PRONOS *signals his agreement.*) Look, you're a painter. Your children will be artists. They'll immortalize your name.

KATAR But think of the education they'll be getting . . . for years and years.

AMIEL Brainwashing, I know. But they'll recover. And their revolt will be even more complete.

KATAR Poor little things . . . alone, abandoned, condemned to live in a hostile world. She'll make apprentice executioners of them!

AMIEL She'll try, but she won't succeed. (PRONOS *shakes his head.*) You can't hide sunlight under a bushel basket. The day will come when they'll see the light. And they'll get such a shock from it that they'll become light and life themselves.

THE LOUDSPEAKER Quiet in the cellblock!

All four sleep. Blackout.

THE LOUDSPEAKER Prisoner Tosan, your lawyer to see you.

PRONOS (*a lawyer*) I'm Captain Fontecha. I've been entrusted with your defense.

TOSAN Delighted.

He extends his hand; PRONOS *refuses.*

PRONOS (*a lawyer*) I should make it clear right away that I've been assigned to this case by the judge.

TOSAN To tell the truth, I didn't think I'd see you before the day of the trial.

PRONOS (*a lawyer*) Yes . . . it's not normal practice in these cases to interview the accused. It's enough to read the indictment. But your case has caused such a stir among the enemies of our Fatherland that I was curious to meet you.

189

TOSAN   I want to speak at my trial. I want to tell them . . .

PRONOS (*a lawyer*)   In court-martial procedure it is strictly forbidden for the accused to speak. I shall speak for you.

TOSAN   Tell them how they tortured me . . . please.

PRONOS (*a lawyer*)   What are you thinking of? Do you really think I'd go along with that—trying to run our country down with some absurd story about being tortured?

TOSAN   It's not absurd. They threw me out of a window. I nearly died. Look, you can still see the gashes on my forehead.

PRONOS (*a lawyer*)   Quiet. I am well aware what happened. While being interrogated, you jumped from the window in an attempt to give the police a bad reputation.

TOSAN   An officer hit me over the head with a typewriter. I passed out. They thought I was dead and they threw me out of the window. I still had my handcuffs on. I broke both my forearms and the base of my skull.

PRONOS (*a lawyer*)   Slanders against the Fatherland.

TOSAN   It's the absolute truth.

PRONOS (*a lawyer*) It's no good your going on like this. I'm warning you now. I saw the judge yesterday. He pulled a pistol out of his pocket and said, "I'll get that one myself. If necessary, I'll get him with this pistol. It served flag and Fatherland in the Civil War."

TOSAN Why bother with a trial?

PRONOS (*a lawyer*) Justice must be seen to be done.

TOSAN What spectators will be there? What journalists?

PRONOS (*a lawyer*) What do you think this is, a theater? There will be no spectators. The doors will be guarded. We're not going to make a spectacle of you. The day, the hour, and place of trial won't be known till a few hours beforehand.

TOSAN What can I say? They must be very unhappy, these people who have rigged this farce to prevent me from talking before they murder me.

PRONOS (*a lawyer*) No one is going to murder you. You will be condemned and executed.

TOSAN So you already know the verdict.

PRONOS (*a lawyer*) What else do you expect?

TOSAN And what is my defense to be—in your opinion?

191

PRONOS (*a lawyer*)   I shall admit the facts.

TOSAN   What facts?

PRONOS (*a lawyer*)   Your crimes.

TOSAN   What crimes?

PRONOS (*a lawyer*)   Those you committed in the Civil War.

TOSAN   Twenty-five years ago. I was seventeen. Anyway what crimes do you mean?

PRONOS (*a lawyer*)   You know very well.

TOSAN   I haven't read the indictment.

PRONOS (*a lawyer*)   The accused may not read it. That's the law.

TOSAN   My only crime was to set up an organization, which would be perfectly legal anywhere else, whose aim it was to see this country freely and justly governed.

PRONOS (*a lawyer*)   If you so much as open your mouth during the trial you will be taken from the room.

TOSAN   And the Director of Prosecutions will be Manuel Fernandez Martinez . . .

PRONOS (*a lawyer*)   As usual.

TOSAN   You know he hasn't even got the necessary diplomas stipulated in the Code of Justice.

PRONOS (*a lawyer*)   He is a patriot.

TOSAN   He is a fraud.

PRONOS (*a lawyer*)   How dare you!

TOSAN   It's common knowledge. He forged his certificates so everyone would think that twenty years ago he passed the bar.

PRONOS (*a lawyer*)   He is a man who thinks only of the good of his country and of God.

TOSAN   He's a man who's sent thousands of his fellows to face a firing squad.

PRONOS (*a lawyer*)   He's purged the country of traitors.

TOSAN   So that's what my trial is to be.

PRONOS (*a lawyer*)   I can see that I can't count on your cooperation.

TOSAN   Certainly not. I'm not going to be an accessory to my own murder.

Lighting change. TOSAN *gets up, holding himself erect.*

PRONOS (*a lawyer*)   I may have been assigned this case, but I refuse to represent you. I shall call upon Captain Redondo to take my place. (*He calls to the guards.*) Put this man on bread and water. He's to be kept in the strictest solitary confinement.

Flashes of light. Lighting change.

KATAR   They put him in solitary.

AMIEL   Afraid he might start something.

KATAR   In solitary . . . do you suppose they'll give him the death sentence?

Pause.

AMIEL   Galileo did right to defy the Inquisition. His theory was founded in reality. That was the first step toward the moon.

KATAR   Are you one of those who thinks they're going to open up the prisons?

AMIEL   We'll come out and there'll be thousands of women waiting for us.

KATAR (*putting him on*)   With flowers, right?

AMIEL   I can see it now . . . I'm already dreaming about it.

KATAR   You and your wet dreams.

AMIEL   My love dreams.

Flashes of light. Lighting change. Fanfare.

DRIMA   Are you the man who just came out of prison?

AMIEL   Yes, why?

DRIMA   I'm madly in love with you. Let me rub your jacket while I emerge from my shipwreck.

AMIEL   Please. Restrain yourself. As you can see, all women want the same as you.

FALIDIA   Please—look at me a moment and I shall be happy the rest of my life. Tell me about those long, bitter years in prison and I shall carry your words with me into all eternity. Spit on my panties and I'll be happy. (*She lifts her skirt.*)

AMIEL   A little decency! I belong to all of you.

FALIDIA   What a man. What a phoenix. How sad he is—like mist rising.

DRIMA   How well he speaks, what underwater bells sound in his voice. Prison is a university for the spirit. Why doesn't he look at us?

AMIEL *dances very grandly, moving in a way half-rhythmic, half-gymnastic, that excites the women's admiration.*

FALIDIA   Can I put a finger up your ass?

AMIEL   Quiet, you're distracting me.

DRIMA   Leave him alone. He's suffered a great deal over the years. Did you invent any theories while you were in prison?

AMIEL   Nothing worth mentioning. Trifles merely. The theory of relativity.

FALIDIA   What a man!

AMIEL   It's not important.

FALIDIA (*anxiously*)   Did you learn to sing?

AMIEL   Yes.

DRIMA   Sing something for us.

AMIEL   If you insist.

He sings an operatic aria, at the end of which he gets a fantastic ovation. He bows.

DRIMA   Did you go in for sports?

AMIEL   Nothing much really. I'm going to break the world record for the pole vault and the hundred-yard dash and I play chess blindfolded.

FALIDIA   What a man!

DRIMA   Could I clean your nostrils with my fingertips?

AMIEL   Please, I'm meditating.

He meditates—the exact image of Rodin's Thinker, *only on a lavatory bowl.*

DRIMA   Look, he's meditating just like Rodin's *Thinker.*

FALIDIA   He's so talented!

DRIMA   Shhhh, you'll distract him.

As they leave, LELIA *comes in and touches* AMIEL's *shoulder. They stare at each other, fascinated.*

AMIEL   Lelia!

LELIA   Amiel!

AMIEL   You haven't changed. Still the same—only more beautiful.

LELIA   I waited for you. You're not the only one, I too have spent all these years locked up in a closet waiting for you to come out of prison.

197

AMIEL Poor love.

LELIA Look. Spiders have spun their webs between my legs and under my arms. (*She shows him her spidered webs.*) It was all for you.

AMIEL You knew I'd come back.

LELIA Yes, I knew. I knew as soon as the age of Pisces was past and we were into the age of Aquarius that you'd come back to me free and serene.

AMIEL Do you love me?

LELIA I close my eyes and I see you as a radiant giant.

AMIEL I knew that if you didn't come to visit me in the last twenty years, it was only because you were saving yourself for me.

LELIA Look, for every year that passed I made a little mark on the palm of my hand with a hot iron.

AMIEL Take off your clothes.

LELIA Take off your clothes.

AMIEL Come closer.

LELIA Wrap your whole body around me.

The two women enter and surround them with a sheet. Organ music. Under the sheet, AMIEL *and*

198

LELIA *remove their clothes and embrace. The women lower the sheet to reveal* AMIEL *and* LELIA *kneeling, touching from knee to breast.*

AMIEL   I've a little bubble of air. It's God. I can feel it quite clearly. When I'm happy it gets very light. I look down and see how beautiful you are beneath me and it's so light it hardly exists. The bubble goes from my heart to my head and from my head to my heart and vibrates in my cock. (*With religious dedication,* AMIEL *puts a glue-like substance [sperm] in* LELIA*'s mouth. She swallows it.*) This is my body which is given for you. Take, eat—forever and ever. So be it.

LELIA   Forever and ever. So be it.

Organ music. Flashes of light. Shouts: "They've sentenced Tosan to death. They've sentenced him to death." Bass drum. Lighting change.

KATAR   They've sentenced Tosan to death.

AMIEL   Sentenced to death? Oh, Christ.

They fall down and weep, PRONOS *more than the others.*

Hey, Pronos . . . maybe you can't talk but you can mourn with us.

PRONOS *gets up. He makes gestures as if he were going to speak. They all look at him. He goes on*

199

gesticulating and moving his lips and tries to speak. At last he does.

PRONOS   Don't kill him. Don't kill him.

AMIEL   You can talk!

KATAR   After twenty years of silence!

AMIEL   You can talk. You've found your voice again.

The light concentrates on PRONOS.

THE APPARITION   Every morning, for years after the war, the reactionary government executed large numbers of prisoners against the cemetery wall. The authorities discovered that these men uttered subversive remarks like "Long Live Freedom" as they fell under the hail of bullets. To put a stop to this it was decided that those under sentence of death should be fitted with muzzles as they left the prison. These muzzles had a wooden peg attached which held the mouth open during the execution, but which prevented the man from shouting.

THE LOUDSPEAKER   Convict Pronos. Report to the grill for execution.

Change of lighting.

KATAR (*a jailer*)   Convict Pronos.

200

PRONOS Don't kill me. It's a mistake. It's not possible. I haven't done anything.

KATAR (*a jailer*) Hold still. We're going to put a muzzle on you so you don't shout things when you get in front of the firing squad.

PRONOS (*trembling with fright*) No, no. I haven't done anything. Don't kill me.

KATAR (*a jailer*) Be quiet. The muzzle's still soaked with spit from the man who was shot yesterday. (*He puts it on* PRONOS *who continues to struggle despite the muzzle*.) And now we're going to put you up against the wall. But first we're going to give you a little truck ride. You Reds can't say we don't treat you right on the day of your execution.

THE LOUDSPEAKER Attention! There has been a mistake. The prisoner Pronos is not under sentence of death. It is the prisoner Tronos . . . with a *T* as in Teresa.

KATAR (*a jailer*) Whew, that was close. Five more minutes and you'd have had it. Well, you were right after all. You didn't do anything. Hang on while I take this muzzle off. That's better. Now you can talk. (PRONOS *is paralyzed*.) What's the matter with you? Say something. (PRONOS *tries, but without success*.) You wanted to talk so bad . . . now, talk! (PRONOS *tries, but can't*.) If you don't say something, I'll kick

201

your ass. (PRONOS *tries again.* KATAR *beats him, but
without success. Pause.*) Oh shit. Never seen anything like it . . . he's gone dumb with fright. (*He
bursts out laughing. Great guffaws.*)

Lighting change. FALIDIA *is standing center stage
in a long cape. A large, blood-stained flag stretches
the width of the stage above the audience's heads.
A patch is spreading in the center. Beneath this
patch is a sort of basin. Blood drips steadily from
the patch to the basin during the rest of the play.
A clock shows four in the morning.*

FALIDIA   Please hurry up and put me through.
(*Pause.*) Yes, I know you're all doing your best.
Thank you. But please make an effort. At five o'clock
my husband will be executed. (*Pause.*) God, how
could something like this happen to me? Here I am,
surrounded by my friends—they're doing everything they can, going from one phone to another,
and still I feel all alone. If only I could be with him.

THE LOUDSPEAKER (*a telephone operator*)   I've got the
President's confessor on the line for you. (*Pause.*)
Hello. One moment please.

FALIDIA (*breaking in*)   Father Mendoza?

*A spot comes up on the basin. The confessor is
seen.*

202

AMIEL (*a confessor; unctuously*) Tell me, my daughter, how can I help you?

FALIDIA At five o'clock—that's less than an hour—my husband will be executed. Please, I beg you, intercede with the President in his behalf. You are the President's confessor.

AMIEL (*a confessor*) All of us here, my daughter, have your husband very much in our thoughts. We all pray for him.

FALIDIA But if you put in an appeal, they won't kill him.

AMIEL (*a confessor*) God in his infinite mercy will pardon even those whose sins are the most heinous.

FALIDIA My husband's only sin was to demand that a representative government be set up. (*Pause.*) Excuse me, but I've no time to lose. I beg you, by all that you hold dear, to appeal for mercy.

AMIEL (*a confessor*) I will remember you in my prayers. God bless you, my daughter.

FALIDIA (*whispered*) Your prayers?

The confessor ostentatiously washes his hands in the basin. He wipes them. The light concentrates on him. Blackout. Pause. A memory. A strange light. A spot lights FALIDIA *and* TOSAN. *A bright sun replaces the clock.*

FALIDIA   Tosan! I'm so happy to see you. It's so long since we had any time together. Bury my legs in the sand.

TOSAN   Falidia!

FALIDIA   I've got a terrible feeling . . . you're going away, aren't you?

TOSAN   Yes. We've work to do, my comrades and I. We must put an end to tyranny once and for all. The people must win back their freedom.

FALIDIA   But what about me and the children?

TOSAN   You're always in my thoughts.

FALIDIA   You know, Tosan, when you're away I set a place for you at the table . . . every morning I get ready for you to come back and at night I never sleep on the left side of the bed—that's your place.

TOSAN   You are my hero, my stream, my childhood, my blue clouds, my light. I love you, Falidia.

FALIDIA   When you come back I'll scrub the ground in front of our house to welcome you and while you're gone the walls will be painted with sadness and I'll lock up my heart in my lonely woman's bones.

They embrace. The telephone rings. Blackout. Lights up. The clock shows a quarter past four.

THE LOUDSPEAKER (*a telephone operator*) Good news, madam. We've just heard that the Pope and foreign heads of state are continually in touch with the President on your husband's behalf.

FALIDIA Thank God. If only they can save him.

THE LOUDSPEAKER (*telephone operator*) Your party is on the line.

FALIDIA Is that General Teran de Rey?

KATAR (*general*) *is standing by the basin.*

KATAR (*a general; very stiff and military*) Dear Lady . . .

FALIDIA I am the wife of . . .

KATAR (*a general; cutting her short*) Madam, as a Christian, you have all my sympathies.

FALIDIA What I'm asking is for you to intercede with the President on behalf of my husband. I beg you, in the name of our common humanity.

KATAR (*a general*) You may rest assured, madam, that as far as your husband is concerned, in my character as a man of honor, prepared to defend our country and all it stands for to the last drop of my blood, I shall conduct myself throughout according to the dictates of my conscience.

FALIDIA   Clemency!

KATAR (*a general*)   Don't let me keep you. Duty calls. My respects, madam.

> *The general ostentatiously washes his hands in the basin. The light concentrates on him. He wipes his hands.*

FALIDIA's VOICE   My Tosan is such a good man. How can they hate him enough to kill him? Oh, Tosan, why should I have to force myself to be polite to them? They're your executioners! I'd like to tell them what I really think . . . but your life comes first.

> *Pause. A memory. Strange light. Spot on* FALIDIA *and* TOSAN. *The sun replaces the clock.*

FALIDIA   You are my life. When you're here I feel so safe just like a little girl under a giant mushroom. Do you suppose they've made dawns just to wrap around us and shower us with kisses? Oh, please, Tosan, don't go, not yet.

TOSAN   Don't think about my journey. I've got to fight.

FALIDIA   I know, but couldn't you stay just one more day?

TOSAN   In the big cities there are two taverns, one for thieves—that's the stock market—and one for murderers—that's the courthouse. We must open the prisons and disband the army. The emancipation of man must be total. And revolution is the only answer.

FALIDIA   Please don't leave me!

TOSAN   I have to go. I have to fight.

FALIDIA   Take me with you.

TOSAN   Alone.

FALIDIA   You know what you must do. You are the root and the mountain and we follow you blindly.

TOSAN   I love you more than anything in the world.

They embrace. The telephone rings. Blackout. Lights up. The clock shows half past four.

THE LOUDSPEAKER (*a telephone operator*)   Madam, I'd like to confirm the report which has reached us from the best-informed sources. The Pope and foreign heads of state interceded for your husband at a quarter past four this morning.

FALIDIA   Thank God. (*She weeps.*)

THE LOUDSPEAKER (*a telephone operator*)   The President of the Bank is on the line for you.

FALIDIA   Thank you. (*Pause.*) Sir . . . I'm calling to . . .

PRONOS (*a banker*)   Please . . . there's no need to call me "sir." That's what they used to call company directors in the old days, but we've come a long way since then. Nowadays, we're much closer to the people. Everything is much less formal. You can call me by my first name. Call me Jack.

FALIDIA   I know you're a close friend of the President and one of the principal financial backers of his campaigns.

PRONOS (*a banker*)   We are blessed with a leader, a man who holds the reins of government firmly in his hands—a reliable guide. We are only his underlings, that is to say we submit of our own free will.

FALIDIA   But the trial . . . the trial only lasted three hours.

PRONOS (*a banker*)   Would you have preferred a trial that dragged on for several weeks—as is the custom in certain decadent countries? Your husband was fortunate enough to be dealt with speedily. Why force him to carry the burden of his shame in public any longer than was absolutely necessary?

FALIDIA   There were no witnesses.

PRONOS (*a banker*)   He was tried before a military court. What good would witnesses have been? Do you suppose they'd have in any way influenced the verdict?

FALIDIA Could you speak to the President?

PRONOS (*a banker*) You should have confidence in him. He will do nothing prejudicial to those principles sacred to the Fatherland.

FALIDIA Would you intercede for my husband?

PRONOS (*a banker*) Whatever happens let no reproaches be levelled against our invincible leader. Believe me, madam, I understand your grief and you will always find in me a man who, out of the kindness of his heart, will do everything in his power to heal those scars that your husband's behavior must have caused. It would be a pity to keep you any longer from your task. I wish you all the best. Goodbye, madam.

He washes his hands ostentatiously. The light concentrates on him. He wipes his hands. Spot on FALIDIA. *She is on her knees, crying, her forehead on the ground. She tries to get a grip on herself. She stands up and covers herself in an enormous black cape which hides her almost completely. Blackout.*

The following conversation takes place during blackout.

THE LOUDSPEAKER (*a secretary*)   It's five to four. Can I speak to the President, please?

THE PRESIDENT'S VOICE   This is the President speaking.

THE LOUDSPEAKER (*a secretary*)   Your excellency?

THE PRESIDENT'S VOICE   What are you waiting for? Go ahead.

THE LOUDSPEAKER (*a secretary*)   About today's execution . . . I've heard that the Pope, the President of the United States, and other heads of state are planning to telephone you to intercede for the condemned man.

THE PRESIDENT'S VOICE   Yes, I'd heard about that.

THE LOUDSPEAKER (*a secretary*)   Had you thought of putting the execution off to give the foreign powers a chance to calm down?

   Pause.

THE PRESIDENT'S VOICE   I've given it a great deal of thought . . . and, no, I will not postpone the execution.

THE LOUDSPEAKER (*a secretary*)   What are your orders then?

Long silence.

THE PRESIDENT'S VOICE He is not to be executed . . .
at five o'clock this morning. (*Long pause.*) He is to
be executed immediately on the stroke of four.

Long silence.

THE LOUDSPEAKER (*a secretary*) The widow will claim
the body.

THE PRESIDENT'S VOICE It must disappear without
trace. There must be nothing left!

> *Music: Saeta. Two executioners in hoods.* TOSAN
> *has been condemned to death by strangulation.*
> *They bring in the garroting chair and place it*
> *center stage. They lead* TOSAN, *who is naked, to the*
> *chair and seat him. A woman weeps.*

THE APPARITION Garroting is death by strangulation.
The condemned man is seated in a chair, his neck in
a collar. The collar is attached to a vice which goes
through the back of the chair. A few turns on the
vice forces it into the condemned man's neck and
kills him.

> *They put straps around his neck, arms, and legs.*
> *The executioner works the handle. Drum roll. A*
> *sharp crack.* TOSAN's *head falls to one side and*
> *hangs. At this moment* TOSAN, *who is naked,*
> *urinates. A woman,* FALIDIA, *catches the liquid in*

211

a bowl. Two women take the bowl from FALIDIA
and hold it before her. She dips her hands into the
bowl. When she removes them they are covered
with blood. The urine is really blood. She washes
her face in this blood. There is a very slow fade to
black.

THE END

THE ARCHITECT
AND THE EMPEROR OF ASSYRIA

translated from the French
by Everard D'Harnoncourt
and Adele Shank

This play was first produced by Lars Schmidt at the Théâtre Montparnasse, Paris, on March 18, 1967. The production was staged by Jorge Lavelli, set and costumes by Roland Deville. The Emperor of Assyria was played by Raymond Gerome and the Architect by Jean-Pierre Jorris.

ACT ONE

SCENE ONE

Airplane noises. Like a trapped and frightened animal, the
ARCHITECT *looks for a refuge. He runs in all directions, digs
in the ground, starts to run again, and finally buries his head
in the sand. Explosion. A bright flash of flames. Trembling
with fear the* ARCHITECT, *his face against the sand, puts his
fingers in his ears.*

A few moments later the EMPEROR *appears. He is carrying a large suitcase. He has a certain forced elegance. He
tries to keep his composure.*

He touches the ARCHITECT *with the tip of his cane.*

EMPEROR: Help me, sir! I am the only survivor of the accident.

ARCHITECT (*horrified*): Fee! Fee! Feegaa! Feegaa! Fee!
Fee! (*For a moment he looks aghast at the* EMPEROR
and then runs off as fast as he can.)

BLACKOUT

215

SCENE TWO

Two years later. The EMPEROR *and the* ARCHITECT *are on stage.*

EMPEROR: It's quite simple, after all. Come on, repeat!

ARCHITECT: Escalator. (*He has some difficulty in pronouncing the "s."*)

EMPEROR (*emphatically*): Now I've lived on this island for two whole years, I've given you lessons for two years, and you still hesitate! It would take Aristotle himself to teach you the sum of two chairs and two tables.

ARCHITECT: I can already talk. No?

EMPEROR: Well . . . yes. At least, if someone drops onto this island some day you can say to him, "Ave Caesar."

ARCHITECT: But today you are to teach me . . .

EMPEROR: Right now listen to my muse singing the wrath of Achilles. My throne!

He sits down. The ARCHITECT *bows low before him.*

That's right, never forget that I am the Emperor of Assyria.

ARCHITECT: Assyria is bordered on the North by the Caspian Sea, on the South by the Indian Ocean . . .

EMPEROR: Stop! That's enough.

ARCHITECT: Teach me, like you promised . . .

EMPEROR: Quiet, quiet. (*Dreamily.*) Ah! Civilization, civilization!

ARCHITECT (*contentedly*): Yes, yes.

EMPEROR: Be quiet! What can you know, you who have lived all your life stuck on this island that the maps have forgotten and that God crapped into the ocean by mistake.

ARCHITECT: Tell me, tell me!

EMPEROR: On your knees! (*The* ARCHITECT *kneels.*) That's all right, it's not necessary. (*The* ARCHITECT *gets up. With great emphasis.*) I will explain.

ARCHITECT: Oh yes! Explain!

EMPEROR: Be quiet! (*Again with emphasis.*) I will explain my life. (*Rising and making large gestures.*) I arose with the first streaks of dawn. Trumpets resounded from all the churches, all the synagogues, all the temples. The day began to break. My father came to awaken me followed by a regiment of violinists. Ah! Music! What a wonder! (*Suddenly alarmed.*) Have you cooked the pork and beans?

ARCHITECT: Yes, sire.

EMPEROR: Where was I? Ah! My awakening by the regiment of trumpeters who came in the morning, the violins of the churches . . . What mornings! What awakenings! Then my divine blind slave girls came running to me and, all naked, taught me philosophy. Ah! Philosophy! Some day I'll explain to you what that is.

ARCHITECT: Sire, how did they teach you philosophy?

217

EMPEROR: Let's not go into details. And my fiancée . . . and my mother . . .

ARCHITECT: Mama, mama, mama.

EMPEROR (*terrified*): Where did you hear that cry?

ARCHITECT: You taught it to me.

EMPEROR: When? Where?

ARCHITECT: The other day.

EMPEROR: What did I say?

ARCHITECT: You said your mother took you in her arms and rocked you and kissed you on the forehead and . . .

The EMPEROR *relives the evoked scene. He curls up in a ball on his chair as if an invisible person rocked him, embraced him, etc.*

And you said she sometimes beat you with a whip and she took you by the hand when you went for a walk and . . .

EMPEROR: Stop! Stop! Is the fire lighted?

ARCHITECT: Yes.

EMPEROR: Are you sure that it stays lighted day and night?

ARCHITECT: Yes, look at the smoke.

EMPEROR: That's all right. Who cares!

ARCHITECT: What do you mean, who cares? You said that some day a ship or an airplane would see us and come for us.

EMPEROR: And what will we do then?

ARCHITECT: Well, we'll go to your country where there are automobiles, phonograph records, and television, and women, and plates of confetti, and miles of thought, and Thursdays longer than nature, and . . .

EMPEROR (*changing the subject*): Have you prepared the cross?

ARCHITECT: There it is. (*Pointing to the bushes.*) Will you crucify me now?

EMPEROR: What! I'm the one who has to be crucified! Isn't it me?

ARCHITECT: We drew by lot. Have you forgotten?

EMPEROR (*angrily*): How could that be! We drew by lot to see who would atone for humanity?

ARCHITECT: Master, you forget everything.

EMPEROR: How did we draw by lot? With what?

ARCHITECT: With a straw.

EMPEROR (*laughing like a madman*): A straw! A straw!

ARCHITECT: Why are you laughing, master?

EMPEROR: I never told you what the word "straw" means.

ARCHITECT: You said . . .

EMPEROR (*changing the subject*): My blind slave girls who taught me philosophy dressed only in pink bath towels! What a memory I have! I remember as if it were yesterday. How they caressed my divine body, how they cleaned its dirtiest corners such as . . . To horse!

ARCHITECT: Shall I be the horse?

EMPEROR: No, I will.

He gets down on all fours. The ARCHITECT *straddles him.*

Say to me: gee-up!

ARCHITECT: Gee-up horsey!

EMPEROR: Beat me with a whip!

The ARCHITECT *whips him with a branch.*

ARCHITECT: Gee-up, horsey! Faster! We have to get to Babylon. Faster!

They trot. They circle the stage several times. Suddenly the EMPEROR *throws the* ARCHITECT *to the ground.*

219

EMPEROR (*beside himself*): What? You didn't put on the spurs?

ARCHITECT: What are spurs?

EMPEROR: How did you expect us to get to . . .

ARCHITECT: To Babylon.

EMPEROR (*terrified*): Where did you get that word? Who taught it to you? Who comes to see you while I sleep? (*He throws himself on the* ARCHITECT *and half strangles him.*)

ARCHITECT: You! You taught it to me.

EMPEROR: Me?

ARCHITECT: Yes, you said it was a city in your Assyrian Empire.

EMPEROR (*recovering his composure, with emphasis*): Ants! (*Looking at a procession of ants on the ground.*) Ants! Miniature slaves! Go and fetch me a goblet of water this instant! (*He sits on the throne and waits. Uneasily.*) Didn't you hear? (*Long silence.*) I said, go and fetch me a goblet of water! (*Furious.*) What! You don't respect the Emperor of Assyria? Is it possible? Die at my feet! (*In a rage, he stamps furiously on the ants. Exhausted, he falls on his "throne."*)

ARCHITECT: Here.

EMPEROR (*throwing the goblet away*): What do I want with water? I only drink vodka. (*A little laugh.*)

ARCHITECT: Didn't you say that . . .

EMPEROR: And my fiancée . . . have I spoken to you of my fiancée?

ARCHITECT (*as if reciting a lesson*): She was very beautiful, very pretty, very blond, with green eyes and . . .

EMPEROR: Are you making fun of me?

ARCHITECT: You've already told me about her.

EMPEROR: Will you do my fiancée?

ARCHITECT: Now?

EMPEROR: You refuse to do my fiancée! (*Furious.*) Savage!

ARCHITECT: The last times it was always me who had to do the fiancée and you didn't do a darn thing!

EMPEROR: I've taught you slang too. I'm lost!

ARCHITECT: When are you going to teach me architecture?

EMPEROR: What for? Aren't you already an architect?

ARCHITECT: All right, I'll do the fiancée.

EMPEROR: But didn't you just now express the desire that I teach you architecture? Ah! Architecture!

ARCHITECT: We said that I should do the fiancée.

EMPEROR: We said that I should teach you architecture today! The fundamental principles of architecture are . . . All right, I'll do the fiancée if you insist.

ARCHITECT: Then what are the fundamental principles of architecture?

EMPEROR (*furious*): I said that today I'll do the fiancée if you're so keen on it.

ARCHITECT: Put on the skirts and petticoats.

EMPEROR: I don't even know where they are. You lose everything. You leave things everywhere. But . . . could it be that you are ignorant of the fundamental principles of architecture, you, an Assyrian architect? Could it be that you have so shamefully abused my confidence in granting you the title of Supreme Architect of Assyria, when you are even ignorant of the rudiments of architecture? What will the neighbors say?

ARCHITECT: You're the one who appointed me. It's not my fault. I'm not the emperor.

EMPEROR: Where are those damned petticoats. Ants! Go and fetch me the skirts and petticoats this instant!

ARCHITECT: They won't obey you.

EMPEROR: What, they won't obey me? Ants, slaves, go and

221

fetch my petticoats. Today I'll play the fiancée . . . Don't you hear me? What? Where's my head? I've already forgotten that I just crushed all of them. (*Very gently.*) Listen, be frank, do you think that I'm a dictator?

ARCHITECT: What's a dictator?

EMPEROR: Well, of course I'm not a militarist. Tell me, my subjects, do you feel crushed under my yoke? Tell me, confess, am I a tyrant?

ARCHITECT: You're not a tyrant. (*Tired of it.*) Is that enough for you?

EMPEROR: I slaughtered the ants! Tyrants do . . .

ARCHITECT: The skirts!

EMPEROR: But aren't we going to play priests today?

ARCHITECT: All right, I see you don't want to.

EMPEROR (*without putting on the skirt, in a woman's voice*): Oh, my love! Do you love me? Together we will go . . .

ARCHITECT: You are so beautiful that when I think of you I feel a flower sprouting up between my legs and its transparent petals spreading over my thighs . . . May I touch your knees?

EMPEROR (*as a woman*): Never have I been so happy. Such a joy inundates me that jets of water spring from my hands to your hands.

ARCHITECT: You with knees so white, so round, so tender . . .

EMPEROR: Caress them! (*He tries to lift his trouser legs to show his knees. He can't.*) Shit! The petticoats! (*Silence.*)

ARCHITECT: I built a canoe.

EMPEROR: Are you leaving? Are you going to abandon me?

ARCHITECT: I'll paddle till I get to another island.

EMPEROR (*emphatically*): Oh! Fortunate young man, Homer has made himself the herald of your virtues.

ARCHITECT: What did you say?

EMPEROR: And your mother?

ARCHITECT: You know very well, I never had a mother!

EMPEROR: You're the son of a siren and a centaur. The perfect union. (*Very sadly.*) Mama, mama. (*He takes a few steps, looking for her, then looks under his throne.*) Mama, where are you? It's me, I'm all alone here, everyone's forgotten me, but you . . .

ARCHITECT (*putting a veil on his head and playing the mother*): My child, what's the matter? You're not alone, it's me, your mama.

EMPEROR: Mama, everybody hates me, they've abandoned me on this island.

ARCHITECT (*very maternally, holding the* EMPEROR *in the shelter of his arms*): No, my child. I'm here to protect you. You mustn't feel alone. Come on, tell your mother everything.

EMPEROR: Mama, the Architect wants to abandon me. He's built a canoe so he can get away and I'll be left alone.

ARCHITECT (*as the mother*): Don't believe that. You'll see that it's for your own good. He'll get help and they'll come to save you.

EMPEROR: Are you sure, mama?

ARCHITECT (*as the mother*): Yes, my child.

EMPEROR: Mama, don't go, always stay with me.

ARCHITECT (*as the mother*): Yes, my child, I'll stay here with you, day and night.

EMPEROR: Dear little mommy, kiss me.

The ARCHITECT *goes to give him a kiss. The* EMPEROR *brutally pushes him away.*

You stink! You stink! What the devil did you eat?

ARCHITECT: The same as you.

223

EMPEROR: Make an appointment with the dentist. Have your teeth filled. You smell rotten!

ARCHITECT: You promised me . . .

EMPEROR: I promised you, I promised you . . . so what? Bring me my cigar box.

ARCHITECT (*with a low bow*): As Your Majesty commands, so it will be done. (*He leaves and returns with a stone.*)

EMPEROR: When I say my cigars, I mean "Geneviève et Michel."

The ARCHITECT *leaves for an instant and returns with the same stone.*

ARCHITECT: Here they are, sir.

The EMPEROR *touches the stone, pretends to choose a good cigar, takes one, smells it, and cuts off the end.*

EMPEROR: Ah! Aroma worthy of the gods! Ah! "Geneviève et Michel" cigars!

ARCHITECT (*starting to light the cigar with a lighter*): Here's a light, sir.

EMPEROR: What? With a lighter? And you are a valet who has studied at the University of . . . What a disgrace! And where did you put the canoe?

ARCHITECT: On the beach.

EMPEROR (*very sadly*): And when did you make it? (*Without giving the* ARCHITECT *time to answer.*) Why did you build it without breathing a word to me? Swear that you won't leave without telling me.

ARCHITECT: I swear.

EMPEROR: On what?

ARCHITECT: On whatever you wish, whatever you hold most sacred.

EMPEROR: On the Constitution of the island.

224

ARCHITECT: Isn't it an absolute monarchy?

EMPEROR: Silence! It is I who speak here and only I.

ARCHITECT: When are you going to teach it to me?

EMPEROR: Now what are you talking about? You spend the whole damn day nagging at me to teach you this and to teach you that.

ARCHITECT: You promised me that today you'd teach me how to be happy.

EMPEROR: Not now. Later, without fail.

ARCHITECT: You always say the same thing.

EMPEROR: Do you doubt my word?

ARCHITECT: When you're happy, what's it like?

EMPEROR: I'll tell you later. Such impatience! Such impatience! Ah! Youth!

ARCHITECT: You know how I imagine it? I think that when you're happy, you're with someone who has a very fine skin and then you kiss her on the lips and everything is veiled in a rose-colored smoke and her body changes into a multitude of small mirrors and when you look at her you're reflected a million times, and you ride with her on zebras and on panthers around a lake and she keeps you attached by a cord and when you look at her it begins to rain dove's feathers which fall to the ground neighing like young colts, and then you enter a room and you walk with her hand in hand on the ceiling (*he speaks hurriedly*) and the heads become covered with snakes who caress you and the snakes become covered with sea urchins who tickle them, and the sea urchins become covered with golden gifts and the golden scarabs . . .

EMPEROR: Enough!

ARCHITECT: Moo! Moo! (*Getting on all fours.*) You see I'm a cow.

EMPEROR: Hold your tongue, you idiot.

225

ARCHITECT: Will you masturbate me?

EMPEROR: Don't you respect me any more?

ARCHITECT: You are the very illustrious and very wise Emperor of powerful Assyria. (*He bows ceremoniously.*)

EMPEROR: What did you dream last night?

ARCHITECT: Assyria, the greatest empire of the Occidental world, in its battle against the Oriental world . . .

EMPEROR: Jackass! It's the other way around.

ARCHITECT: I am talking about the yellow peril.

EMPEROR: So you have become a reactionary?

ARCHITECT: It's not like that?

EMPEROR: Let's make war.

> *They get ready. They crouch down. They seize "machine guns." They shoot: tac-tac-tac-tac. They find themselves face to face, camouflaged. They each carry a "helmet" and a "flag."*

ARCHITECT (*camouflaged; only his "flag" can be seen*): This is the Radio of the Victorious Forces. (*In the voice of an announcer.*) Enemy soldiers! Don't be deceived by the false propaganda of your officers. This is the Commander-in-Chief talking to you. Yesterday we obliterated with hydrogen bombs the civilian population of half of your country. Surrender like soldiers. You have claim to the honors of war. For a better world!

EMPEROR (*in the same voice*): This is the official Radio of the Future Victorious Forces. This is the Marshal-in-Chief talking to you. Enemy soldiers, don't let yourself be seduced by the demagogy of your superiors. Yesterday our rockets wiped out the entire civilian population of your nation, (*sounding like a scratched record*) civilian population of your nation, civilian population of your nation . . .

The ARCHITECT *emerges from his camouflaged sector. He cries. The* EMPEROR *emerges, also in tears. They turn back to back, both dressed as soldiers and "armed." They cry while they look at photos of their dead civilian relatives. All at once they turn around, scrutinize each other, and take aim.*

EMPEROR *and* ARCHITECT (*shouting*): Hands up, traitor!

Hands in the air, they throw down their "machine guns" and look at each other with terror. A pause.

ARCHITECT: Are you an enemy soldier?

EMPEROR: Don't kill me.

ARCHITECT: Don't kill me.

EMPEROR: So, is this how you fight for a better world?

ARCHITECT: To tell the truth, the war scares me. I cower deep in my trench and . . . I hope it'll end soon.

EMPEROR: I put up my hands because of you! It's disgusting! Fine soldiers the enemy has.

ARCHITECT: And you?

EMPEROR: Me, I'm not much of a soldier. Here in my sector we all want this to end soon. What're those photographs you were looking at?

ARCHITECT (*on the verge of tears*): All the members of my family that you've killed with your big fat bombs.

EMPEROR (*condescendingly*): Come on, buddy, don't cry. Look at mine, you killed them.

ARCHITECT: Them too? Well, we really don't have any luck. (*He dissolves into tears.*)

EMPEROR (*majestically, throwing down his soldier's equipment*): What a life I led! Every morning my father came to wake me with a cortege of ballerinas. All of them danced for me. Ah! Dance! Some day I'll teach

227

you about dance. The entire population of Assyria witnessed my getting-out-of-bed ceremony, thanks to television. Then came the audiences. First the civilian audience which I granted from my bed while my hermaphrodite slaves combed my hair and poured all the perfumes of Arabia on my body. Then began the military audience which I granted from the height of my toilet chair, and finally the ecclesiastic audience . . . (*Very concerned.*) What is your religion?

ARCHITECT: The one you taught me.

EMPEROR: Then you believe in God?

ARCHITECT: Are you going to baptize me?

EMPEROR: What? You aren't baptized? You are doomed! For all eternity you'll roast day and night, and the most beautiful she-devils will be chosen to excite you but they'll push red-hot irons up your rectum.

ARCHITECT: You said I'd go to heaven.

EMPEROR: Child! How little you know of life.

ARCHITECT: Hear my confession.

The EMPEROR *sits on the throne. The* ARCHITECT *kneels at his feet.*

Father, since my last confession I have been guilty of . . .

EMPEROR: What idiotic farce is this? I am doing the confessor again! Out of my sight, ludicrous knave. I'll not confess you. Because of me you shall die, crushed by the weight of your sins and you'll roast for all eternity.

ARCHITECT: I dreamed that . . .

EMPEROR: Who asked you to tell me your dream?

ARCHITECT: You just asked me.

EMPEROR: What do I care about your dreams . . . All right, tell me.

ARCHITECT: I dreamed I was alone on a deserted island and all of a sudden an airplane fell and I was in a terrible panic and I ran everywhere. I even tried to bury my head in the sand and then someone called from behind me and . . .

EMPEROR: Don't continue. What a strange dream! Freud, come to my aid!

ARCHITECT: Is this one erotic too?

EMPEROR: How could it be otherwise?

ARCHITECT (*bringing a whip*): Are you going to beat me?

EMPEROR (*condescendingly*): All right. What role shall I play?

ARCHITECT: I don't care.

EMPEROR: Shall I do your mother?

ARCHITECT: Come on, quick, beat me, I can't stand it any longer. (*He bares his back and waits to receive the blows of the whip.*)

EMPEROR: Why this haste? So now the gentleman must be obeyed instantly. No sooner said than done.

ARCHITECT (*in a tone of supplication*): Come on, beat me. Only ten blows. Come on!

EMPEROR: "Only" ten blows! At my age! Perhaps you imagine that I'm young Hamlet leaping over the tombs of his rotting ancestors?

ARCHITECT: Whip me, whip me, I can't stand it any longer, it hurts there.

EMPEROR: Now, now, let's not have a nervous breakdown. I'll whip you. But . . . how many times?

ARCHITECT: As many as you want, but make it fast. If you hit hard, one will be enough.

EMPEROR: Where to whip the gentleman? (*With emphasis.*) On his rosy behind? On his ebony back? On his thighs —elegiac columns of immortal Sparta?

ARCHITECT: Beat me, beat me!

EMPEROR: All right, here I go!

Solemnly he hits the ARCHITECT *once very lightly and with extreme gentleness. The* ARCHITECT *hurls himself on the* EMPEROR, *pulls the whip away from him, and whips himself twice with great violence. He falls on the ground like a madman. Then he gets up and goes off.*

ARCHITECT: I'm leaving forever.

The EMPEROR *paces majestically.*

EMPEROR: So be it. Let's be Shakespearian. This provides me with the occasion for a monologue. (*He sobs. He blows his nose into a large handkerchief.*) Ah! Alone at last. (*He walks up and down with an air of agitation.*) But how can I manage to atone for humanity all by myself? (*He mimes the crucifixion. Suddenly he shouts.*) Architect! Architect! (*Softer.*) Forgive me. (*He sobs and blows his nose. He mimes the crucifixion.*) The feet, yes. I can nail the feet better than a centurion, but . . . (*He shows with gestures the difficulty of nailing the hands.*) Architect! Come back, I'll whip you as many times as you want and as hard as you want.

He cries. The ARCHITECT *enters. Very dignified, the* EMPEROR *stops sobbing.*

How come you're here? You listen at doors? You spy on me?

ARCHITECT: Aren't you mad at me?

EMPEROR: Shall I beat you?

ARCHITECT: Don't bother.

EMPEROR: Have I sometimes regaled you about my fourteen secretaries?

ARCHITECT: The–always–naked–fourteen–secretaries–who–wrote – the – masterpieces – which – you – dictated–to– them . . .

EMPEROR: You have the audacity to jeer at my literature? Know that I was offered the . . . what's the name, let's see . . .

ARCHITECT: Nobel–Prize–and–you–refused–it–because . . .

EMPEROR: Be quiet, babbler! What do you know about morality?

ARCHITECT: Morality is bordered on the North by the Caspian Sea, and the South . . .

EMPEROR: Animal! You jumble everything up. That's Assyria. Confusing Assyria with morality! What a barbarian! What a savage!

ARCHITECT: Should I put out the light?

EMPEROR: Do whatever you please.

ARCHITECT: Le-lo-mil-loooooo-loooo.

As the ARCHITECT *is saying these words the sky becomes dark and night falls. Total darkness.*

EMPEROR (*in the dark*): Another one of your jokes! I've had enough. Let day return. Make the light come back. I haven't brushed my teeth yet.

ARCHITECT: But you said I could do whatever I please.

EMPEROR: Anything you please except making night fall.

ARCHITECT: All right, I'll do it.

EMPEROR: Quick!

ARCHITECT: Mee-tee-rreeee-teeee!

The day returns as it went away.

EMPEROR: Don't frighten me like this any more.

ARCHITECT: I thought you wanted to sleep.

EMPEROR: Don't meddle with that. We have enough to do as it is. Leave the responsibility for the sun and the moon to nature.

ARCHITECT: Are you going to teach me philosophy now?

EMPEROR: Philosophy? Me? (*Sublimely.*) Philosophy? What a wonder! Some day I'll teach you this human treasure. This divine fruit of civilization. (*Alarmed.*) But tell me, how do you manage to make day and night?

ARCHITECT: Oh! . . . It's very simple. I don't know myself how I do it.

EMPEROR: And those words you mutter?

ARCHITECT: I say them like that without knowing why. But night can also fall without those words. It's enough for me to wish it.

EMPEROR (*intrigued*): And those words . . . (*Catching himself.*) Ignorant brute! You've seen nothing! Have I regaled you with my stories about television, Coca-Cola, tanks, the museums of Babylon, our ministers, our popes, the immensity of the ocean, the profoundness of our theories . . .

ARCHITECT: Tell me, tell me!

EMPEROR (*majestically, as he sits down on the throne*): Bird! Yes, you who perches on this branch, fetch me immediately a leg of venison. Do you hear me? I am the Emperor of Assyria. (*He waits in the pose of a great lord. Alarmed.*) What? You dare to rebel against my unlimited power, against my science and my supreme eloquence, against my word and my grandeur? I have given you the order to fetch me immediately a leg of venison. (*He waits. He picks up a stone and throws it in the direction of the branch.*) All right, you die. I only reign over obedient subjects . . .

232

ARCHITECT: Who throw themselves at the feet of the most powerful of the emperors of the Occident. (*He prostrates himself at the Emperor's feet.*)

EMPEROR: Of the Occident, you say? Of the Occident and the Orient. Don't you know that Assyria has already launched several manned satellites to Neptune! Tell me, has there ever been a feat that could compare to that?

ARCHITECT: No one on our beloved Earth is more powerful!

EMPEROR: Uhhhh! My heart! . . . The stretcher!

The EMPEROR *writhes in pain. The* ARCHITECT *brings a stretcher.*

My heart! Listen to it. I am stabbed by a great pain. Alas, my poor heart . . .

The ARCHITECT *stoops to listen to the Emperor's heart as if he had a stethoscope.*

ARCHITECT: Don't worry, Emperor, I don't think it's anything. Rest and the pain will go away as it has gone away many times.

EMPEROR (*panting*): No, this time it's serious. I feel faint. I am sure it is an infarctus of the myocardium.

ARCHITECT: Your pulse is nearly normal.

EMPEROR: Thank you, my son. I know that you're trying to reassure me.

ARCHITECT: Sleep a little while and you'll see that it will pass.

EMPEROR (*troubled*): My last words? I have forgotten them. Tell me, tell me quickly, what are they?

ARCHITECT: "I die and I am content; I leave a perishable world to enter into immortality." But don't worry about that.

EMPEROR: I want to confide something to you, something I

233

have never told you before. I would like to die disguised. (*A pause.*) Disguised as the Bishop of Chess.

ARCHITECT: As what?

EMPEROR: The Bishop of Chess . . . a bishop in the game of chess. Accede to my wishes. It's very simple: you place a little stick between my legs so that I can stand up like a chess piece and you cover me with the mad Bishop's armor.

ARCHITECT: Your wish shall be done.

EMPEROR: Uhhhhhhh! I'm dying, I'm dying! Do what I ask you.

The ARCHITECT *brings the stick and the armor: a sack. He disguises the* EMPEROR. *He leaves an opening in the sack for the face to appear.*

Uhhhhhh! Dear mama, I'm dying!

ARCHITECT: There, there. You'll be cured. Now you're dressed as the Bishop of Chess.

EMPEROR: Kkkk-iiii-sssssss me. (*They kiss. The* EMPEROR, *out of breath, says.*) "I die satisfied: I leave this mortal coil for . . ."

His head falls back. The ARCHITECT *sheds bitter tears. He takes the Emperor's hand and kisses it.*

ARCHITECT (*sobbing*): He's dead! He's dead!

He finally puts the body disguised as the Bishop into a coffin and closes the lid. In tears he begins to dig a hole. Suddenly the lid raises and the EMPEROR *comes out, removing his disguise.*

EMPEROR: Skunk, trash, shit-head! You were going to bury me. Bumpkin, hermaphrodite, triple blockhead!

ARCHITECT: But isn't that what you ordered me to do?

EMPEROR: To put me in the ground? Simpleton, clodpole. I would have awakened in my tomb and who'd have gotten me out of there? With three feet of earth on my stomach?

ARCHITECT: Last time . . .

EMPEROR: I told you to cremate me . . . (*Sublimely.*) And to throw my ashes into the sea like those of Byron, Shakespeare, the Phoenix, Neptune, and Pluto.

ARCHITECT: Last time you got furious when I wanted to cremate you. You said that you'd wake up, your balls half burned, dancing the jig and shouting "Vive la République!"

EMPEROR (*very seriously*): I yield to all your caprices, but be careful about my death. No errors. This time it's all been nothing but a string of errors. What immense distress is mine!

ARCHITECT: I'll take my canoe and go.

EMPEROR (*humbly*): Where to?

ARCHITECT: The island opposite. I'm sure it's inhabited.

EMPEROR: What island? I've never seen one.

ARCHITECT: That one, over there.

EMPEROR: I don't see anything.

ARCHITECT: The mountain's in the way. I'll open it. (*He claps his hands. There's an enormous noise.*) Do you see it now?

EMPEROR: You move mountains? You move mountains too? . . . (*Sincerely.*) Don't leave. I'll do whatever you want. I'll proclaim you Emperor of Assyria; I'll abdicate.

ARCHITECT: I'll leave you and I'll find a fiancée . . .

EMPEROR: I'm not enough for you?

ARCHITECT: I'll walk through the cities and I'll scatter the streets with bottles to intoxicate the teenagers and I'll hang swings everywhere so that the grandmothers can show their behinds and I'll buy a zebra which I'll shoe in tight doeskin so that it'll have blisters and I'll be very happy because I'll know everyone and I'll see . . .

EMPEROR: Architect, admit you hate me.

ARCHITECT: No, I don't hate you at all.

EMPEROR: I'll give you my dreams for a present, if you want.

ARCHITECT: You always dream the same thing, always the garden of happiness, always Bosch, and I'm tired of women with roses planted in their posteriors.

EMPEROR: You're not an artist, you're nothing but a boor. You ignore all that's sublime, you only like scum.

ARCHITECT: What's better? You never told me anything about it.

EMPEROR: Run to my Imperial Wardrobe and take the costume you want.

ARCHITECT: When I leave I'll have all the costumes I want: I'll dress myself with matches, in a vague and indefinable style; I'll have tin trousers and electrical neckties, jackets like coffee cups, and pearl-gray shirts encircled by an infinite chain of trucks loaded with houses . . .

EMPEROR (*a pause*): Should I circumcise you? I'll keep your foreskin on an altar and it will perform miracles like the fifty-six of Christ.

ARCHITECT: Will you teach me philosophy?

EMPEROR: Ah! Philosophy! Philosophy! (*Brusquely he gets on all fours.*) I am the sacred elephant. Climb on my back and we'll reach the sacred year of Brahma.

The ARCHITECT *climbs on him.*

Coil the chain around my trunk.

He hands the chain to the ARCHITECT.

And now make me move forward and pray.

ARCHITECT: Forward, white elephant . . .

EMPEROR: I'm a sacred elephant, I'm pink.

ARCHITECT: Forward, sacred pink elephant, we go on a pilgrimage to see Brahma of the fourteen hands, we are going to be blessed fourteen times per second. Long live God!

The EMPEROR *throws him to the ground.*

EMPEROR: What sacrilegious words have you uttered?

ARCHITECT: Long live God!

EMPEROR: Long live God? Ah! Then I don't know if it's a sacrilege. One would have to read the *Summa Theologica* or at least the Bible in comic-book form.

ARCHITECT: Before leaving I'd like to confess something to you.

EMPEROR: Tell me everything . . . I'm your father, I'm your mother, I'm everything to you. (*Pause.*) One moment, I'm called to the red telephone. (*Ceremoniously he mimes the telephone scene.*) Yes, this is the President. (*A pause.*) Speak! Speak! Dear President, how are you? (*A pause.*) How understanding you are, and always joking. (*Pretending to blush.*) A proposition! President, we are no longer at school! (*A pause.*) Don't speak to me in this tone, I didn't know you were homosexual. To make a proposition to me! Old lech, little hussy! (*A pause.*) What? You propose to declare war on my country?! (*Furiously.*) From the height of these skyscrapers ten thousand centuries are looking down at you. I'll crush you like a fly crushes a wild elephant, my people will invade yours and make of

237

you . . . What did you say? A hydrogen bomb will explode above our heads in thirty seconds? Mama, mama! (*To his secretary.*) An umbrella! (*The* ARCHITECT *opens an umbrella and both take shelter under it. Into the telephone.*) Lout! War criminal! Assassin of mothers-in-law! (*To the* ARCHITECT.) To think that we'd prepared everything to surprise them with our bombs tomorrow morning at five o'clock. A phoenix, a phoenix, my kingdom for a phoenix!

They mime the explosion of the bomb. They die, victims of the bombing. They fall into the bushes. Soon they reappear imitating two apes: they scratch their heads. They contemplate the state of desolation into which all was plunged after the fall of the bombs.

ARCHITECT (*as a female ape*): Hum, hum. There isn't a single human alive after the atomic explosion, mm!

EMPEROR (*as a male ape*): Mmm, mmmmm! Papa Darwin!

The two apes embrace passionately.

ARCHITECT (*as the female ape*): We'll have to start from scratch.

They seek cover in a favorable spot nearby.

EMPEROR (*changing his tone, very angry*): I forbid you to leave, I forbid you to confess one more thing to me, I am in command here and I order you to destroy your canoe.

ARCHITECT: Right away.

EMPEROR: Why such a hurry? Hair-brained youth, quicksilver! Tell me, aren't you happy with me?

ARCHITECT: What does happy mean? You never taught me.

238

EMPEROR: Happy . . . happy means . . . (*Angrily.*) The devil! I don't know. (*Softly.*) Did you have your b.m. today?

ARCHITECT: Yes.

EMPEROR: And how was it, hard or soft?

ARCHITECT: Well . . .

EMPEROR (*concerned*): What, you don't know? Why didn't you tell me? I so much enjoy watching you do it.

ARCHITECT: It was rather soft and it smelled . . .

EMPEROR: Skip the smell. (*More calmly.*) I'm always constipated. (*A pause.*) Everything'd be different if you had a bachelor's degree, if you'd studied at a university, no matter what. We don't understand each other. We belong to two different worlds.

ARCHITECT: Me . . . (*Sincerely.*) I love you.

EMPEROR (*very touched, on the edge of tears*): You're making fun of me.

ARCHITECT: No.

The EMPEROR *blows his nose, turns around and speaks in a new tone, very emphatically.*

EMPEROR: You can't imagine: every morning Assyrian television transmitted my awakening, my people contemplated this spectacle with such devotion that the women cried and the men repeated my name in a murmur. Then three hundred naked and mute girls came to admire me. They attended to my delicate body and, perfuming it with the essence of rose . . .

ARCHITECT: Tell me what the world's like.

EMPEROR: You mean the civilized world. What a wonder! During thousands of centuries man has stored knowledge and has enriched his intelligence until he has attained this marvelous perfection that has become life.

Everywhere, happiness, joy, tranquility, laughter, understanding. All is conceived to render man's life easier, his happiness greater, and his peace more durable. Man has discovered all that's necessary to his well being and today he's the happiest and most serene being in all creation. A goblet of water!

ARCHITECT (*addressing himself to a bird that the audience can't see*): Bird, bring me a goblet of water!

A brief wait. The ARCHITECT *watches the bird take flight and then return. He stretches out his hand and then takes the goblet the bird delivers to him.*

Thank you.

EMPEROR (*after drinking*): What's that? Now you talk to the birds in my language.

ARCHITECT: That doesn't matter. What's important is what I think: there's a transmission of thought between us.

EMPEROR (*thoroughly frightened*): Tell me seriously, do you read my thoughts too? Can you see into my mind?

ARCHITECT: I want to write. Teach me to be a writer. You must've been a great author.

EMPEROR (*flattered*): I've written some famous sonnets! And what plays, with their monologues and their asides. No writer has succeeded in equaling me. The best have copied me! Beethoven, d'Annunzio, James Joyce, Charles V, Shakespeare himself, and his nephew Bernstein.

ARCHITECT: Tell me, how did you kill her?

EMPEROR: Who?

ARCHITECT: Well . . .

EMPEROR: When? How? When did I tell you about that?

ARCHITECT: Have you forgotten?

EMPEROR: I, forget? (*A pause.*) Listen. You know I'm going to retire from life. I want to consecrate myself to solitary meditation. Chain me.

ARCHITECT: Why do you want to retire now?

EMPEROR (*with religious solemnity*): Listen to me, these are my last words: I am tired of living, I want to remove myself from all that still ties me to the world. I want to separate myself from you. And above all don't talk to me anymore. I'll remain alone, plunged in my meditations.

ARCHITECT: Is this a new game?

EMPEROR: No, it's the truth. Besides, I have to get used to it because you're going to leave in the canoe.

ARCHITECT: I won't go away.

EMPEROR: Enough talk! The chain.

The ARCHITECT *brings the chain. The* EMPEROR *passes it around his ankle. He attaches himself to a tree.*

ARCHITECT: Where're you going?

EMPEROR: I'm going into my hut. Never talk to me again.

ARCHITECT: But . . .

EMPEROR (*solemnly, as he enters the hut*): Farewell! (*He disappears inside.*)

ARCHITECT: All right, I understand, it's a game. Come out of there.

Silence. One by one the Emperor's clothes appear through the dormer window.

But . . . why're you undressing? You'll catch cold.

He looks through the window. The EMPEROR *shuts it from the inside.*

Listen to me, let me see you at least! Open the window! (*Silence. He listens at the door.*) What, you're pray-

241

ing? Open, once and for all. Do you hear me? Now stop that murmuring. Why would you be praying now? Are you going to die? I'll tell you my dream.

Listen: I dreamed I was a Sabine and that I lived in a very ancient city. One day the warriors arrived, led by Casanova and Don Juan Tenorio, and they carried me away. Does this interest you? (*He looks around. He gestures in the direction of the bushes.*) Snake! Bring me a suckling pig. (*He goes into the bushes and bends forward.*) What service. Thank you, thank you. (*He returns with the leg of a suckling pig.*) Emperor of Assyria, your admiring females have brought you a suckling pig. Smell it. (*He holds it at arm's length.*) After all, it's what you like best, why not come and get it? (*Silence. He leaves the stage and returns dressed as a woman: it is a scanty costume that can easily be removed or put back on.*) Look through the crack in the hut, admire the pretty girl who's landed on the island. (*He walks to and fro coquettishly. He speaks as a woman.*) Emperor! Come out, I'm your humble slave. I offer you presents of the most delicious dishes and liqueurs, and my sculptured body belongs to you. (*Silence.*) Architect, what can I do to make this man of my dreams come out to look me over? (He speaks as the ARCHITECT.) You're the woman, you should know better than I. Besides, he's so jealous that I hardly dare stand next to you. (*As the woman.*) Emperor, come out for a moment! Let my lips brush your divine lips, let my hands caress your ebony body, let our bellies be joined in an eternal union. (*As the* ARCHITECT.) You who are so beautiful! You who so much resemble the Emperor's mother, why doesn't he yield to so many charms? (*As the woman.*) O Emperor, cruel as the hyenas of the desert! If you abandon me like this I'll have to go with the Architect. (*As the* ARCHITECT.) Don't embrace me so passionately, the Emperor is as jealous as a tiger. (*As the woman.*) Oh beautiful young man, I close my eyes and when I embrace you I think I'm in the arms of the Emperor. How young you are! How seductive you are! How right the proverb is when it says: like emperor, like slave. Let me embrace your flaming abdomen. (*As the* ARCHITECT.) Oh! Enough, I can't resist. How bewitching you are, how beautiful! I surrender, the victim of your charms, even if the Emperor himself comes out and kills me in a fit of jealousy. (*There is the sound of kisses, of passionate murmurs. Suddenly furious, he goes to the window.*) I won't talk to you anymore! I won't talk to you anymore! Don't tell me afterward that you want to be my friend. I never want to see you again. I'm going to get my canoe. I'm leaving forever. I won't even say good-bye to you. In a few minutes I'll paddle toward the island over there.

He leaves with furious determination. Long silence. The EMPEROR *is heard murmuring some prayers. The murmurs crescendo. The door opens. The* EMPEROR *appears naked, or dressed in a minuscule loincloth.*

EMPEROR (*meditating*): . . . and I will build myself a cage of wood and I'll shut myself inside it. From here I will pardon humanity for all the hate that it has always shown against me. And I'll pardon my father and my mother for the day when their bellies united to beget me. And I'll pardon my city, and my friends, and my neighbors for having always underestimated my worth and ignored who I am, and I'll pardon . . .

(*Troubled, he looks around. While he speaks he makes a scarecrow which he places on the throne.*) Ah! In chains! And alone at last! No one will contradict me anymore, no one will make fun of me anymore, no one will witness my foibles. In chains! What happiness! Long live the padlock! My universe: a circumference which has for its radius the length of the chain . . . (*he measures it*) . . . let's say three yards . . . (*he measures it again*) . . . say two and a half yards, unless it's three and a half. Therefore, if the radius is three yards, say four—I don't want to cheat—the area is πR^2, that is to say 3.1416, R equals three, when squared it's nine, multiplied by π, that makes twelve square yards. What more could be asked of a low-cost housing project. (*He whines. He blows his nose. Without interrupting his monologue he dresses the scarecrow with his Emperor's garments. He tries to climb a tree but fails. He jumps, trying to see as far as possible. Finally he shouts.*) Architect! Architect! Come back, don't leave me alone. I'm too much alone. Architect! Archi . . . (*He pulls himself together.*) I have to get organized. No negligence. Wake up at nine A.M. A touch of grooming. Meditation. Think about the squaring of the circle, perhaps write a sonnet or two. And the morning will pass without my noticing. At one o'clock lunch, ablutions, then a little nap. Shake myself once—only once, but well. All that shouldn't take more than three-quarters of an hour. What a loss not to have the *Story of O* at hand. I'll think about that actress, what's-her-name, I have her name on the tip of my tongue, with her strangely curved legs, so sexy, and her beautiful blond hair, and her prominent belly . . . Stop! After the nap . . .

(*He takes great pains with the details so that the scarecrow reproduces his own silhouette exactly.*) There you are, already talking to yourself! You're becoming schizophrenic. You can't do that. Your equilibrium. (*A pause.*) In the afternoon, one hour to think of my family, another for the Architect, well, a half-hour, or rather, he deserves a quarter of an hour. Dinner. Ablutions. And finally to bed at . . . let's say ten P.M. Three or four hours to get to sleep and then tomorrow will be here! And what savings I will make: no movies, no newspapers, no Coca-Cola. (*While he is talking he removes his chain. He looks all around and cries sadly.*) Architect! Architect! Come back! (*Imitating the voice of the* ARCHITECT.) Escalator, escalator, escalator! (*Humbly, to the scarecrow.*) Don't scold me. I know very well you've been teaching me for a year to speak and I still can't pronounce the "s" properly. (*He bows very low.*) Tell me, Emperor, how you woke up in Assyria to the sound of music played by a legion of flutists. Television carried your awakening, didn't it, and a hundred thousand slave girls, chained and marked with your seal, scurried around to wash and rub every cell of your divine body with syrups from Afghanistan. (*He pretends to listen to the scarecrow-emperor's reply.*) Oh! No, my life's of no importance. (*A pause.*) No, I don't have to be asked twice, but my life isn't the least bit interesting. (*A pause.*) What I've been? My profession? Of no importance. (*Ashamed.*) Well, toward the end I had a good salary, strange as it may seem. How happy my wife was when they finally gave me a raise. If I'd stayed I would have received the key to the executive washroom. (*A pause. He leaves. He*

245

returns with a grass skirt and ceremoniously slips it over his head while he goes on with his story.) Who told you? When I came in, they were together naked on the bed. He said, "Come see how I take your wife." (*A pause.*) She resisted with all her strength and it seemed to me that she cried. She pleaded, "No, no." Then she stopped struggling and she panted regularly as she held him to her shoulder; you could only see the whites of her eyes. When it was all over, she started to cry again and he roared with laughter. (*A pause.*) The same thing was repeated several times. Finally, he got up smiling and said to me: "Well, there's your wife." Then I had to console her and stroke her back, she let out a cry which almost . . . (*He sits crosslegged on the ground. He cries.*) But we loved each other, she was so good to me. When I had the slightest cold she always applied poultices. (*A pause.*) And my superiors loved me too, and one day they even told me they would make me . . . (*A pause. He cries.*) My mother? (*A pause.*) Sometimes we spent all afternoon quarreling. (*A pause.*) She didn't love me anymore like she did when I was a child, she had a deadly hatred for me. No, my wife, she truly loved me. (*A pause.*) Friends . . . yes, I had some but . . . evidently they envied me. They had reason to be jealous of me! (*He tries to climb a tree but fails. He jumps, trying to see as far as possible. Finally he shouts.*) Architect! Architect! Come back. Don't leave me alone. I'm so very lonely! Architect! Archi . . . I ought to call him Archi . . . that's more elegant. (*He resumes his former tone.*) Well, certainly in the end I no longer saw my friends . . . I had a lot of work to do and I couldn't spend my time with them.

When you work eight hours a day and when you take the train, the subway, and . . . I had no time left to do anything and I'd become indispensable, that's what my superiors told me. (*A pause.*) When I was little it was different. What dreams I had! One time I had a fiancée and I had begun to fly, but she didn't believe it, and I knew that one day I'd be emperor, like you. Emperor of Assyria, that's what I thought I'd become, emperor, like you.

Who'd have thought that I was going to meet you. I dreamed that I'd be first in everything. That I'd write and that I would be a great poet: but believe me, if I'd had the time, if I hadn't had to work all day long, what a poet I would have been. And I'd have written a book like Voltaire's *Candide* and I'd have gotten even with all my enemies who were so jealous of me. No one would've been left unscathed! (*A silly little laugh.*) Emperor, what do you want me to do? I'm your subject. Command me. (*Silence.*) You're bored? (*Silence.*) I'll do it right away, you'll see how that'll cheer you up. (*He leaves and returns with a chamber pot. He lifts up his skirt and sits down on the pot. He tries.*) Impossible. I'm constipated. (*Long moment of silence. He is still sitting on the pot. He looks very distressed. He gets up and takes the chamber pot with him. He comes back without it. He starts to cry.*) I could have become a watchmaker. I'd have been free, I'd have made money. All by myself, at home, I would have repaired watches, without a boss, without superiors, without anyone to make fun of me. (*He sobs.*) When I was little it was different. (*He cheers up.*) You know, I nearly took a mistress. How dashing I would have been, me with a mistress. She was very blond, very beautiful . . . we were happy . . . we met in a park . . . and we talked for a long time, a long time. And we agreed to meet again the next day. I spent the night drawing a heart with an arrow for her—a large heart like those in the churches. For the red I used my own blood. I pricked my finger very hard. How it hurt! (*He cries. He looks in the distance and calls, disconsolately.*) Architect! (*He calms himself.*) All right. Let's get back to the subject. I continue. Where was I? (*A pause.*) And I thought of her constantly: she was very blond, very beautiful, when I looked at her scales seemed to be growing all over my body, and I felt like a big fish gliding between her legs. I did pretty well with the heart . . . Perhaps it was a little too round. And I drew an arrow and I wrote my name. While I was drawing I thought I was flying in the air with her and we lost each other in the sky and her body was nothing but hands and lips for . . . Anyway it was very nice: the heart, the arrow, the drops of blood. It was a symbol. The annoying thing is that later the blood turned black . . . She was so beautiful, so blond, we talked at least half an hour in the park . . . banalities, you could say, about the weather, she asked me where such and such a street was . . . but she was very well aware that behind all these words we really spoke of our . . . love. She loved me without a doubt. When she said to me "it's not as cold as last year" I knew that she wanted to tell me, "We'll leave together and we'll eat sea urchins while I heap cameras into your hands and your pubic area." And when I answered her, "Yes, last year at this time one couldn't walk in the park at this hour," it was as if I had said, "You are like all the sea gulls of the world at the hour of the siesta, you sleep on me like a bird entering a bottle, I feel your heart beat and I feel the rhythm of your respiration on all the pores of my skin and from my heart spurts a jet of crystalline water with which to bathe your white feet." And I thought of still more things, that's why I spent the whole night making the heart for her. And since I didn't know her name I decided to call her Liz. The next day I ran to the meeting place. How excited I was! I hardly worked at the office. My superiors thought I was acting strange. What a day I lived through thinking of her. I asked myself if I should tell my wife. I didn't tell her anything. When I got to the park . . . (*he is on the edge of tears*) . . . well, she must have made a mistake, she hadn't understood . . . For an entire week I went to the park for at least five hours every evening . . . She must have been run over by a car. It couldn't be anything else . . . (*Changing his tone.*) I'm going to dance for you . . . (*He does a grotesque dance.*) I could have danced like a god. What do you think? Am I boring you? (*He recites.*)

> *Breathes there a man with soul so dead*
> *Who never to himself has said*
> *This is my own, my native land.*
> *Whose heart has ne'er within him burned*
> *As home his footsteps he hath turned*
> *From wandering on a foreign strand* . . .

I shouldn't have landed here. When is His Majesty going to grant audiences? (*He takes off the skirt and is in his loincloth.*) Do you want me to get dressed? (*He leaves and returns with a black-lace woman's slip. He smells it.*) How good it smells! (*He puts it on.*) And then God and his creatures: us! (*He judges the effect of the slip.*) That's not bad, eh? Emperor . . . do you know I played for God's existence at a pinball machine. God existed if I won one out of three games. I didn't make it too difficult. And then I play very well . . . and it was a machine I knew. I lit the colors in a jiffy. I play the first game: 670 points and I need 1,000. (*He leaves and returns with a garter belt.*) I begin the second game: first ball, enormous mistake, it slips between my legs. Sixteen points. A record. (*He takes the garter belt and adjusts it around his waist.*) I launch the second. I felt inspired, let's say divine. The customers of the café were there panting. I made the machine vibrate like a Negro dancing with a white woman. It responded to everything: 300, 400, 500, 600, 700 points. I got all of it—the bonus, the refund, the points, the extra ball. At the end of it all I had got . . . (*He looks at himself. He adjusts the garter belt.*) That's not bad on me, huh? How do you like my garter belt? Ah! If the Architect were here, we would build Babylon and its hanging gardens again. 973 points, 973! That means if I take off the 16 points from the first game, 957 points, and that with a single ball! Once I reached a thousand then God existed. I got impatient, God was in my hands. I held the irrefutable proof of his existence. Farewell the great watchmaker, the supreme architect, the great master-of-ceremonies: God would exist and I was going to demonstrate it in the most definite way, my name would be spread in all theology manuals. An end to the councils, the lucubrations, the bishops and the doctors, I alone, I was going to discover everything. They would write about me in all the newspapers. (*He leaves and returns with a pair of black stockings.*) I prefer them black, don't you?

(*He puts them on coquettishly and attaches them.*)
Architect! Architect! Come back. I'll talk to you! I
won't lock myself in the hut anymore. (*He sobs.*)
Birds, obey me! Go and call him, tell him I'm waiting!
(*Furiously.*) Did you hear me? (*He changes his tone.*)
What did he say? Clu-clee-clee-clu-clee . . . no, that's
not it. To think that he talks to the birds. What a fellow.
When he moves the mountains . . . Mountain! Move!
(*He nervously watches for something to happen.*) Nothing, not a breeze. Mountain, I order you to fall into the
sea. (*He watches. Silence.*) And what a character . . .
he can make it be day or night anytime. (*He leaves. He
comes back with a black lace brassière which he puts
on. He puts peaches in the cups.*) If my mother could
see me! Where was I? Nine hundred and seventy-three
points! God was, so to speak, at my mercy, I only have
to get twenty-seven more points. Even on my worst
days I make more than that. I launch the ball artisti-
cally and it falls right into the bonus triangle. One point
for every time they touch—and with my style . . .
I start to shake the ball which moves around like
I want it to. Do you realize, Emperor! Do you realize, Your Majesty. (*Suddenly he shouts.*) Architect!
I'm going to have a baby, don't leave me alone
. . . poor little woman! (*He starts to pray.*) "In this
valley of tears . . ." (*The rest is inaudible.*) Emperor, my mother hated me, believe me, believe me, I
swear, it was her fault, only her fault! (*He leaves. His
voice comes from off-stage.*) I can't find it . . .
Where did that slovenly wretch put it? And it's certainly not because I haven't told him: "Put everything
in order. Every object in its place." Just look where
he leaves his things. A comb! Ugh! A prophylactic on

our island? Birth control has got this far? I'll put it on! Ah! It's my size. (*He shouts.*) Architect! Where'd you put the dress? He's rowing now like a galley slave or like one of the bastards in the Olympics. Ah! Youth! What a pig. Look where he's put it. Such a nice dress in the butterfly collection drawer. (*He thinks it over.*) What did he mean by that? Emperor, I'll be right there. (*He appears with a dress over his arm.*) All the customers of the café surrounded me and I shook the machine like a devil. It obeyed me submissively: 988, 989, 990, 991, 992, 993 . . . and I only needed a thousand points . . . and the ball was still up there. I couldn't lose now: when the ball drops it automatically counts ten points. I was crazy with joy. God had chosen the most humble of mortals to prove his existence. (*He coquettishly adjusts his stockings, his garter belt, his slip, and his brassière. He puts on high-heeled shoes and walks for a moment.*) How do they manage to walk in these? (*He advances hesitatingly.*) It must be a question of getting used to it. *Cum amicis deambulare.* What a Latin scholar I could've been! I'm sure that if I start walking in these heels in no time at all I'll run the marathon. How deeply moving, my arrival in Athens—was it Athens?—in high heels and a garter belt. "Athenians, we have won the greatest victory of modern times," then I'd sell my memoirs to some weekly magazine. Architect! (*He shouts.*) Listen to me, I'm going to be a mother, I'm going to give birth to a child. Come to my side. (*He changes his tone.*) What a skunk, with his little canoe out to . . . what does he know about life? (*He holds out the dress. It's a nun's habit. He puts it on.*) Listen to this, you won't believe it. With my ball I scored points again and again: 995, 996, 997, 998, 999 and at that moment a drunk knocks the machine and TILT! The machine stays stuck like that. The game was finished, and like an idiot it showed 999 . . . 999! (*He looks at himself in the nun's habit.*) What a Carmelite I'd have been! But barefoot, no, out of the question. (*He shouts.*) 999! Do you realize, Emperor? What should one believe? Should I count the ten automatic points as valid? The third game . . . better not talk about it! What a shock! 999 points. (*He walks up and down looking at himself.*) And if I performed miracles? The Carmelites do make miracles. (*He quotes.*) "And you find it miraculous to nourish a crowd like Christ did with two miserable sardines and a crust of bread? Christian capitalism had done much better than that." What a man who wrote that! He's my kind of man. Emperor, are you listening? You're not very talkative. Say something. It seems to me I'm hitting my head against a stone wall. Are you angry with me? Don't you like me as a Carmelite? (*He throws himself at the feet of the scarecrow-emperor. He takes one of its legs and caresses it.*) Emperor, I am in love with you. For a word from your lips . . . (*He gets up and paces.*) I'll have to deliver all by myself. (*He shouts.*) Architect, it's starting, starting. (*Indeed, his belly is expanding abnormally.*) They are very inventive, the good Sisters. With a dress like this you almost can't tell when they're pregnant. My father, I have been guilty of . . . of having . . . I mean . . . of letting myself do wicked things. (*He speaks as a confessor.*) What, you wretched creature! How could you dare to commit so enormous a sacrilege! Miserable cursed bitch! (*He speaks as a Carmelite.*) Yes, my Father, the devil has horribly tempted me. (*As the confessor.*) With whom did you do it, harlot? (*As the Carmelite.*) With that poor little old man who lives all alone on the fifth floor. (*As the confessor.*) Trollop, you're pressing more thorns into the flesh of Christ with this human squalor. How many times did you do it, you filthy profaner? (*As the Carmelite.*) What, how many times? How many times could it be. (*As the confessor.*) That's what I'm asking you, sinner. (*As the Carmelite.*) But only once . . . he's quite old, the poor man. (*As the confessor.*) No human penitence can redeem your sin. Infidel! Atheist! (*As the Carmelite.*) What can I do, Father, to receive absolution? (*As the confessor.*) Sacrilege! Come to my cell tonight with chains and whips. I'll undress you and I'll spend the night whipping you. Your sins are so abominable that I too will have to ask God to give you his pardon, and to obtain it I will also undress and you'll whip me, cursed bitch. (*Changing his tone.*) Architect! Come, come quickly, I need you. (*He shouts.*) I'm pushing, I'm pushing! Where's the stretcher? (*He lies on it.*) Tell me, doctor, will I suffer much? (*Silence. As the doctor.*) Breathe like a dog. (*As the woman, he pants. As the doctor, annoyed.*) Haven't you learned to deliver without pain? Breathe. Like that. Ah! Ah! (*He pants like a dog, but badly. As the doctor.*) No, not like that. Like this: Ah! Ah! (*He breathes badly.*) Doctor, I'll never learn. Help me. I'm alone . . . abandoned by everyone. (*As the doctor.*) All you know is fornication! That's the only thing you know how to do without an apprenticeship. Ah! Ah! (*He pants like a dog, but well. As the doctor.*) You see how easy it is. (*He pants badly. As the doctor.*)

Wretch. To think you got on all fours with that man like an animal in heat and now you don't know how to bark. Humans! Christ should have been a dog crucified on a street lamp and the entire canine humanity would have come to piss on the lamppost. Pant, dog! Ah! Ah! (*As the woman.*) Doctor, help me. Give me your hand. (*As the doctor.*) Noli me tangere! (*As the woman.*) I'm pushing! It's coming! I'm sure of it! (*As the doctor.*) Ah, here's the head, a good head . . . The shoulders are coming. Good shoulders. (*Out of breath he moans, screams, and foams. As the doctor.*) There's the chest, a good chest! One last effort. Another push. (*As the woman.*) I can't anymore, Doctor. Put me to sleep. Give me a shot. (*As the doctor.*) You think you're Thomas de Quincey. Give you a shot! One push and right now! (*A piercing scream.*) There it is. All of it. A beautiful specimen of an earthling. (*He moans, cries, and calms himself. As the doctor.*) A new member of the race. There it is. No one can deny that you're collaborating in the defense of our civilization. (*As the mother.*) Is it a boy or a girl? (*As the doctor.*) What did you want? A girl. There're only girls now. Lesbians one and all. No more wars, religions, pandering, automobile accidents! Happy humanity. The best of all possible worlds! They'll spend all their money on knickknacks. (*As the mother.*) Doctor, let me see her. (*As the doctor.*) Here she is. (*As the mother.*) How beautiful she is, how cute, what a love! His spitting image! How happy I'll be. I'm going to make her baby clothes myself. (*He sits up on the stretcher, rocks the baby, and hums.*) His spitting image, so pretty, so adorable. The very face. (*As the doctor.*) What face? (*As the mother.*)

The cathedral clock's. When the clock laughed it laughed like she does. Therefore I'll call her Geneviève de Brabant. (*As the doctor.*) What profession are you going to choose for her? (*As the mother.*) Swedish masseuse, that's most up-to-date. Her hands will massage the backs, the sides, the stomachs of all the men on earth. She'll be the reincarnation of Mary Magdalene. (*Short pause. Addressing the scarecrow-emperor in another tone.*) Emperor, Emperor . . . (*Crying painfully.*) Architect! Architect! Archiiiiiiii! (*To the scarecrow-emperor.*) You see what he's like. He detests me, he left me to my sad fate. He set forth for other islands in quest of adventure and God knows what he'll find. (*He gets on all fours.*) Emperor, I'm a sacred camel of the desert, climb on my back, I'll take you to see the most fascinating male and female slave markets of the entire Occident. Climb on my back, Emperor. Whip me with your imperial riding crop so that my pace will be swift and straight and so that your divine person can soon be purified by the contact with the straight, young, vigorous bodies of these boys and girls. (*Straightening up again.*) What a brute! In a canoe! In our century of progress, of civilization, of flying saucers—to travel in a canoe! If Icarus, Leonardo da Vinci, or Einstein could see him! Why have we invented helicopters? (*A pause.*) 999 points . . . Without the drunk I would automatically get ten points more; the game, God, the angels, heaven and hell, the blessed and the wicked, the holy foreskin and its miracles, the hosts mounting to heaven in chalices pulled by golden chains, the council measuring the wingspread of the angels, the statues of the Virgin shedding tears of blood, the miraculous pools and fountains, the donkey, the cow, the pitcher . . . (*A pause. Quoting.*) "All that is atrocious, nauseating, putrid, and vulgar is contained in one word: God." (*He laughs.*) This guy's my kind of man, too. What a character! (*A pause.*) Believe me, Emperor, with all the respect I owe to your person, with all the veneration I have for you, that a man like the Architect—by the way, the Supreme Architect of Assyria—could travel in a canoe! He didn't even take out an insurance policy. The world's rotten indeed. (*He shouts.*) Scarab, go and get me this minute a golden scepter for the Emperor! (*He waits. Nothing comes. He looks around, troubled.*) I've let them develop bad habits. They do whatever they please. How can I punish them with the cat-o'-nine-tails? Modern education. Progress. The Society for the Prevention of Cruelty to Animals! Everything goes down the drain. Some day the flying saucers will descend to earth. (*He mimes their arrival.*) Mr. Martian, sir . . . (*Aside.*) Assuming that they are Martians . . . Welcome to earth. (*As a Martian.*) Glu-tree-tro-peeeee. (*To the scarecrow-emperor.*) Martians talk like that. (*To the Martian.*) What did you say? (*As the Martian.*) Tru-tree-looo-peeeeeeee. (*To the scarecrow-emperor.*) You see, he's talking about educational systems. (*To the Martian.*) Yes, I understand. You're right. With our system we're cutting our own throats. (*As the Martian.*) Flu-flu-flu-flu-flu-jeeeee. (*As the* EMPEROR.) You want to take me along to your planet? (*Terrified.*) No, no, mercy! I want to stay here. (*As the Martian.*) Tree-clu-tree-clu-tree . . . (*As the* EMPEROR.) I'm the funniest earthling you've seen? (*Blushing.*) Me? Little old me! But I'm like everyone else. (*As the Martian.*) Plu-plu-plugreeeeee. (*As the* EMPEROR.) You're not going to put me in a zoo?! (*As the Martian.*) Plu-ple. (*As the* EMPEROR.) Oh! Thank god! (*As the Martian.*) Jlu-flu-gne-gne-poooo. (*As the* EMPEROR.) The daughter of the Martian king is in love with me? She loves me? (*As the Martian.*) Kee-ko-looooo. (*As the* EMPEROR.) Oh! Excuse me, I misunderstood. Yes, you're cute. A little . . . well . . . (*As the Martian.*) Gree-gree-treeeeee. (*As the* EMPEROR.) How funny. To you we look strange and ugly. I hope you don't say that about me . . . you must be talking about the others. People wash so little nowadays! But let's not argue. I won't go to your zoo, nor to your city. (*Gradually building to anger.*) I want to stay on earth, whatever you say concerning things of the spirit. We have just reached the point where we can sustain grief, and as nice as it might be to live on Mars, I'm sure without ever having set foot on it that it can never equal the earth. (*As the Martian.*) Tree-tree-tree-trooooo. (*As the* EMPEROR.) What, I'll die an atrocious death during a war, burned by radiation? Well, listen carefully: in spite of the fact that I don't know and have no desire to know Mars, I a thousand times prefer to live on earth in spite of our wars and our difficulties, rather than leave for your (*ironically*) dream planet. (*To the scarecrow-emperor, changing his tone.*) Imagine, every morning he gets the crazy idea to wash himself in that ice-cold pool. And I tell him, Architect, you're going to catch pneumonia. But he doesn't give a damn and stays under the fountain even if it rains cats and dogs. He splashes himself with the water and what's more has the gall to ask me to do the same thing. Past forty . . . he's forgotten how to count . . . he doesn't understand a thing! Past forty . . . in fact, he's never admitted his age to me. How can he know his age, I wonder. What can he be—twenty-five, thirty-five . . . He's such a poet! Could he be my son? Perhaps. My son. I ought to have had a son. I'd have taught him to play chess at three, or at four; and to play the piano. We would've walked in the park, a child—that appeals to women. What flirtations I would have had! (*He stops and shouts.*) Architect! Come back! Stop paddling. It's bad for the lungs. You'll get asthma. (*To the scarecrow-emperor.*) Speak to him of asthma, to him, a joker who always bathes in the coldest pool on the island, always in the same one. I don't say that it's too risky in the summer, if you're well covered and near a stove at high noon when the sun's strongest . . . but naturally taking many precautions. He jumps in headlong like a madman. So young and already balmy. And then this business of cutting his hair once a year, on the first day of spring. How did he manage to calculate it without my help? (*He stops in the middle of the stage and shouts.*) Architect, come! We'll be friends. We'll build a house together. We'll erect palaces with labyrinths, we'll dig pools for sea turtles to bathe in, I'll give you an automobile so that you can tour through all my thoughts (*very sadly*), and pipes streaming liquid smoke in spirals that change into alarm clocks. I'll drain the swamps and out of their mud will emerge a flock of pink flamingos with tin-foil crowns. I'll season the most delicious dishes and you'll drink liqueurs distilled from the essence of my dreams . . . Architect! (*He shouts.*) Architect! . . . (*Half crying.*) We'll be happy! (*He lowers his head and remains like that for a long moment. He pulls himself*

259

together and speaks with emphasis.) I imagine you as
Emperor. I imagine your awakening, Assyrian television transmitting close-ups of the first fluttering of
your eyelids on your closed eyes . . . in all the
boroughs and hamlets the women can't keep from
crying watching you . . . (*Changing his tone.*) No,
he's not more than thirty-five; I'll give him thirty-five
at the most. He's such a child, such a poet, of such
high spirituality. What an idea to appoint him architect. (*He has a brilliant idea.*) Emperor, we can find
out his age. We can figure . . . (*He goes toward the
hut.*) Here's his sack. (*The audience cannot see what
he is doing.*) I'll explain. You'll see how simple it is.
He cuts his hair once a year, and because of I don't
know what superstition and sorcery, he wraps the hair
in a large leaf and puts it into the sack. Therefore I've
only to count the leaves to find out how old he is. Do
you realize, Emperor, what brilliant ideas I have! My
mother used to say: "what a bright boy I have!" (*He
goes into the hut. His voice comes from inside the
hut.*) One, two, three . . . but there're so many
leaves . . . (*Troubled.*) Four, five, six, seven . . .
(*He stops. Long silence. He comes out flabbergasted.*)
It's impossible, there're hundreds of leaves . . . Is it
possible that this fountain . . . Hundreds of leaves,
perhaps a thousand . . . Bathing every day . . . at
least a thousand. (*He goes into the hut. A long wait.
He comes out.*) And all of them with hair, his hair,
some of them already half decayed . . . The fountain of youth . . . (*Aghast.*) But how . . . He
never told me . . . and surely I recognize his hair,
always the same color, the same shade . . . How can
it be that . . .

Terrified, he runs out. Silence. The ARCHITECT *enters.*

ARCHITECT (*shouting*): Emperor!

The EMPEROR *soon appears, stunned. They are at opposite sides of the stage.*

EMPEROR: Tell me, how old are you?

ARCHITECT: I don't know. A thousand five hundred . . . two thousand years. I don't know exactly.

THE CURTAIN FALLS SLOWLY

ACT TWO

SCENE ONE

The ARCHITECT *enters cautiously, without making noise. He goes to the door of the hut.*

ARCHITECT (*very gently*): Are you sleeping? Emperor?

> *He comes out and exits stage right. A pause. A large table appears stage right. The* ARCHITECT *pushes it to the center of the stage. He brings out a tablecloth and puts it on the table. He sets a large plate and a gigantic knife and fork. He sits down at the table. He pretends to carve a gigantic creature which is lying on the table. He mimes eating a morsel of it. He puts everything into the table drawer and reverses the table-cloth. It becomes the cover-cloth for a judge's bench. He takes several masks, a small bell, and a large gilt-edged book from the drawer. He puts on a kind of toque and a judge's mask and shakes the bell.*

EMPEROR (*from inside the hut*): What's going on, Architect? (*He comes out.*)

ARCHITECT: Accused, approach the bench and repeat: I swear to tell the truth, the whole truth, and nothing but the truth.

EMPEROR (*raising his right hand*): I swear. (*In another tone.*) And for that you wake me at this hour?

ARCHITECT (*lifting his mask*): I won't tolerate any asides, do you understand? (*He puts his mask back on emphatically.*) Accused, you may sit down if you wish. Try to be precise in your statements; we are here to aid justice and to shed light on your life and the offense with which you are charged.

EMPEROR: What offense?

ARCHITECT: Is the Accused married?

EMPEROR: Yes, your Honor.

ARCHITECT: For how long?

EMPEROR: I don't remember . . . ten years.

ARCHITECT: Are you aware that all your statements can be held against you?

EMPEROR: But . . . you're accusing me . . . well . . . you're alluding to . . . to my mother?

ARCHITECT: The Court asks the questions.

EMPEROR: But my mother's disappeared.

ARCHITECT: We haven't gotten to that yet.

EMPEROR: Is it my fault that she's gone God knows where?

ARCHITECT: We will take into account all the mitigating circumstances that you can present for your defense.

EMPEROR: That's the limit. (*In another tone.*) Architect, don't continue this game. The tone you're using hurts me very much. Do you understand? (*With great tenderness.*) I know how to speak with my feet as you taught me. Look! (*He lies on the ground, legs in the air, and begins to wiggle his feet.*)

264

ARCHITECT (*taking off his mask and his toque*): Are you being obscene again? (*The* EMPEROR *wiggles his feet.*) Always the same thing.

EMPEROR: Did you understand?

ARCHITECT: Everything. You're the one who never understands a thing!

EMPEROR: I understand everything!

The ARCHITECT *lies down on the ground behind the table. Only his wiggling bare feet can be seen.*

ARCHITECT: I'll bet you can't understand what I say.

EMPEROR (*laughing*): Take it easy. You'll see that I can read everything. "At this point my imagination lacks the strength to keep the memory of so lofty a spectacle."

The ARCHITECT *continues to wiggle his feet. The* EMPEROR *interprets.*

"And as two wheels respond to a single impulse, my thought and my desire, steered with a single accord, are carried elsewhere by the sacred love which sets the sun and other stars in motion."

The ARCHITECT *reappears, furious. He puts on the toque and mask.*

ARCHITECT: The Court will learn everything. The first witness we are going to call will be your own spouse.

EMPEROR: For heaven's sake, don't involve her in this. She knows nothing. She can't tell you anything.

ARCHITECT: Silence. Let the first witness take the stand.

Putting on a mask, the EMPEROR *disguises himself as the "wife."*

Are you the wife of the Accused?

265

EMPEROR: Yes, your Honor.

ARCHITECT: Did you love each other?

EMPEROR: Oh, you know, we've been married a long time.

ARCHITECT: Did you love him?

EMPEROR: I saw him so little. He left very early in the morning and came back very late. It's been a while since we talked to each other.

ARCHITECT: Has it always been like that?

EMPEROR: Oh, no! He was a wild fellow in the beginning. He said he knew how to fly. He talked incessantly. He dreamed he'd be Emperor.

ARCHITECT: And later?

EMPEROR: He didn't even beat me anymore.

ARCHITECT: There was a time when he beat you?

EMPEROR: Yes. To assert his virility. To avenge the innumerable humilities he suffered. Later he came home from his office so tired that he didn't even feel like it.

ARCHITECT: What were your feelings toward him?

EMPEROR: It was never a grand passion, of course. I put up with him.

ARCHITECT: Was he aware of it?

EMPEROR: Oh yes. He didn't set the world on fire, and in his enthusiasm he made horrendous mistakes, but he didn't have any illusions about me.

ARCHITECT: Have you deceived him with other men?

EMPEROR: And what was I supposed to do all day long? Wait for him?

ARCHITECT: Did you have any children?

EMPEROR: No.

ARCHITECT: Did you plan it that way?

EMPEROR: No, it was more like an oversight.

ARCHITECT: What was your secret wish?

EMPEROR: To play the lute in a period costume while a

266

Machiavellian cavalier caressed me. Perhaps he would kiss my naked back which was revealed to him by my generously cut bodice. Also, though I'm not in the least inclined to deviations, I would have loved to have been surrounded by a harem of women who would take care of me. I would have liked to have had scholarly chickens and butterflies to wear on a ribbon, and I don't know what—a thousand things. I also think that I would have taken a liking to surgery. I imagine myself operating, dressed all in white, a large window behind me. (*A short pause.*) Anyway, he loved only his mother.

ARCHITECT: Who do you mean?

EMPEROR: My husband. Can I tell you something?

ARCHITECT: Speak, the Court is here to listen to you.

EMPEROR (*after looking around to be sure that no one can hear*): I'm sure he married me only to cross his mother.

ARCHITECT: Did he hate her?

EMPEROR: He hated her like a devil and he loved her like an angel. He lived only for her. Do you think it's normal for a man of his age to hang by his mother's apron-strings day and night? He needed a mother, not a wife. When he hated her he'd do anything to annoy her, even get married. I was the victim of that vengeance. (*He removes the wife's mask.*) Are you out of your mind! You've gone crazy!

ARCHITECT (*raising his judge's mask*): What's the matter with you?

EMPEROR: You've gone crazy like him.

ARCHITECT: You frighten me.

EMPEROR: Me?

ARCHITECT: Who?

EMPEROR: What do you mean?

ARCHITECT: Who's gone crazy like me?

EMPEROR: God.

ARCHITECT: Oh!

EMPEROR: But when, before or after?

ARCHITECT: Before what?

EMPEROR: I want to know when he went crazy, before or after creation.

ARCHITECT: Poor fellow.

EMPEROR: You think He's at the center of the earth?

ARCHITECT: We've never checked.

EMPEROR: He must be there, precisely at the geometric center, spending his time looking up women's slips.

ARCHITECT: We've never checked.

EMPEROR: Well, let's, just to make sure. Ah! I imagine Him peacefully in the center embedded on all sides by the earth, like a worm, happy, completely mad, and thinking He's a transistor.

ARCHITECT: Should I lift the ground off?

EMPEROR: Yes, yes.

The ARCHITECT *lifts a piece of earth as he would pull out a drawer. Both look in. They lie down in order to see better.*

I'm going to get the binoculars.

He comes back with the binoculars. They look curiously toward the center of the earth.

You can't see a thing. Funny how dark it is.

The ARCHITECT *nods his head and gets ready to close up the earth. The* EMPEROR *speaks, suddenly very uneasy.*

Tell me, are you sure no one can see us?

ARCHITECT: Yes, of course, absolutely sure.

EMPEROR: You think the hut is camouflaged well enough?

ARCHITECT: I'm sure of it.

EMPEROR: Don't forget the spy satellites, the planes with photo-electric cameras, radar, radio-electric detectors . . .

ARCHITECT: Don't worry, no one'll discover us here.

EMPEROR: And the fire and smoke. Have you put out everything so that no smoke will escape?

ARCHITECT: Well, sometimes there's a little smoke.

EMPEROR: You miserable wretch! They'll discover us, they'll discover us!

ARCHITECT: No, absolutely not.

EMPEROR: We'll be discovered because of you and your sloppiness. Who asked you to cook meals? You Babylonian Sybarite! Haven't you heard of Sodom and Gomorrah? You'd deserve it if God destroyed our island like he destroyed the cities that surrendered to vice. To cook meals! To make smoke! You ignore the hygienic virtues of cold meat. You casserole, you turnip boiler, you chowder-head, you fly gawker. May my wrath of Achilles fall on you.

ARCHITECT: All right. I agree. (*On his knees.*) Tell me, do you love me? (*He quickly sits down at the table and puts on the judge's mask.*) Let the second witness take the stand. Call the brother of the Accused.

The EMPEROR *puts on the "brother" mask.*

EMPEROR: I know, I must swear to tell the truth . . . of course. In my profession we have a great respect for justice. My brother, the poet!

ARCHITECT: You are being ironic.

EMPEROR: Why ironic? If he were a poet we'd all know

269

about it: it's a public profession, isn't it? We'd have seen him on T.V. Anyway, I think so. The poet. Always with his head in the clouds. Does Your Highness know—excuse me, your Honor—how the poet amused himself when he was a child?

ARCHITECT: Speak, we are here to bring everything into the open.

EMPEROR: My apologies to the ladies, but I must report that my brother had a special talent which he performed in front of the whole school: he drank his classmates' urine.

ARCHITECT: Although the deed itself may constitute a certain issue of grave concern, don't you think that . . .

EMPEROR: Excuse me for interrupting you. If that isn't serious, what're you going to think about what he tried to do to me. Let me explain. (*He furiously tears away the "brother's" mask.*) No, not that! Leave my brother out of this! I forbid you! My brother is a numbskull who doesn't understand anything! You don't have to let him talk, send him away! You're betraying me! Besides, I won't play anymore. That's the end of this trial. (*He sits on the ground and has a tantrum.*)

ARCHITECT (*shaking the bell*): No more childishness, on with the trial. I won't tolerate interruptions!

The EMPEROR *stops the stamping and straightens himself, full of dignity. He speaks in the solemn tones of Cicero.*

EMPEROR: *Quo usque abutere, Catilina, patientia nostra? O patientia mea* . . . Yes, for how long, Catilina, are you going to abuse my patience. Our fatherland Rome . . . (*He breaks off and takes on a familiar tone.*) You're a dirty dog: I'll permit you everything,

270

except the interrogation of my brother. My brother is an aquatic animal, kin of the crocodile, the shark, and the hippopotamus. I picture him in the swamps primeval swimming half submerged in search of prey. And me, like the exterminating angel, contemplating his motions. Look at his face and mine. (*He stops.*) Architect, we'll make Assyria an avant-garde country in our image. The underdeveloped countries will live sheltered from misery.

ARCHITECT (*raising his mask*): Emperor, I think that . . .

EMPEROR: Be quiet, wretch! Listen to the breeze of the centuries proclaiming our work imperishable. (*Silence.*) From the height of these . . . (*He hesitates.*) You will be Architect, the Supreme Architect, the Great Organizer, a pocket-size god, so to speak. Facing you, supporting you, myself, in all modesty the great Emperor, governing the destiny of Assyria and leading humanity toward triumphant tomorrows.

ARCHITECT: I feel as if a large eye . . .

EMPEROR: Me too . . . the large eye of a woman . . .

ARCHITECT: It watches us.

EMPEROR: That's right.

ARCHITECT: Why?

EMPEROR: Look at it. (*They look at the sky.*) It watches over us. See how its eyelashes are long and curled. (*With great violence.*) Cruel Desdemona, cruel like the hyenas of the desert, out of our sight! (*They look, disconsolate. To the* ARCHITECT:) It doesn't move.

The ARCHITECT *violently seizes the bell and puts on his mask. The* EMPEROR *puts on his.*

ARCHITECT: Witness, you are going to tell what your brother did with you.

EMPEROR: When I was only ten and he fifteen, my brother the "poet" amused himself by violating me and by forcing me to do the same to him. (*Tearing the mask away.*) Children's games! Of no importance.

ARCHITECT: Silence! Let the witness continue his testimony.

EMPEROR (*putting on his mask*): As I said. Must I draw you a picture? I'll tell you how it happened. (*Furious, without his mask.*) Enough, enough! That's enough!

ARCHITECT: The Court demands silence! Let the witness continue.

EMPEROR (*with his mask*): He waited for our mother to leave. We stayed alone at the house. He filled the bathtub half full of olive oil and the entertainment began. Afterward came the strangest part. When it was all over, he began to tremble and to beat himself against the bathtub. I remember one day he ended by cutting his hand badly and he sprinkled the blood on his sex while humming a hymn and sobbing. (*He pulls off his mask, sits down to cry, and hums.*)

> *Dies irae, dies ira*
> He who dies will fret, ha, ha!
> *Dies irae, dies ira*
> Shit on God, etcetera.

ARCHITECT (*removing his judge's mask and putting on the hat of the mother*): My son, why are you sitting here crying and blaspheming?

EMPEROR: *Dies irae, dies ira* . . .

ARCHITECT: You're covered with oil. What've you done?

EMPEROR: *Dies irae, dies ira*

The dead are dead from cholera!

ARCHITECT: My son, it's me, mama, don't you recognize

me? You're a child, how can you dream of death? What's happening? You're all bloody. Why did you make yourself bleed there? We have to call a doctor.

EMPEROR: Mama, I want you to buy me a very deep well, very deep, and to drop me down and to come every day for only an instant and to bring me just enough food so I won't die.

ARCHITECT: My child, what're you talking about?

EMPEROR: And only on Sundays you'll bring me the radio so that I can find out the baseball scores. Will you?

ARCHITECT: My son, what've you done that makes you so sad?

EMPEROR: Mama, I'm perverted.

ARCHITECT: Your brother?

EMPEROR (*standing up brutally*): Your Honor. With the consent of the Court I wish to assume my own defense. A great poet has said, "Little bastard, big bastard, we are all bastards." There's the real truth. I'd like to know in whose name you're judging me.

ARCHITECT: We are justice.

EMPEROR: Justice? What justice? What is justice? Justice is a certain number of men like you and me who most of the time escape this very justice by hypocrisy or subterfuge. To try for attempted murder someone . . . who has never wished to kill anybody! Besides, I don't want to do like everyone else. I forget all the advice, I forget that they recommended I should cry and look repentant to create a favorable impression. The devil with all that advice. Most of all, why all these courtroom tricks? So that the grand comedy of justice can continue. If I cry, or if I look contrite, you aren't going to be fooled either by my tears or my repentance, but you'll understand that I play my part

273

in this puppet show and you'll take that into account when you deliver the sentence. You're here to teach me a lesson, but you know very well that this lesson can be taught to anyone at all, yourself to begin with. I don't give a damn for your courts, your operetta judges, your puppet tribunals, and your prisons of vengeance!

The ARCHITECT *suddenly pulls off his robe and his toque.*

ARCHITECT (*clapping his hands*):

> With Alice I always agree.
> With Alice I always take tea.
> The last one to get to the tree . . .
> (*Very slowly and at the same time starting to leave.*)
> A cuckold will be!

They exit running.

EMPEROR (*from off-stage*): You cheated. You've been practicing!

In the distance is heard chuckling and the sound of a fall. Soon the ARCHITECT *enters.*

ARCHITECT: I'll wait for you here while I eat my dromedary egg with pheasant sauce. Don't be afraid, I'm not going to bullfight you. Eh! Toro, toro!

EMPEROR (*from off-stage*): Mooo! Moooo!

ARCHITECT: A beautiful pair of horns can sprout even in the best of families.

The EMPEROR *enters, his head decorated by a pair of horns.*

EMPEROR (*plaintively*): To think that once you were like a grandmother to me, you loved me, you couldn't do anything without me. I taught you everything. You don't respect me anymore, not at all. If my ancestors saw me! Horns! A pair of horns that the gentleman has planted on my forehead by witchcraft and why? Because I got to the pine tree in the clearing after he did. (*He moos and cries.*)

ARCHITECT: Oh, bull of gold, of bronze, bull descendant of Taurus . . .

EMPEROR: You're my sacred cow.

ARCHITECT: I'm your cow and your blushing camel.

EMPEROR: Then scratch my legs.

He puts a leg forward. The ARCHITECT *scratches it for a moment.*

No, not like that. Scratch better. From underneath.

The ARCHITECT *scratches him better.*

ARCHITECT: I've had enough of scratching you. The minute I start, you get heavy.

EMPEROR: Me, heavy? Is that the way you treat the Emperor of Assyria? Moreover, an Emperor of Assyria with horns, which is really something. Long live the Monarchy!

ARCHITECT: Every night it's always the same thing: "Scratch me a little until I fall asleep." Right away you start to snore like a blacksmith's bellows, but as soon as I stop scratching you—silence, you open an eye and say, "Scratch me, I'm not asleep yet."

EMPEROR: Take these horns off me! Don't forget that I have my dignity too. Besides, they're heavy and I can't move my head freely.

ARCHITECT: How do you want them to disappear? Should I clap my hands once?

EMPEROR: You're crazy! Clap your hands! Never! Do you

know what I dreamed last night? . . . Someone whipped me and I complained. In the dream a girl said to me: "Don't complain . . ." I answered: "Can't you see I'm suffering, that I'm enduring terrible pain?" She laughed and told me: "How can you suffer if this is only a dream? It isn't real." I said she was wrong. She answered that to convince myself that she was right all I had to do was clap my hands. I did it and I suddenly found myself with my hands together, awake, sitting on my bed within the four walls of the hut.

ARCHITECT: Yes, I saw and heard you.

EMPEROR: Imagine, if you clap your hands now and I wake up from this dream I take to be life . . . to be . . . Can you imagine us in another world? Better to have a little at home than a lot abroad. (*Suddenly, he very ostentatiously brings his hands together as if to clap. He hesitates a few seconds, waiting. He's going to clap his hands. Slowly. He stops and turns his head toward the* ARCHITECT.) In the name of God, when are you going to make these damn horns disappear?

ARCHITECT: Now, now, don't get excited. It's very simple. Rub your head against the trunk of the cocoa tree and they'll fall off.

The EMPEROR *runs out.*

No, not that one. Yes, the other one.

A pause. Confused noises. The EMPEROR *comes back without the horns, still rubbing his forehead with a leaf.*

EMPEROR: Don't I look younger without horns?

As he speaks, the ARCHITECT *furiously moves to the Court table, puts on the robe, and adjusts the judge's mask.*

ARCHITECT: Having heard the brother of the Accused, the Court calls the next witness: Mr. Samson.

The EMPEROR *puts on the mask of Mr. Samson.*

EMPEROR: I swear to tell the whole truth.

ARCHITECT: Where did you meet the Accused?

EMPEROR: While playing a pin-ball machine.

ARCHITECT: Is that the only time you saw him?

EMPEROR: No, one day he asked for my assistance. Well, he invited me to dinner and I agreed to help him.

ARCHITECT: Doing what?

EMPEROR: The angel.

ARCHITECT: The angel?

EMPEROR: Yes, in a church.

ARCHITECT: Please explain.

EMPEROR: When the church was empty, always about eleven o'clock at night, we went into the choir, way up. He took his clothes off and stuck a few feathers on his back, ten or twelve. Then he rigged himself with a lot of ropes and I pushed him over the edge. He swung to and fro, like an angel or an archangel, and when he couldn't go on any longer I pulled him back. He always lost half his feathers. I wonder what the church personnel must have thought when they found them on the floor in the morning.

ARCHITECT: Did you know his mother?

EMPEROR: Yes, the Accused told me he would give me all the treasures of the world if I would do her in.

ARCHITECT: You refused, of course.

EMPEROR: As if I were a criminal! To do the angel, all

right. A game from time to time, why not? But to kill
. . . And then, you ought to have seen them one day
at the movies! I saw them by chance. One would have
sworn they were lovers!

ARCHITECT: Thank you very much for these clarifications.
The Court wishes to recall the wife of the Accused.

The EMPEROR *changes his mask.*

EMPEROR: You need further testimony?

ARCHITECT: The Court wishes to know your opinion of the
nature of the intimate relations between the Accused
and his mother.

EMPEROR: I told you already: they loved each other, they
hated each other. It depended upon the moment.

ARCHITECT: Do you think there was something equivocal,
let's say incestuous, between them?

EMPEROR: On that point I am absolutely positive: I don't
believe a word of it.

ARCHITECT: Have you heard the testimony of the preceding
witness?

EMPEROR: Gossip! My husband was a spirited and impetu-
ous man, but he never had incestuous relations with
his mother. And here's the proof: shortly before her
disappearance they went through a period of violent
hatred. Then his mother requested a meeting which
my husband agreed to under the following conditions:
first, that his mother pay him a very large sum for
every minute of the conversation; second, that she
suck him with what he called her "maternal mouth,"
thereby committing the most infamous sin. That's
what he said; he was always so innocent.

ARCHITECT: And what does all this prove?

EMPEROR: This clearly proves that there was never anything equivocal between them or else he wouldn't have demanded what I just told you as something exceptional. By the way, I remember a detail that might interest the Court.

ARCHITECT: Please speak.

EMPEROR: Lately when she came to visit him, he would ask me to cover his eyes with adhesive tape and cotton. What's more, he sometimes consented to speak to her, but with each of them in separate rooms. (*Ripping his mask off.*) I'll bet you're going to condemn me! Answer me!

ARCHITECT: An eye for an eye, a tooth for a tooth.

The EMPEROR, *very sad, walks around the stage and sits down on the ground, turning his back on the* ARCHITECT. *He puts his head between his hands. The* ARCHITECT *looks at him with annoyance. Then, deciding that the matter seems serious, he walks over and looks closely at the* EMPEROR, *finally taking off his own mask.*

ARCHITECT: What's the matter with you now? (*The* EMPEROR *whimpers weakly.*) Come on, calm down, it's not that bad. Do you want to blow your nose? (*The* EMPEROR *nods. The* ARCHITECT *addresses himself to the highest branches of a tree invisible to the audience.*) Tree, give me one of your leaves. (*Indeed, a rather large leaf falls immediately. He takes it.*) There, blow! (*The* EMPEROR *blows his nose and angrily throws the leaf-handkerchief away. Then he turns even further away from the* ARCHITECT.) Does the gentleman wish anything else? (*The* EMPEROR *whines.*) All right, I know. It's true. You were the Emperor, you're still the Emperor of Assyria; when you got up

279

in the morning all the trains and all the sirens blew to announce to the people that you had just awakened. (*Having said these words, he goes to see how the* EMPEROR *is reacting. The* EMPEROR *is still not listening.*) Ten thousand Amazons, with sculptured bodies, naked, in your rooms . . .

Suddenly the EMPEROR *gets up and breathes deeply as if he were aping an actor of melodrama.*

EMPEROR (*with supreme eloquence*): Ten thousand Amazons, which my father imported directly from the Oriental Indies, came running naked in the morning into my room and kissed the tips of my fingers while intoning in chorus the imperial hymn, the refrain of which goes as follows:
> Long live our immortal Emperor
> May God keep him forevermore.

What echoes! Ten thousand . . . (*Aside.*) Even if my room had been a stadium . . . (*Again with emphasis.*) My life has always had the imprint of a unique fate within the great universal destiny. It was an example for future generations; in a word, for posterity. (*A pause. He sits down.*) You're right, I tried to kill my mother. Samson told the truth. (*Getting up brusquely, full of vigor and conviction.*) So what? I tried to kill her. Well? If you think you're going to give me a complex, you're dead wrong. I couldn't care less. (*A sudden anxiety comes over him again. He crawls on his knees to the* ARCHITECT.) Do you still love me in spite of that?

ARCHITECT: You never told me about this attempted crime.

EMPEROR (*getting up again, very dignified*): I have my secrets.

ARCHITECT: So I see!

EMPEROR: If you want to know the truth, I only loved one single being: my German shepherd. He came to me every day. We took walks together, like two lovers: Pegasus and Paris. I didn't need an alarm clock: every morning he came running to lick my hands. Sometimes he saved me the trouble of washing them. Thanks to him I stopped telling my secrets to my billiard pals. He was very faithful to me, isn't that what one says?

The ARCHITECT *gets on all fours, fastens a leash around his neck, and puts a gas mask on his face.*

ARCHITECT: I'm your German shepherd of the islands.
EMPEROR: Hey! Pluto! Dig, dig!

The ARCHITECT *immediately begins to scratch the sand like a dog.*

Let's see what my good doggie will find.

The ARCHITECT *continues to dig, barking. At last he pulls a living partridge out of the ground. He takes it between his jaws and happily runs out with it. He comes back right away. The* EMPEROR *pets him tenderly and gives him little pats on the back.*

"In the scale of creatures only man can inspire sustained disgust, the repugnance caused by an animal is short-lived."

The dog approves, barking happily.

The man who said that sure is my kind. That's right, always stay by my side like a dog and I'll love you for all eternity. Together, like the dog Cerberus and Homer, we will traverse the abysmal kingdoms of the ocean! (*He puts on a blindman's glasses and takes a*

281

cane. *The dog guides him. He speaks solemnly.*)
"Sing, O muse, the wrath of Achilles." I think I've
said that already. Alms, alms for a poor man blind
from birth who can't earn his own bread. Alms, alms!
Thank you, madam, you're very kind. May God give
you long life and preserve your sight for many years.
Alms for the love of God. For the love of God . . .
Oh my, now that I'm blind I've never seen God more
clearly. O Lord! I see you with the eyes of faith now
that my eyes are blind. O Lord! how happy I am! I
feel, like Saint Theresa of Avila, that you have in-
serted a fiery sword into my behind.

ARCHITECT (*in dog language*): Into my entrails.

EMPEROR: That's it, into my entrails, and it fills me with
sublime joy and pain. O Lord! I also feel like the
Saint, that the devils play ball with my soul. O Lord!
At last I have found faith. I want all humanity to be
witness to this event. I also want my dog to have faith.
Dog, tell me, have you faith in God? (*Incomprehensible barking from the dog.*) You apostate Turk, you
don't believe in God?! (*He tries to beat the dog, but it
escapes. Like a blindman he's reduced to groping to
the right and left with his cane.*) Damned animal!
Come here! I'm the voice of the revelation of faith.
(*He strikes with his cane in all directions, trying to
beat the dog who mocks him.*) I'll form a crusade of
faithful blindmen to fight with great bayonnet thrusts
all the atheist dogs of the world. Cursed beast! Come
here. Kneel down with me, I'm going to pray. (*He
strikes with his cane in all directions. The dog defies
him, barking.*) You're still making fun of me! Damned
coyote of the pampas. Poor animal, he'll never understand the very lofty virtues of pimpism.

The ARCHITECT *removes his gas mask and goes back to the judge's bench.*

ARCHITECT: Let the next witness take the stand.

The EMPEROR, *disgruntled, takes off his blindman's glasses.*

I said, let the next witness take the stand. Madame . . . Olympia de Kant.

EMPEROR (*as Olympia*): Can I be of use to you?

ARCHITECT: Did you know the mother of the Accused?

EMPEROR: How could I not have known her? She was my best friend. We've been friends since we were children. We were expelled from the same school . . .

ARCHITECT: Why were you expelled?

EMPEROR: Children's pranks. We played doctor, naked of course. We took each other's temperatures, we performed all kinds of operations, we turned ink pots upside down on our heads and the ink dripped slowly all the way down to our feet . . . in that era of old-fashioned morals you can guess what they imagined. Certainly, we hugged and kissed each other, why shouldn't we? We were two little girls at the brink of life. Nevertheless, they threw us out of school.

ARCHITECT: How old were you?

EMPEROR: She was a little older than I. Two little girls, I tell you. Games, nothing but innocent games. But then I suppose we're not here to discuss that subject.

ARCHITECT: A subject not without interest. How old were you when you were expelled?

EMPEROR: Who? Me? (*Very grave.*) Barely twenty.

ARCHITECT: Oh! (*An uneasy silence.*) Of course you knew the Accused.

EMPEROR: He was his mother's great love; she lived only for him. And I always believed that he loved her with the same fervor.

ARCHITECT: They never quarreled?

EMPEROR: Every day they had violent disputes. That's what love is. You could see them walking in the park like lovers. They quarreled at the top of their lungs without caring in the least that you could hear them. I would never have believed that things would go so far.

ARCHITECT: So far?

EMPEROR: A few days before his mother disappeared forever, "disappeared" . . .

ARCHITECT: What are you insinuating?

EMPEROR: I believe that no one ever disappears, somebody makes you disappear.

ARCHITECT: Are you aware of the gravity of your accusation?

EMPEROR: I never intrude in other people's affairs. What I was going to say is that a few days before her disappearance something happened which she told me about and which is worth recounting. While she slept her son crept in and carefully placed a fork, salt, and a napkin next to the bed—and a butcher knife. He carefully lowered it to his mother's throat and at the moment when he dealt the terrible blow which was to decapitate her, she moved aside. It seems that the Accused, instead of feeling ill at ease, laughed like a madman. (*He stops, takes off his mask, and shakes with hysterical laughter.*) Beautiful mother steak! The butcher's masterpiece, the weekly special. (*He explodes into laughter. Suddenly he becomes serious and turns to the* ARCHITECT. *He speaks very sadly.*) I never told you, but you know, when I go away from

284

you . . . (*Very happy.*) To think that I could have struck her a good blow with the carving knife and sold her as beefsteak. My mother in fillets! (*Very sad once more.*) You don't know it, but if I leave you to go (*very dignified*) to the bathroom it's because . . . (*He laughs.*) My mother, what a story! I suppose you didn't believe a word of what Madame Olympia de Kant said. (*Sadly.*) Well, today you'll know everything. I'll tell you the truth. I leave you so that I can blaspheme.

ARCHITECT: But why? Don't you want to blaspheme with me?

EMPEROR (*sadly*): Don't make me cause a scandal. Don't forget these historic words: "And if thy right hand offend thee, cut it off and cast it from thee. And if thy right foot . . . " Perhaps that's why you see so many one-legged people nowadays?

ARCHITECT: There isn't going to be a scandal. If you want to, we can blaspheme together right now.

EMPEROR (*worried*): Together? You and me? Blaspheme?

ARCHITECT: Certainly, that'd be great.

EMPEROR: What do you say we blaspheme to music?

ARCHITECT: Excellent idea!

EMPEROR: What music would piss God off the most?

ARCHITECT: You should know better than I.

EMPEROR: If we blaspheme to military music it should be as much fun for him as a kick in the ass. (*Sadly.*) Do you know exactly what I do when I leave? I defecate in the most distinguished manner and with great euphoria. Then, with the product, using it as paint, I write: "God is a son of a bitch". . . Do you think that someday he'll turn me into a pillar of salt?

ARCHITECT: Is he turning you into a pillar of salt now?

EMPEROR (*with great eloquence*): Poor moron. You haven't read the Bible. It's unbelievable!! Ah, youth! You didn't know it: God can change you into a pillar of salt as easily as he can cast fire upon you or inundate the earth in an instant. Be very careful!

ARCHITECT: All right, are we going to blaspheme together, yes or no?

EMPEROR: What, aren't you afraid?

ARCHITECT: But you yourself . . .

EMPEROR: Don't remind me of my petty youthful errors. You know nothing about the weaknesses of the flesh, how could you know? Listen to me. (*He takes the stance of a tenor and sings to an opera aria.*)

> Shit on God.
> Shit on His divine image.
> Shit on His omnipresence.

(*To the* ARCHITECT.) At least add tralala-tralala. (*Singing.*)

> I hate God and all His miracles.

ARCHITECT: Tralala-tralala.

EMPEROR (*furious*): Animal! How dare you interrupt me!

ARCHITECT: But you asked me . . .

EMPEROR: Be quiet! Can't you see that I was following my inspiration? Do you think it's so easy to sing opera? (*A pause.*) About that trial, where were we?

ARCHITECT: So now you're the one who's interested?

EMPEROR: Go back to your seat immediately. Aren't you ever going to render justice on this damn island? If Cicero came out of his grave, what Catilina-like speeches he would come up with!

The ARCHITECT *puts on his judge's mask.*

ARCHITECT: Justice will be done. Let the next witness take

286

the stand. One moment. The Court rules that it has heard all the witnesses. We're going to hear what the Accused has to say in his defense. We found this letter. What do you think of it? "Like the bird flying to the shore over the heads of rowing fishermen . . ."

EMPEROR: Don't go on, I recognize my mother's style.

ARCHITECT (*murmuring while he reads to himself*): Ah! This seems more interesting. "I've always been like a rock, like a library, like a radio-electric detector for my son, for him . . ."

EMPEROR: Always the same old story: all the love she gave me, etcetera . . .

ARCHITECT (*murmuring, then reading*): . . . "when he was a child, I had to lay him down on the sidewalk and put a blanket over him, then raise the blanket and say 'My baby, my treasure, you've died far away from mama. . .'"

EMPEROR (*impatient*): Games, nothing but innocent games. There isn't anything extraordinary about it.

ARCHITECT: Don't forget that she wrote that letter a few days before her alleged disappearance.

EMPEROR: What do I have to do with her disappearance?

ARCHITECT (*reading*): "I suspect the worst. Lately he has become very strange, he reprimands me for every little thing. When we go to the woods on clear nights, he doesn't dance the farandole anymore. I have the feeling that he watches me furtively, that he . . ."

The EMPEROR *runs off. The* ARCHITECT *takes off his judge's mask, puts on the mask of the mother, and then wraps himself in a scarf which covers his head. The* EMPEROR *enters and executes a diabolical dance, singing.*

EMPEROR:

    In the night all the stars
    Slip into women's garters and fine high-heeled shoes
    In the night all the stars
    Deep inside my brain bid me heed.

The mother dances a kind of farandole with him. He stops, brusquely.

    I'll throw you to the German shepherd.

ARCHITECT: What'd you say, my child?

EMPEROR: I'll kill you and make the dog eat you.

ARCHITECT: My son, what's gotten into you, my poor little darling baby?

EMPEROR: Mama, I'm so unhappy.

ARCHITECT: Child, I'm here to comfort you.

EMPEROR: Will you always comfort me?

ARCHITECT: How can you have ideas like that? Don't you love me anymore?

EMPEROR: Oh, yes. Look! I'm a banana. Peel me and eat me if you want to.

ARCHITECT: My child, you're losing your marbles. You're going crazy. You're alone too much. You should go out more, go to the movies once in a while.

EMPEROR: Everybody hates me.

ARCHITECT: Come, I'll rock you on my bosom. (*The* EM-PEROR *puts his head on the mother's bosom.*) My child, don't cry. Poor little thing. Everybody hates him because he's better than they are. They all envy him.

EMPEROR: Mama, let me sit at your feet like when I was little.

ARCHITECT: Yes, my child.

The mother raises her feet. The EMPEROR *sits with his back turned to his mother and leans his neck*

*against the insteps of his mother's feet—a very diffi-
cult position to get into and to hold. The mother sings
a lullaby.*

> Sleep long my tiny little one,
> For in your mother's arm,
> No devil or no bogyman
> Can do you any harm.

The mother sings the song softly while the EMPEROR
*falls half asleep. Suddenly he wakes up seized by a
violent frenzy.*

EMPEROR: Let all the centuries hear me: it's true I killed
my mother, I alone, without anyone's help.

The ARCHITECT *runs to put on his judge's robe.*

ARCHITECT: Are you aware of the consequences of your
confession?

EMPEROR: What does it matter? May all the punishments
of heaven and earth fall on me, may I be devoured
by a thousand carnivorous plants, may a squadron of
giant bees suck all the blood out my veins, may I be
hung by my feet in the infinite spaces millions of
light years away from this planet, may Satan's drag-
ons roast my buttocks until they are nothing but two
scarlet tambourines.

ARCHITECT: How did you kill her?

EMPEROR: I hit her on the head with a hammer while she
slept.

ARCHITECT: Did she die immediately?

EMPEROR: Right away. (*Dreamily.*) What a strange sight,
it looked as if vapors were escaping from her shat-
tered head, and I thought I saw a lizard crawl out of
the wound. He got on the table facing me and stared
at me fixedly, his goitery throat moving up and down.

Examining him more closely, I could see that his face was my face. Then when I tried to catch him he disappeared as if he were only a phantom.

ARCHITECT: But when . . .

EMPEROR: And then, I don't know why, I had this great longing to cry. I felt unhappy. I kissed my mother, and my hands and my lips got all bloody. I called in vain, she didn't answer, and I felt sadder and sadder, and even more unhappy. (*He calls her.*) Darling mother. It's me. I didn't mean to hurt you. What's the matter? Why don't you move? How you bleed. Do you want me to do a dance just for you? (*He begins to do contortions and pirouettes very awkwardly. He recites.*)

> "The March Hare and the Hatter were having tea. A Dormouse was sitting between them, fast asleep, and the other two were using it as a cushion, resting their elbows on it . . ."

Darling mother, I didn't want to hurt you, I only gave you a little tap with the hammer, quite gently.

> ". . . and talking over its head. 'Very uncomfortable for the Dormouse,' thought Alice, 'Only as it's asleep, I suppose it doesn't mind.' "

Did you like it, Mommy? Did I say it good? Talk to me. (*A pause.*) Say something.

ARCHITECT (*rapping on the table*): What did you do with the body? How can you explain that it has never been found?

EMPEROR: Well . . . (*he timidly lowers his head*) . . . it's not important.

ARCHITECT: Justice must know everything.

EMPEROR: The German shepherd that we had . . . the dog . . . the dog . . . well, he ate her.

ARCHITECT: And you didn't stop him?

EMPEROR: Me . . . actually, what's wrong with that? It took him several days. Every day he ate one piece . . . I let him into the room.

ARCHITECT: Did he devour everything, even the bones?

EMPEROR: I threw the ones he couldn't chew up into the incinerator at the medical school.

ARCHITECT: The Court will judge your actions . . .

EMPEROR (*in a very false tone*): Like a ship with billowing sails that stops at all the ports on its route, my grief will know all the degrees of martyrdom. (*Sincerely.*) Architect, sentence me to death, I know I'm guilty. I know I deserve it. I don't want to live another minute of my botched-up life. I think I'd have been happy in an aquarium, sitting on a chair, surrounded by water and fish and the little girls would have come to see me on Sunday. Instead of that . . . Architect, tell me that you're still . . . my friend, tell me that, in spite of everything, you won't throw me out tonight.

ARCHITECT: We're here to judge you.

EMPEROR: Architect, tell me once and for all that you've condemned me. (*A pause.*) Look here, I'm your Phoenix. (*He imitates the Phoenix.*) Climb on my back and I'll carry you to the paradise of obscure enlightenment.

ARCHITECT: No stories. You stand before a court.

EMPEROR: The pieces of evidence against me are your round swans during the last period of the full moon.

ARCHITECT: You'll be judged with extreme severity.

EMPEROR: May I ask what my punishment will be?

ARCHITECT: Death.

EMPEROR: May I choose the method?

ARCHITECT: Speak!

EMPEROR: I would like you to kill me with a hammer blow. Architect, will you kill me yourself?

ARCHITECT: I suppose the Court can grant your request.

EMPEROR: But most of all . . . I don't request, I demand, it's the last wish of a condemned man that . . .

ARCHITECT: Speak for the last time.

EMPEROR: After my death . . .

ARCHITECT (*taking off his toque*): Emperor, are you serious?

EMPEROR (*gravely*): Very serious.

ARCHITECT: This was just another farce—your judgment, your trial . . . but you seem to be taking it seriously. Emperor, you know I love you.

EMPEROR (*moved*): Are you serious?

ARCHITECT: Yes, very serious.

EMPEROR (*changing his tone*): But today we haven't been playing.

ARCHITECT: Today was no different from any other day.

EMPEROR: It was different. You learned many things I didn't want you to know.

ARCHITECT: So what? Will you kiss me?

The ARCHITECT *closes his eyes. The* EMPEROR *comes to him and kisses him very ceremoniously on the forehead.*

On the forehead?

EMPEROR: I respect you. What do you know about these things?

ARCHITECT: Teach me about them, like you've taught me everything else.

EMPEROR: Today you will kill me: you condemned me to death and you have to carry out the sentence.

ARCHITECT: But dying isn't a game like the others, it's irrevocable.

EMPEROR: I demand it. It's my punishment. I was going to tell you my last wish.

ARCHITECT: Speak.

EMPEROR: I want . . . I want you to . . . well . . . to eat me . . . to eat me. I want you to be you and me at the same time. You'll eat all of me, Architect, you understand?

BLACKOUT

SCENE TWO

Some hours later. On the table, which before served as the judge's bench, lies the naked body of the EMPEROR. *The table is set for a meal. When the lights come up the* ARCHITECT, *a big napkin tied around his neck, is in the process of cutting off one of the Emperor's feet with a knife and fork. As the end of the play approaches the* ARCHITECT *gradually takes on the voice, the tone, the traits, and the expressions of the* EMPEROR.

ARCHITECT: Good gracious! He has very tough ankles. (*He tries to saw the foot off, but fails. He speaks to the head of the dead* EMPEROR.) Ah! Emperor, what the hell have you done with the bones of your feet that makes them so hard to cut? (*He goes into the hut and returns with a primitive saw. He saws with this improvised tool. It doesn't work.*) To kill him . . . to eat him . . . And me here all alone. Now who'll carry me to Babylon on an elephant? Who's going to caress my back before I go to sleep? Who's going to whip me when I want it? (*He moves toward the bushes.*) Moles, go and fetch me a hatchet, we'll see if

I can manage to get the damned foot off. (*He holds out his hand. Nothing happens.*) What's going on? You don't obey me? It's I who speak to you. I'm the Architect, I'm not the Emperor. Bring me a hatchet. (*He holds out his hand and waits uneasily. After a long moment of expectation a hatchet appears between the bushes.*) They took their sweet time about it, nincompoops! Won't they obey me anymore? We shall see. Let the thunder and lightning strike at once. (*He waits in anguish.*) What? Not this either? I feel very funny. It's very alarming. I've showered in the Fountain of Youth, I've done all the exercises, and now they won't obey me. (*Thunder and lightning.*) Ah! Good! Better late than never. (*Hatchet in hand, he walks to the* EMPEROR. *He strikes a formidable hatchet blow on the foot and succeeds in cutting it off. He takes it in his hands and examines it closely.*) His five toes are there. His callouses. It's a good foot, rather large, thank God. He shouldn't be ticklish anymore. (*He tickles the sole of the foot and then laughs himself.*) To eat him like this, without gravy . . . A little salt would do wonders. (*He salts it. He bites into it and devours the mouthful.*) Ah, it's not so bad. It's going to be an excellent meal. (*Suddenly he stops eating, frightened.*) I hope it's not a fast day. Is it Friday? I don't think so. Anyway, what kind of religion is it that forbids you to eat meat on Friday? That bastard, oh, excuse me, the Emperor didn't even tell me. In one of them there's a story about Friday and about the . . . crusades. Tsk, I don't remember anything. In another there are harems? What a mess in my head. If I remember right, all of them forbid masturbation . . . unless . . . where are those catechisms? In fact, what's my religion? Well . . . perhaps I'd better leave that alone. (*Suddenly very uneasy.*) The paper, where's the paper? (*He goes into the hut and returns reading a small piece of paper.*) "I want you to dress like my mother when you eat me. Don't forget to put on her large whalebone corset." Good God, I almost forgot the most important thing. (*He goes into the hut and returns with a large suitcase which has painted on it in big letters: "Clothing of my adored little mother." He opens the suitcase.*) What a smell! My God! That lady must have pee-peed on herself. She smells even worse than the Emperor did, and when he took a fancy to touch his sex you could smell it for a mile. What habits: handling it all day, airing it out, contemplating it . . . (*Suddenly he bursts out laughing.*) And when he hid it between his legs you wouldn't believe he had one! What a little brat. (*He takes out the corset, puts it on, and begins to lace it.*) What are all these laces good for? Wait a minute. I sound almost like the Emperor. What's happening to me? I'm talking to myself too. Like he used to say: I'm alone, this provides me with the occasion to be Shakespearian. Damn corset! Who could have invented such a thing! Why did he order me to dress in his mother's clothes? Well, better not interfere with his affairs. (*To make pulling the laces easier he loops them over a branch and pulls them brutally.*) I'm suffocating! How did they manage, wrapped in this contraption? (*At last he has the corset laced. He wraps himself in a shawl and puts on a quaint hat.*) What a splendid mother I make! Agrippina is nothing compared to me. My womb is ready to beget Nero himself . . . (*Troubled.*) But didn't the Emperor say that?

296

Down with Monarchy! I've had it up to here with you and your mother. The last thing I'm going to do for you is to eat your cadaver dressed as your mother and then I will travel toward other shores in my canoe. From the waves I hear the call of the ten thousand trumpets of Jericho. From my belly will grow the light to guide me toward a country where I will live overcome with happiness, where the children rove with the queens of Sheba, and where the old men rule the women with caressing hands. (*He has finished dressing as the mother; he sits down at the table and ceremoniously eats another piece of the Emperor's foot. He stops chewing and, crying, speaks to the Emperor's head.*) You know, I'm very sorry . . . I feel very lonely without you. You were good company. Promise me that you'll come back to life . . . Why don't you talk to me? At least say you still like me. (*He waits a moment.*) Tell me something, I implore you. Make a miracle. The saints speak after they're dead, you told me that yourself . . . Make a miracle for me. It doesn't matter what . . . as long as I can feel your presence, that's all I ask. (*He raises a glass.*) See this glass of water? Change it into whiskey. Come on, try. It's only a little glass. If I had asked you to cast a big bell and to make fertile the sterile women who would come to ring it—but only whiskey . . . Try, try . . . Or even easier: turn the water into white wine! (*He waits; nothing happens.*) That's child's play . . . All right, watered down wine! (*Furious.*) Very well, I won't speak to you anymore . . . I won't pay any attention to you. Kick off by yourself. (*He bites furiously into the Emperor's foot. He takes the glass of water that he has just raised, puts it to his lips, and violently throws it away*.) Son of a bitch, pig! You turned it into ammonia! You're nothing but a phony, a carnival saint! If that's a miracle I'm Sarah Bernhardt. (*He devours a large piece of foot*.) What did he mean by that? Ammonia! So there must be an afterlife . . . a beyond. If I had a tripod to sit on I would communicate with him. Anyway, there's one choice morsel for me. Once I've eaten his brain with all its nucleic acid, we'll see what we'll see. With his nucleic acid in my pot, I'll be capable of anything. (*He goes to the hut and returns with a sculptor's chisel and a straw*.) May I? First I'm going to suck up your nucleic acid. Thanks to it . . . Now I understand! The ammonia was for his mother, for his mother . . . (*He laughs*.) Thanks to your nucleic acid I'm going to be master of your memory and your dreams—and therefore your thoughts. (*He places the chisel behind the ear of the* EMPEROR *and makes a hole. He puts the straw in and sucks the brain. Some of the substance, which is similar to yoghurt, slides down his jaws, and when he finishes, he licks it away*.) Yum! I feel like a new man. Ahhh! I deserve a little nap. Gorillas, go and get me a hammock. (*He waits confidently*.) What's happening? Didn't you hear me? I asked for a hammock. (*He waits impatiently*.) What? Are you refusing to obey me? (*He goes toward the bushes*.) Hey, gorilla! Yes, you. Go and get me a hammock this instant! (*He waits for some time*.) Not only do you refuse to obey me, but you run away! That's the limit. (*He sits down, complaining very sadly*.) I've lost all my authority.

BLACKOUT

SCENE THREE

Only the Emperor's bones are left on the table. The ARCHITECT *now has the same intonation and manners as the* EMPEROR.
When the lights come up the ARCHITECT *is sucking the last bone.*

ARCHITECT: Now that I can no longer command the animals, I'll train a goat. When I tell it to make its signature with its hoof it will scribble with a flourish; when I tell it to imitate Einstein, it will stick out its tongue; when I tell it to do the bishop, it will get on its knees. Emperor, where are you? How could I have eaten you so easily? Dust you are and to dust you shall return . . . And the sun? Does the sun still obey me? We'll check: Let night fall. (*Nothing happens. He sucks the last bone again and puts it on the table.*) Now I can truthfully say that I am finished. (*The bones remain on the table where they form a kind of dislocated skeleton.*) I'm all alone and talk as if I were with him. I've got to stop that. (*He hits the table with his hand and a bone rolls to the ground. He gets down under the table to pick it up and completely disappears from sight.*) Where the hell is that bone?

When he reappears it is the EMPEROR *who comes out from under the table, dressed as the* ARCHITECT.

EMPEROR: Ah! Here it is. Here's the damn bone, subject of our concern. I have to be very careful; I knock everything on the ground. A goat, that's it. A learned goat who will become Princess of Chaldea or Empress or a lascivious nun. (*He pushes the table with the bones on it and it disappears stage right.*) Let all the scraps of the imperial orgies disappear. Alone at last! This time I'm certain I'm going to be happy. A new life begins for me. I'll forget all the past. Better still, I'll forget the past in such a way that I'll have it all the more present in my mind, so that I won't fall back into any of my past errors. No sentimentalities. Not a tear for anyone else. (*He cries, then pulls himself together.*) I said not a tear for anyone else. Serene. Tranquil. Happy. Without complications, without interference. I'll study and all alone I'll discover perpetual motion. (*He stretches out a leg and looks in the opposite direction.*) Scratch my leg, tickle me. (*Slowly, his face turned away, he moves one hand toward his leg. When he touches his knee he says voluptuously.*) That's it, there, scratch well, slowly, a little lower, with your nails. Harder. With your nails, I tell you. Harder, scratch harder. Still harder. Lower. Harder. Harder. (*Suddenly a frenzy overcomes him and with his other hand he seizes the hand which has been scratching. He looks at it, surprised, as if it were lifeless.*) What orgies I'll have. Me, all alone. I'm going to be the first, the only, the best! I have to be careful

300

so no one will see me. Hidden day and night. No fire. No cigarettes. The light of a butt can be seen on a radar screen for ten thousand miles around. I'll have to take every precaution. I'll sing arias. (*He sings.*) Figaro—Figaro—Figaro—Figaro—Figaro . . . What a guy. And since I'm alone humanity won't envy and persecute me. No one will know what talent he possesses—this unique inhabitant of a planet, I mean of a solitary island. And now, since nobody can hear me (*crazy with joy*): Long live I! Long live I! Long live I! And shit on everyone else! Long live I! Long live I! Long live I!

He dances in happy ecstasy.

At this moment an airplane noise is heard. Like a trapped and frightened animal, the EMPEROR *looks for a refuge. He runs in all directions, digs in the ground, starts to run again, and finally buries his head in the sand. Explosion. A bright flash of flames. Trembling with fear the* EMPEROR, *his face against the sand, puts his fingers in his ears.*

A few moments later the ARCHITECT *appears. He is carrying a large suitcase. He has a certain forced elegance in his freshly ironed clothes. He tries to keep his composure.*

He touches the EMPEROR *with the tip of his cane.*

ARCHITECT: Help me, sir! I am the only survivor of the accident.
EMPEROR (*horrified*): Fee! Fee! Feegaa! Feegaa! Fee!

For a moment he looks aghast at the ARCHITECT *and then runs off as fast as he can.*

FAST CURTAIN

GARDEN OF DELIGHTS

translated from the French
by Helen Gary Bishop and Tom Bishop

Characters

LAIS, *beautiful actress*
TELOC, *a man*
MIHARCA, *childhood friend of* LAIS
ZENON
MC'S VOICE
VOICE OF POLICEMAN
and NINE YOUNG SHEEP (EWES)

Décor

A huge space with many columns as far as the eye can see: they form a kind of labyrinth.

Every here and there, rather far apart, one can distinguish a few small balconies between columns.

A circular moving platform allows for the entrance and exit of a small green for the NINE YOUNG SHEEP. *A gate keeps them from getting out.*

Act One

Darkness.
A single spot grows brighter on LAIS *until she is*
entirely visible. The remainder of the stage remains in
the shadows. LAIS *seems to have stepped out of an old*
engraving: her arms are bare, a plunging décolletage,
a tiered gown, a rococo chapeau on her head. She sings
very sweetly and sentimentally.

LAIS (*singing*)   Such is life, seeming so delectable,
   Like a siren, affected and mutable,
   She envelops and plunges us into her sweetness,
   Until death comes to break the oar and cable,
   And of us remains but a fable,
   Less than wind, smoke, dream, and darkness.

   Or she might sing the following song.

Sadness surrounds me, mute like stupidity
I cannot even escape misunderstandings
When betrayal accuses me with its black heart
of electrolysis, of Wednesdays, and tempests.
I will speak out for a million lemons instead of for
   glory
And I feel a bubble rising into my brain
From my pained heart screaming of madness.

   Another spot suddenly lights up a corner of the
   stage where the live baby SHEEP *bleat timidly.*
   LAIS *talks to them.*

305

LAIS (*with love and tenderness*) Hush there, my
pretty ones. I'm right here with you, you're not alone.

A few of the SHEEP *continue to bleat.*

Don't be afraid of anything. The big bad wolf doesn't
exist. No one will slaughter you. Those are stories invented by men. Poor little things. (*She sings the song
to herself again, then hums it softly.*) Are you
calmed down now? But you must have your dinner,
it's getting late. Tomorrow I'll buy you anything
you want. I'll give each of you a wrist watch so you'll
know exactly when I'll return. Poor little darlings,
have your dinner in peace. I don't want you to have
nightmares. My poor little ones, my darlings! And
I'll even buy you a television set if you'd like. . . .
All right now, it's dinnertime!

*Suddenly a tremendous roar is heard, like the
lamentation of a savage beast.* LAIS *runs to turn
on a light. She seems frightened. The stage lights
up entirely. Above we make out a cage, and inside
it the beast who roared. The cage is suspended
about fifteen feet above the stage by means of a
thick rope which is worked by a pully.* LAIS *grabs
hold of the rope and brings the cage down. At precisely this moment the phone rings. Another roar
is heard from the cage.* LAIS *hesitates: she doesn't
know whether to bring the cage down entirely or
answer the telephone. She decides to answer the
telephone.*

LAIS Hello.

MC'S VOICE   Good evening, I'm the emcee of the TV show.

LAIS   Oh yes.

MC'S VOICE   The program will begin in a féw minutes. Are you ready?

LAIS   Yes, I'm here.

MC'S VOICE   Now here's how we shall proceed: first we'll show a fast film resumé of your extraordinary acting career. I must reiterate that it will be very difficult to make our audience understand why you refused to come to the studio to tape the interview part of the show yourself. Uh, in case you've changed your mind about that I assure you that I can get a crew over to your home in a matter of minutes to tape your answers to the audience's questions, and . . .

LAIS   No, please don't start that again.

MC'S VOICE   Very well, we'll do it your way, but I assure you the show without your presence just won't get the same ratings.

LAIS   Well then, it might be better if we canceled it.

MC'S VOICE   No! uh no, no, I assure you, it'll work out fine. I have a tendency to exaggerate things, pay no attention to me. Well, now, as agreed, we'll phone you four or five times during the show and one member of the studio audience will ask you questions. And you will reply from the privacy of your own home.

LAIS   I don't see any other way of doing it.

MC'S VOICE   Very well. Stand by!

A roar of impatience from the cage. LAIS *runs to the rope and brings the cage all the way down.*

*Inside is a creature which resembles a man, but is
hairy like an animal, with gestures like an ape:*
ZENON. *He is in his natural state, half naked. Now
he is groaning with pleasure. Once the cage touches
the floor,* LAIS *opens the door.* ZENON *laughs and
shows his teeth; he comes out of his cage, happy.*

LAIS (*very tenderly*) Easy there, little boy. Give me
your hand. Come out, come on. Give me your hand.

> ZENON *jumps all around her, happily. He makes a
> huge leap and tries to take her in his arms.*

LAIS Be careful, you'll crush me.

> *He does seem to be squeezing her too strenuously.*
> ZENON *moans with happiness and jumps from one
> column to another. From the top of one of them
> he cries:*

ZENON Me . . . see . . . me . . . see . . . me see you
. . . you . . . p . . . pre . . . pretty.

> *He expresses himself with great difficulty, stutter-
> ingly. He seems to know only a few words. It is
> clear that he has an adoration for* LAIS. *She seems
> to have a tender affection for him.*

LAIS (*very tenderly*) Now come on, get down from
there. Acting like a baby at your age.

> *He goes on jumping from column to column. Be-
> tween moments of joyful laughter, he murmurs
> almost unintelligibly:*

ZENON Very . . . very . . . pr . . . pretty . . . you . . .
very . . . very . . . pre . . . pretty.

LAIS Now calm down, come put your head in my lap,
and I'll tell you the story of the princess whose heart
was full of skyscrapers.

ZENON *jumps down from a column and falls upon*
LAIS *as he tries to take her into his arms; instead
he knocks her to the floor and hurts her.*

LAIS (*angry*) Look what you've done! You struck
me in the breast. I could get cancer. You brute! I
can't let you out for two minutes. You break everything and hurt me. I should keep you locked up all
day long!

ZENON *is contrite, he knows he's done something
wrong, and he scratches the floor, head lowered.*

ZENON Me . . . bad. (*He picks something up from
the floor.*) Take . . . now . . . me . . . me . . . good
. . . gift . . . gift . . . (*He offers* LAIS *something
he holds between his huge fingers.*)

LAIS (*disgusted*) A fly? Is that your gift?

ZENON Fly . . . pr . . . pretty . . . (*Seeing that she
won't accept it,* ZENON *examines the fly carefully and
eats it with satisfaction.*)

LAIS Don't eat that!

ZENON (*laughs*) . . . Already . . . ate . . .

LAIS The things you do!

The telephone rings.

(*To* ZENON) And now you be quiet, be good, don't
make any noise. Do you hear?

ZENON (*laughs*)   Yes.

LAIS   I'm not joking. While I'm on the phone, I don't want to hear a peep out of you.

ZENON (*laughs like a child*)   Yes.

LAIS (*picks up the telephone*)   Hello . . .

MC's VOICE   This is WITI-TV calling.

LAIS   Good evening.

MC's VOICE (*very sophisticated*)   Lais, the greatest actress of the century and the most secretive, will reply to questions from our audience. Are you ready, Lais?

LAIS   Yes.

MC's VOICE   Thank you. A lovely young lady with charming pigtails will start with the first question.

VOICE OF GIRL FROM AUDIENCE   I'd like to ask you, if you don't mind, how you live? Is it true, as they say, that you live alone in like a huge castle away from everybody, except for when you act?

LAIS   I'm not actually alone . . .

GIRL   Who do you live with?

Long silence.

LAIS   Uh, well . . . (*Pause.*) With my memories, my ghosts too. I speak to them and they live with me as though they were flesh-and-blood people.

MC's VOICE   Thank you very much, Lais, for your frank answer to our first question. We shall be returning to you later.

LAIS   Very well.

She puts down the phone. The SHEEP *bleat in the background.*

310

My little ones, what's the matter? Haven't you had dinner yet?

> LAIS *sets the platform into motion and the sheep move onstage.*

Oh what a silly I am! You want me to feed you, don't you?

> LAIS *grabs a pitchfork and goes toward the sheep pen and their feeder. She feeds them their "dinner" with the fork and the* SHEEP *bleat with pleasure.*

How beautiful you are, my sweet ones!

> LAIS *caresses them and kisses them.* ZENON *growls furiously.*

You keep still! (*To the* SHEEP.)   That's right, you eat my darlings. You are my most precious treasures. You're my warm and moving hopes and dreams.

> *Pause. Sound of hand bells. Darkness. The platform turns, the* SHEEP *disappear. Sound of hand bells.*

The light returns, very different. Onstage, MIHARCA *and* LAIS.

MIHARCA (*playing a nun*)   You are a stubborn and willful child.

LAIS (*as a young girl*)   But Sister . . .

MIHARCA   You are all the same and you are worse than the others. You all deserve to be whipped.

LAIS   I didn't do anything.

MIHARCA   What's that in your hand?

LAIS   Nothing.

MIHARCA   Is that so? Give it here.

LAIS   No Sister, please.

MIHARCA   Open up your hand, Celestine!

LAIS   Sister, please . . .

The nun snatches the piece of paper from LAIS' *hand savagely.* LAIS *closes her eyes tight.*

MIHARCA   What does this mean? What are all these sketches? (*She reads.*) "I swear that one day I'll be free, I swear that God does not exist, I swear that my name is not Celestine but Lais, I swear . . ." You will be punished for this. Put her in the cell!

LAIS   No Sister, please, not that.

MIHARCA   Just look at the way you revolt against us. Such gratitude! You who have neither mother nor father. If it weren't for us you'd be a beggar girl on the streets!

LAIS, *in the cell. She's crying. She interrupts her crying and exclaims fiercely:*

LAIS   I'll show them . . . I swear that I'll be free, I swear that my name is not Celestine but Lais . . .

A knock is heard from the other side of the wall.

MIHARCA'S VOICE   Are you all right?

312

LAIS Yes.

MIHARCA's VOICE Listen, raise the loose board on your side of the wall and I'll be able to come visit you.

LAIS *raises the board and* MIHARCA *appears. She is one of* LAIS' *girlfriends.*

MIHARCA Poor little Lais, always being punished.

LAIS I'll show them, I'll show them.

MIHARCA Calm down. Here, have a drink (*She extends a drinking horn full of water.*)

LAIS The sisters hate me. No one loves me.

MIHARCA Don't say silly things. One day we'll get out of here and we'll be happy. And I love you.

LAIS When I get out of here I'll be freer than free. I'll have everything: transparent eggs full of harps and tricycles, earthworms and zebras, and I'll go out walking with them in French gardens, with a bouquet of pansies for my parasol and I'll have, I'll . . . (*Furious.*) I'll have an enormous caldron of boiling shit where I'll throw all those people who've made me suffer up to now . . .

MIHARCA I'll give you a gift of a pencil to draw all your plans with and its eraser will wipe away all your nightmares.

Pause.

Have you tried any new experiments?

LAIS Yes, look! (*Very ceremoniously.*) Look at my hand. (*In her closed hand a small intense light shines.*)

MIHARCA What's that?

313

LAIS   I don't know. But keep looking because it'll soon disappear.

MIHARCA   What a bright light! . . . Maybe it's God hiding in your hand in order to love you better.

LAIS   God . . . then you think that God doesn't hate me, that He hasn't forgotten me? (*Dreamily.*) You think that God is watching me and protecting me as though I were a lost sheep in a forest of wolves?

At that moment the light disappears for good.

He's gone.

MIHARCA   You're wonderful. I really do love you.

They embrace each other lovingly.

LAIS   I love you too.

MIHARCA *raises her skirt abruptly and shows her buttocks.*

MIHARCA   If you love me so much, kiss my ass.

LAIS   Me?

She hesitates. The telephone rings. Darkness.

The action resumes in the "habitual" décor. The lights become "normal" again. The phone rings. LAIS, *adult, picks up the telephone.*

MC'S VOICE   Dear Lais, whom we all admire, one of the ladies in our audience would like to ask a question. Are you ready?

314

LAIS Yes.

VOICE OF LADY Rumor has it that you once committed a crime. In fact I heard that it was horrible and that you . . .

MC'S VOICE I have to interrupt you, Madame, and ask you not to ask questions based on malicious gossip which certain unscrupulous papers and magazines will publish merely for their sensation value.

VOICE OF LADY Oh, I'm so sorry. May I ask another question?

MC'S VOICE Go ahead.

VOICE OF LADY They say that you were an orphan, is that true?

LAIS Yes, it's true.

VOICE OF LADY I can imagine how much you suffered.

LAIS I'm sorry to disappoint you, but actually my parents became a marvelous dream. I have always felt sad and sorry for all those people who have had to endure the dull reality of their real parents, most of whom are banal and boring. But I was free to imagine mine as being strange and fascinating; I could be the bastard daughter of Einstein, or the child of Neptune and a Roman slave, a creature come alive from the imaginings of a mad genius of a poet.

MC'S VOICE Thank you very much, Lais, for your answer . . . (*Slightly affected tone.*) which was so . . . poetic. We'll be right back.

LAIS *puts down the telephone.*

ZENON Me . . . me . . . be . . . your pa . . . papa . . . and . . . your mama . . . (ZENON *takes her into his huge arms and rocks her like a baby. With a flashlight which he finds next to him he tries to give*

315

her a baby bottle.) Bo . . . bottle . . . for . . . my
. . . ba . . . baby girl . . .

LAIS (*breaking free*)   You're so stupid!

ZENON   Spank . . . for little girl . . . ba . . . bad
little . . . girl.

> *They chase each other between the columns. Darkness.*

Lights up, different. The nun reappears.

MIHARCA (*as nun*)   Don't think that we dislike you,
my child. God has taught us that we must love each
other and even the most depraved of creatures. One
day you will leave here since it seems that God has
not decided to call you into His service.

> LAIS, *as young girl, listens.*

We will place you in a fine home and you will be a
perfect house servant, since we have taught you how
to do everything. Now you must not forget the
prayers which every object in the home has inspired. Repeat with me.

> *They pray together.*

MIHARCA   The refrigerator.

MIHARCA *and* LAIS (*together*)   Blessed art thou for
my brother, the refrigerator, who is responsible for
conserving the fragile life of my sisters, the vita-
mins. Oh, if only I were more careful about conserving life, less impressionable to the ideas of cor-

ruption, conservative enough to cherish traditions.

MIHARCA   The thermostat.

MIHARCA *and* LAIS (*together*)   Blessed art thou for my brother the thermostat, obedient gadget of atmosphere. He suggests a humble and discreet role to me: that I maintain the tone, without subterfuge, which is required, not more not less.

> *We continue to hear the murmur of their prayers.* LAIS *runs in the countryside, flowers in her hand; she seems very happy and she rolls around on the grass. She cries out.*

LAIS   May I be blessed a thousand and one times, may I have the most beautiful face in the world, may my body produce ten thousand tiny alligators, all white and shining to illuminate my happiness. May I be blessed a thousand and one times . . .

> *She continues to roll around and finds herself suddenly at the feet of a man* (TELOC) *who stands, legs apart, and laughs aloud. He holds a trumpet in his hands.* LAIS *tries to run away, but* TELOC *catches her.*

TELOC   Where are you going, you who run in these woods?

LAIS   Don't tell the sisters!

> TELOC *laughs.*

TELOC (*with authority*)   Sit down here at my feet. (*He laughs again.*)

LAIS   You won't tell anyone that I ran away?

317

TELOC   Don't worry, little girl . . . tell me what happened.

LAIS   The sisters beat me and I ran away.

TELOC   Do you see those fields?

LAIS   Yes.

TELOC   Do you see those mountains?

LAIS   Yes.

TELOC   Do you see those birds flying?

LAIS   Yes.

TELOC   Well, you are just as free as they are. And like them your eyes sing of your love for liberty.

LAIS   They do?

TELOC   Yes. Now clean my shoes with your skirt, they're very dirty.

LAIS *seems a little frightened, but she executes the order very attentively.*

Look at my chest!

LAIS   It looks very strange.

TELOC   My chest has hair on it and yours doesn't. (*He laughs.*)

LAIS   That's not all . . . I seem to see stairs?

TELOC   Oh, you saw them. Well on those stairs my thoughts climb from my heart to my head, also my desires descend from my brain to my belly.

LAIS   How pretty they are! (*Silence. She looks carefully at his chest.*) And those ropes . . . and those shelves with little books . . . and those pots . . .

TELOC   Be careful, they're very small.

LAIS   There's one that's very shiny with a sign on it: pear jam.

TELOC (*angrily*)   Don't touch that, my soul is in there.

LAIS   Your soul is the pear jam?

TELOC   And yours, what is it?

LAIS   Well, I don't know. But what difference does it make? The sisters tell me that since I am bad my soul will go to Hell anyway.

TELOC   Don't believe it. (*He takes a normal-sized jar of jam out of his pocket.*) Look at this jar . . . I'll make you a gift of it and as soon as you can, put your soul in there.

LAIS   How beautiful it is! How big it is! What beautiful designs on it. How strange they are!

TELOC   You will put your soul in there.

LAIS   But I don't know whether mine is pear jam or something else.

TELOC   You should know. My soul does everything I want it to.

LAIS   Is that so?

TELOC   Absolutely.

LAIS   Let's see. (*Abruptly.*) At this very moment make a red parachute with a purple fringe fall with a crystal ball holding a goldfish with wings inside it.

TELOC   At this very moment.

The chute falls. LAIS *is stunned as she realizes that the chute has fallen as she asked.*

No need to say anything. It's perfectly normal. But since you're a very sensitive little girl, I'm going to do something very special for you . . . that other people would certainly not understand.

LAIS   What's that?

TELOC   What is your favorite tune?

LAIS   I love Schubert's "Ave Maria." The sisters taught it to me. I sing in the choir.

TELOC   Go ahead and sing it then; I'll accompany you.

LAIS   On the trumpet?

TELOC   The trumpet is too common . . . I'll do much better. Only you will be able to appreciate it.

The duo which follows should be one of great exaltation. LAIS *sings the "Ave Maria" and* TELOC *accompanies her with his farting. He manages all the notes.*

LAIS   But . . .

TELOC   Yes, I'll accompany you with my farting.

LAIS   That's marvelous.

LAIS *sings the "Ave Maria" and* TELOC *accompanies her. They look at each other happily, in ecstasy. Then* TELOC *plays the "Ave Maria" at a much faster pace on the trumpet, solo. We hear the music a long time. Darkness.*

The action continues.

LAIS' VOICE (*adult*)   Where are my darlings?

Bleating of the SHEEP. *The rotating platform brings them back.*

Don't be impatient, my pretty ones, I'm coming to see you.

ZENON *becomes excited and growls.*

ZENON   Me . . . Me!

LAIS' VOICE   Be quiet, don't act like an animal.

ZENON Everything for . . . sheep . . . No . . . Nothing for me . . .

> LAIS *appears. Her head is covered with electric wires.* ZENON *goes to see her.*

LAIS Leave me alone. I'm giving myself an encephalogram.

> *We see that the wires do in fact lead to a machine.*

Help me . . . (*To the* SHEEP *as she caresses them.*) Poor little things, my darlings. Tomorrow I'll give you sardines for breakfast, you love them so. Now go to sleep for a while. (*She puffs up their pillows. She makes them disappear.*) God, I'm going mad . . . giving pillows and sardines to sheep . . . ah, why not?

> ZENON *is furious to see* LAIS *giving so much attention to the* SHEEP; *he grabs a pillow and rips it to pieces and tries to get others.*

What are you doing? Calm down.

> ZENON *is wild.*

ZENON Everything . . . for sheep. (*He goes on tearing apart the pillows, feathers fly everywhere.*)
LAIS Calm down or I'll lock you up in your cage.

> *His destructive rage continues.*

All right . . . it's the cage!

LAIS *threatens him with a stick.* ZENON *crouches and throws himself at her feet . . . he tries to lick them.*

I've told you not to lick my feet.

ZENON, *at her feet, seeks forgiveness.*

Well then, be good and help me. I want to know what I'm like. When I give you a sign, tell me what's showing on the encephalogram.

ZENON *goes to the machine.*

LAIS   Good. (*She gets into a chaise longue and closes her eyes.*) All right, I'm ready . . . now let's see, I'm going to think of . . . Miharca.

Long silence, she seems lost in meditation. All at once she becomes agitated, bad-tempered. ZENON *is intrigued, runs back and forth, excitedly.*

What did you see?
ZENON   Where?
LAIS   On the sheet coming out of the machine?
ZENON   Small lines . . . sma . . . small lines.
LAIS   What kind of lines, straight ones or crooked?
ZENON   Not crooked . . . str . . . straight . . . pretty . . . lines.

He jumps for joy. She goes over herself to read the sheets.

LAIS   It looks as though . . . I . . . I'm going to

think of Teloc now. (*Long silence. She meditates, seems joyous, in ecstasy, smiles.*) Teloc!

ZENON *peering at machine with attention.*

LAIS   What's happening?

ZENON   Sma . . . small lines . . . small . . .

LAIS (*tears off the electrical wire furiously*)   What the devil use is this damn machine now that I think of it? . . . I am neither going to give birth nor become Prime Minister that I know of. What difference does it make? Am I going mad or what? Tomorrow I'll hook up the sheep. (*She sobs all of a sudden.*) Lord, my God . . . I am alone on this earth . . . I'd give up everything, I'd stop acting, I'd retire. But please look my way, I, the most humble of creatures, the saddest and loneliest. I'm here doing the best I can with this life which depresses and horrifies me and for which I am not prepared. God, make me like the others so that I may find peace and resign myself to my fate. Lord, don't forget me, your most unworthy servant. Now I realize very clearly that nothing I do makes any sense, that my life is a total failure, that nothing is worth the effort, and that I have known no love for anyone. (*She cries.*) I'll put a string of thorns around my thigh, I'll wear a hair shirt and I'll do penance. And if you ask me to I'll take a teaspoon and scoop out my eye in order to offer it to you. (*She mimes this scene in so realistic a manner as to be horrible. All at once, hysterical.*) Enough! Stop! Idiot! Stupid Lais! Dumb bitch! Take out your eye! Are you crazy or what? You are a famous actress. The *best!* And God let you get born thoughtlessly, with the help of two pairs of

323

asses run through with a dart. (*To* ZENON.) Come! I'll start my life over with you, we'll get married, the two of us.

ZENON *runs to her joyously.*

We'll get married and I'll live a normal life. We'll give dinner parties, we'll go to the races, I'll have lovers, we'll buy a TV set and a country house, we'll practice yoga and acupuncture . . . Yes, I'll open wide my door and the whole world will see how I live. My secret life is over: I have nothing more to hide. (*She screams.*) I'm so happy . . . bring the costumes, we'll get married at once.

ZENON *goes to get costumes.*

The sheep will be our witnesses. They'll sign with a lick from their tongues.

ZENON *returns, thrown together in what looks like a bride's gown. Upon seeing him,* LAIS *laughs, awkward, uncomfortable.*

Are you going to be the bride?
ZENON (*happily*) Yes, yes, me . . . bri . . . bride . . . you . . . husba . . . band.

LAIS *steps into tuxedo pants which she wears over her gown and puts on a top hat. In the background we hear the* SHEEP *bleating and the wedding march. In a grotesque and yet touching manner, they walk arm in arm toward one of the columns.* ZENON *looks exactly like a gorilla covered with a*

324

*bridal veil. This scene should be played grandi-
osely, full of music and sounds.*

LAIS (*playing priest*)   Zenon, do you take this man
Lais as your husband, to honor and feed, to give him
your groin of flames and honey, til death do you
part?

ZENON *grunts "uh huh" happily.*

Say "yes, I swear."

The phone rings. LAIS *goes toward the phone as
she takes off her tuxedo.*

MC's VOICE   Are you ready, Lais?
LAIS   Go ahead.
MC's VOICE (*to a woman in the audience*)   You may
ask your question.
WOMAN's VOICE   First of all, I would like to tell you
that your performance in *Fando and Lis* was wonderful.
LAIS   Thank you.
WOMAN's VOICE   Although I must say I didn't like the
play at all . . . I thought it didn't make much sense,
it was cold, and much too close to *Romeo and Juliet,*
which inspired it.
MC's VOICE   Please, Madáme, we are not here to do
theater criticism.
WOMAN's VOICE   But in that play you were a woman
in love, and very convincingly. Have you ever been
in love?
LAIS   There have been . . . men.
WOMAN's VOICE   I've heard that during your adoles-

325

cence, while you were still with the sisters . . . a man uh . . . and uh that he disappeared forever afterward.

LAIS   He . . . he was . . . an exceptional person, blessed with many magic powers I never understood . . . I'll make the usual statement: everything I know, even in the theater, is thanks to him.

MC's VOICE   Thank you very much for your reply, which I am sure has satisfied the lady.

WOMAN's VOICE   I'd like to know . . .

They are cut off. LAIS *remains pensive a few moments, then exits.*

The lights change.

LAIS (*offstage, as young girl*)   Miharca! Miharca!

Silence.

Miharca! Miharca!

MIHARCA *as young girl appears, then* LAIS.

LAIS   We've got to get out of here.

MIHARCA   What for? The sisters love us, we're together, we're happy.

LAIS   Let's do something; travel around the world, be free . . . let's do it now!

MIHARCA   What's the matter with you?

LAIS   Come with me. You're the only one who really understands me . . . here . . .

MIHARCA   What do you mean *here?*

LAIS Well . . . uh . . . here.

MIHARCA You know someone on the outside?

LAIS You won't tell?

MIHARCA No, promise.

LAIS I met a man, a beautiful person . . . with stairs on his chest and his soul in a jar of jam . . .

MIHARCA You're crazy.

LAIS Come with me, you'll see.

They run together in and out of the archways between the columns, giggling and squealing like two mischievous little girls.

LAIS Teloc! Teloc!

No one appears.

Teloc! Teloc!

Still no one.

MIHARCA You see! You made it up, there's no one.

LAIS No, there is . . . *Teloc!*

MIHARCA You made me sneak out of school, take a chance on getting punished, for nothing.

LAIS Well then, let's run away for good, now.

MIHARCA No, we can't.

LAIS Let's do it, let's escape.

MIHARCA Don't leave me.

LAIS (*change of mood, euphoria subsiding*) Then Teloc isn't real . . . he doesn't exist . . . oh, I feel sick. I'm afraid . . . do you think I'm going to die?

MIHARCA Don't be silly!

LAIS But I feel like I'm going to die . . . oh, I don't

want to die, even if I have to go on being a rotten apple all my life, I don't want to die.

MIHARCA You won't, don't worry. We'll always be together. We'll play all our games and have fun. (MIHARCA *mimes playing a flute for* LAIS.)

LAIS I don't want to play games. I want to crawl into a cage with a flower pot and you'll come to water us both every day.

MIHARCA Look! The lions!

MIHARCA mimes snapping a whip, lions roaring, but LAIS won't play.

LAIS Miharca, do you think we're like Adam and Eve in Paradise or Botticelli's virgins? I want to spend my life with a dove sitting on top of my head and a gossamer scarf flowing around my neck.

MIHARCA (*playing*) I'm going to give you an injection.

LAIS No!

MIHARCA Lift your skirt and take down your pants. I'm going to vaccinate you against the evil eye.

LAIS No, I don't want to.

MIHARCA You see how you treat me! I do everything for you and you don't even care. I hate you. Goodby! (*She runs away*.)

LAIS Miharca! Miharca!

LAIS cries alone. Enter TELOC, clothed half as a football player, half as a lumberjack.

TELOC Little girl with little faith.

LAIS (*delighted*) Oh you *were* here. I was sure you were.

328

LAIS *rushes to* TELOC *and tries to clean his shoes with her skirt.*

TELOC   Don't touch me!

LAIS (*intimidated*)   I wanted my friend Miharca to meet you. We sneaked out of school to see you.

TELOC   Tell me what you would like most to do now?

LAIS   Oh I'm so happy . . . tie me to a tree and make me afraid.

TELOC   How about if we played football?

They jump around and play. They grapple for the ball on the ground. TELOC *jumps* LAIS *and pins her down.*

LAIS   Uhhh you're so heavy . . . I can't breathe.

TELOC   Poor little thing . . .

LAIS   You're hurting me with your helmet.

TELOC   Ah, my helmet is magical.

LAIS (*fascinated*)   How?

TELOC   With *this* I can travel into the past and into the future.

LAIS   Oh, I want to travel.

TELOC   Where would you like to go?

LAIS   Into the future *and* the past too. I want to see Cleopatra, Christ with Mary Magdalene. I want to see Breughel, I want to see the astronauts a thousand years from now, I want to see Buddha, Bosch . . .

TELOC   Ha, ha, ha, you'll see them all. But first, tell me how many doves there are in one wish?

LAIS (*thinks*)   Seven and eleven. But in my wish right now there's only room for you.

329

TELOC   Well, since you're good at guessing, you might go very far. You'll be an actress.

LAIS (*wonderment*)   An actress?

TELOC   Wouldn't you like that?

LAIS (*quickly*)   Oh yes, I'd love to be an actress only I have a bad memory . . . and I'd be ashamed to show my legs . . .

TELOC   You'd do as you liked about that.

LAIS (*relieved*)   Oh really?

TELOC   Would you be so ashamed to show your legs?

LAIS   Yes, very. The sisters told me that God sees all the bad things we do and that we should never take all our clothes off, not even to go to bed. When we take a bath, we wear a long nightshirt slit up the side so we can soap ourselves without being . . . naked.

TELOC   Show me your legs.

LAIS   My legs?

TELOC   Right up to the thighs.

LAIS (*shocked*)   The thighs . . . but it's a sin.

TELOC   Forget it!

LAIS   No, I'll do it . . . for you. (*Raising her skirt slightly.*) Is that enough?

TELOC   I can't even see your knees.

LAIS   But if I raise it higher . . .

TELOC (*angry*)   Never mind.

LAIS   Don't be angry.

TELOC   I'm not angry.

LAIS   You looked as if you were.

TELOC   All I know is that if you really trusted me . . .

LAIS   I do . . . look. (*She raises her skirt quickly and uncovers her thighs for a moment.*)

TELOC   But I didn't see anything.

LAIS   I have to show them longer?

TELOC   Of course. I want to *see* your thighs.

LAIS   Oh, that's really bad.

TELOC   You must close your eyes and show me your thighs until I say "enough."

LAIS   . . . All right, but afterward I'll have to go to Confession. I'll say it was windy and . . . no, I mustn't lie . . . oh, here goes.

Resigned and resolved like a person taking a plunge, she shows her thighs for a good while. TELOC *comes close to her, and with a colored crayon writes the word "hope" on her thighs. "Ho" on one side and "pe" on the other.*

TELOC   Enough. Open your eyes and let down your skirt.

LAIS   What did you do?

TELOC   I wrote on you.

LAIS   Oh, write some more, that felt nice.

TELOC   Quiet! We're going to go on a trip through time.

LAIS   You said I would be an actress.

TELOC   You will be an actress; the reincarnation of God on earth. You will be the Messiah; you will assume all the worries and wonders of the whole world. You will be beaten, tortured, loved . . . and then you'll remove your mask, just like in real life.

LAIS   Oh please, the tortures right away.

TELOC   What kind do you like?

LAIS   I don't know.

TELOC   You'd better decide.

LAIS   You know, there are times when I become very devout and I really believe in God and I speak to him and I put on a hair shirt in the morning, and I

331

go from the dormitory to the church with my hair shirt and a string of thorns around my thigh, and I feel great pain and during Mass I understand that I am doing it for God and God smiles at me, and I can feel him right there in my thigh; I feel that He thanks me and that He and I will be friends forever. And when Mass is over, I rush back to the dormitory for the most painful, the most beautiful moment of all, when I take off my hair shirt and undo the string of thorns. My thigh is all swollen and when I pull out the tiny thorns which stick in my flesh, the blood spurts out and I feel great pain and pleasure at the same time and I know that God is all around me and I feel him taking me into his arms and once I'm there, warm and safe, I can cry without being afraid of Hell or Purgatory or any of the thousands of punishments I'll receive for my countless sins and because I ran away from school and talked back to the sisters and because I hate them even though they took me in when my parents didn't want me and had left me an orphan . . .

TELOC   Oh stop that drivel, you stupid girl.

LAIS (*hurt*)   You're making fun of me.

TELOC   I don't want you leafing through your dreary family album in my presence.

LAIS   Then tell me, what kind of an actress shall I be?

TELOC   Didn't you want to go on a trip?

LAIS   Oh yes, I still do.

TELOC   Well then, put on the helmet.

LAIS   Tell me, will I sing, will I dance?

TELOC   No, you'll be an actress.

LAIS   Will you let me do a dance just for you?

TELOC   Do you know how to dance?

LAIS   I dance sometimes when I'm by myself, and

332

sometimes I sing too. I make believe I'm in a palace ballroom . . . like this. (LAIS *goes through a frantic dance, very different from any kind of real dancing. She does a sort of hysterical, convulsive movement. At first she moves about a great deal; then she slows down. With deliberate innocence she rubs her belly with her hands, throws herself back like a mad creature. All of this seems insane and hysterical. She ends up, rear up, head down.*)

TELOC   So that's your dance?

LAIS   Yes, now come dance with me.

TELOC   No, singing the other day was enough. I'm no good at acrobatics.

LAIS   Oh, our song was so beautiful. Do you know I haven't told anyone about it, not even Miharca?

TELOC   Very good. For that you get a kiss on the forehead. (*He kisses her forehead.*)

LAIS   More!

TELOC   What a little glutton you are.

LAIS   Look, I'm putting on the helmet. (*She does.*)

TELOC   And you will start your trip in time.

LAIS   Oh, oh, oh, my head's spinning. Oh!

A kind of cone of transparent light falls on LAIS. *Vague images begin to become distinguishable. They flash on a sort of screen which has just fallen between two columns.*

TELOC's VOICE   Press the buttons on the helmet and you'll be able to go into the future and the past.

LAIS *presses the buttons. Like a magic lantern, a series of projections flash on and off as* LAIS *presses on. The stage is bathed in a strange at-*

333

mosphere created by real fireworks. Strange music over a background of boots, explosions, bombs, etc. Suddenly the following images appear on the screen: Superman running with girlfriend in arms. Goya's dog. A battleground from World War II, devastation. A giant Alice in Wonderland. The professor and the nightclub singer, Blue Angel. Hundred Years War, devastation. Two lovers of Chagall. An advertising poster. The painting "The Birth of Arrabal." The painting "The Garden of Delights" by Bosch. The same images come on again at a dizzying speed until LAIS *rips off the helmet. Everything returns to normal.*

LAIS I don't know how to use it. Everything went too fast.

TELOC With these buttons you go forward or backward.

LAIS I'm so afraid. It's awful . . . war is awful.

TELOC You have to learn to use it. The red button goes into the past and the little needle shows you the place and the century. If you want the future, it's the black button. You were making the needle jump in all directions.

LAIS I didn't know . . . but I don't want to see the past, I'm too afraid.

TELOC Why?

LAIS There are so many dead, so many wars, so much suffering.

TELOC Weren't you asking for torture a while ago?

LAIS But that was different. If you torture me, it's because you love me. When you're close to me I can feel how alive you are, and . . .

334

TELOC   All right, let's throw the helmet away then.

LAIS   No! Please, I'd like to see more. I'd like to watch some of the ceremonies of my life . . . like my first Communion . . . and those to come . . . my wedding . . . my death.

Phone rings. Darkness.

The phone rings. The action resumes. The lights become "normal." The stage is empty: in a corner, the phone rings. ZENON *enters, he tries to pick up the receiver. He grabs the phone books and tears out pages as he laughs. The* SHEEP *bleat: they have just reappeared. The phone keeps ringing insistently and* ZENON, *more and more frenetic, continues to rip pages out of the phone books. Bleating of* SHEEP.

LAIS' VOICE (*adult*)   Hush there, my poor little things, this evening I shall read you the story of *Alice*. But right now be quiet; they're phoning me again.

The SHEEP *bleat.* LAIS *enters.*

LAIS   Look what you've done, you beast. (*She seems very nervous; she would like to pick up the ringing phone, but at the same time wants to scold* ZENON, *tie him up, and keep him quiet.*) I can't leave you out two minutes before you start doing something stupid, you break everything, you tear my clothes, rip up my shoes, and now my phone books. (*She is on the verge of tears.*) God, what have I done to deserve such punishment, why must I be deprived of any happiness or peace? And now you be quiet!

I'm going to tie you up so you'll quiet down. And if you go on jumping around I'll put you in your cage and you'll stay there all night long.

ZENON *drops his head; he seems to be very sorry.*

ZENON Me . . . bad . . . me . . . love you. (*He tries to kiss her, to put his arms around her.*)

LAIS Stop that and be still. You can hear the phone, can't you? Leave me alone, I'll send you to a zoo, to the pound, to an institution. I don't see why I have to go on sacrificing my life for you.

She ties him to a column. ZENON *tries to kiss her.*

And now keep still and be quiet!

The phone has gone on ringing. She finally picks it up.

MC's VOICE Here we are back again with you, Lais, I hope we're not disturbing you.

LAIS No, no, not at all.

MC's VOICE Another lady from our audience would like to ask a question.

LAIS Go right ahead.

LADY's VOICE I think you are the most beautiful woman I have ever seen.

LAIS Don't say things like that. There are many beautiful women and I . . .

LADY's VOICE Well, then how does it affect you to know that you are one of the most beautiful?

LAIS I never found myself beautiful, on the contrary, when I was little I thought myself ugly. The, uh, place where I spent my youth, the people who raised me, told me I wasn't pretty. And for many years I really believed I was one of the most repugnant beings on earth. I was sure that I would never be able to have . . . a lover . . . and that if one day I wanted to become a woman, I would only be able to do it with some sort of monster or an exceptionally ugly man whom I would pay for his services. For a long time . . . (*She hesitates.*)

At that very instant, we hear ZENON *say very distinctly as he takes advantage of the silence and with unusually good elocution:*

ZENON   I want to . . . bugger you.

LAIS *cups the receiver with her hand and angrily orders* ZENON *to shut up, and in a stage whisper says:*

LAIS   You'll pay for that!

MC's VOICE   Is anything wrong, are you not feeling well . . . ?

LAIS   No, it's all right . . . I was saying . . . uh.

MC's VOICE   Oh, your reply was more than adequate. Isn't that right?

LADY's VOICE   Yes, thank you so much and I want you to know I'll always admire you.

LAIS *puts down the phone. She storms over to* ZENON, *near tears.*

LAIS   Do you realize what you've done? What are they going to think of me? Oh my God, what humiliation!

337

What torture! But why me, why, God, why! (*She takes hold of* ZENON *and makes him get into his cage and pulls the pully till he has ascended, at stage center.*) And I'll never take you out of there, you'll stay locked up forever, I'll forget all about you. You are a monster. You're determined to destroy me.

ZENON Me . . . love . . . you.

LAIS Leave me alone with your stupid declarations. If you loved me, if you really loved me . . .

ZENON *cries like a baby with loud sniffling sobs.*

That's right, go ahead and cry, cry! I'm the one who should be sobbing. I've got a right to cry. My life is hell because of you! From now on I can only trust my sheep.

The SHEEP *bleat.* LAIS *goes to them. She disappears from the view of the audience.*

LAIS' VOICE My poor little darlings, I love only you, my sweet ones. You alone are good to me. You never say a thing. I'll always love you. I'm going to write a hundred sonnets for you and I'll read them to you before I go to sleep. Come here, I have a kiss for each of you.

We hear the kissing. Darkness.

"Different" lights up. MIHARCA (*as young girl*) *enters.*

MIHARCA Lais! Lais! Where are you hiding? What are you doing, Lais? (MIHARCA *disappears.*)

We hear a prayer being murmured. It sounds like LAIS *praying. As a light comes up on her we see her in a kneeling position. Actually what we see is an almost life-sized Frankenstein standing before her, which turns out to be a dummy. As the light concentrates on them,* LAIS *stands up. She places candles all around the Frankenstein and lights them all with great ceremony.*

LAIS (*as young girl, to Frankenstein*) And I know that you understand me and love me truly even though I am ugly . . . I know that you would never feel the disgust I would surely inspire in other men. We shall be secretly engaged. And one day, if you still haven't found me repulsive, you'll let me become your wife: to make love to you. You know that I'm very ugly and disgusting. That is I go to the toilet at least once every day and that's very disgusting I know and I'm very ashamed of it. I think that's the main reason other men don't want to have anything to do with me . . . And then, once a month . . . and sometimes I even have bad breath too, oh nobody says anything about it, not my friends or the sisters, so as not to hurt my feelings, but I'm sure I smell exactly like Mother Catherine. I don't notice it myself, of course, but that's because day and night I'm so used to my own mouth's smell. And then I have an awful body, misshapen. My bones stick out all over instead of being covered with smooth, soft flesh which I know is so attractive . . . and I don't think my nose is well shaped either. I guess when people see me they must say "What a catastrophe, what a nose, all crooked," and I feel so ashamed and I don't know where to run and hide. But I know that you understand and love me despite my monstrous appearance. Every now and then I remind myself that I must remain a worthy fiancée for my Frankenstein and so I let a week or two pass without even washing my hands. And I end up with my nails black and my face full of dirt and I take such pleasure in thinking of you and how much you'd love me that way.

MIHARCA's VOICE   Open up!

LAIS *opens after having blown out the candles and covered her Frankenstein with a sheet.*

MIHARCA   Why did you lock yourself in?

LAIS   I was just . . . uh . . .

MIHARCA   Do you know that I dreamed of you?

LAIS   You did?

MIHARCA   I dreamed that you killed me, but after I was dead I came back to see you and you gave me a piece of white bread.

LAIS   How could you dream of something like that?

MIHARCA   It was awful to see myself dead and eating your white bread. It was really awful.

LAIS   But why did I kill you?

MIHARCA   You killed me in order to win, to enter into the garden of delights . . . It was sacrificial. . . . Swear that you don't hate me.

LAIS   Me hate you?

The bells ring.

Listen, it's bedtime.

MIHARCA   Let's go then.

LAIS   No, stay.

MIHARCA   But it's forbidden.

LAIS   So what, let's pretend we're already free.

MIHARCA   Let's play a game.

LAIS   All right, which one?

MIHARCA   I'd like to play the part of chaste St. Joseph and you can be Jesus.

LAIS   That will be difficult.

MIHARCA   Lie down, I'm going to rock you. My poor little cherished son who is going to save the world through his sufferings, with those huge nails in his hands . . .

LAIS   But I shall accomplish miracles, I'll make paralytics walk and the blind see.

MIHARCA   Now that you will become a man, look what I have brought you. (MIHARCA *takes out a huge knife with a shining blade.*) Now lie down.

LAIS   That frightens me.

MIHARCA   Never mind, just lie down.

LAIS *lies down on the floor with great apprehension.* MIHARCA *kisses the tips of* LAIS' *fingers, her forehead, and her feet.*

LAIS   What are you doing?

MIHARCA   Keep still, it's a rite. (MIHARCA *proceeds as if with a ceremony; she raises the knife high.*) Now you must scream very loud.

LAIS *screams without conviction.*

Louder!

LAIS *screams with all her might as* MIHARCA *pretends to stab her in the lower abdomen.*

341

That's good, look at that. (MIHARCA *proudly shows off a tiny bit of something which shines.*)

LAIS   What did you do?

MIHARCA   I circumcised you.

Cannon shots ring out. Then violin music. Darkness.

The scene changes to a prison. The shadows of bars are projected across the stage. We hear LAIS *crying. She is alone on the stage.*

LAIS (*murmuring*)   I don't want to live in a prison. I want to get out of here. What have I done? Why must I stay here day and night with that electric-light bulb staring at me constantly? Poor Lais, poor miserable Lais. (*She screams.*) I want to be free. (*After a moment.*) I'm locked in a prison in secret, nobody knows or cares, I've been forgotten, I have only one visit a day from the guards who bring me water, bread, and soup. (*After a moment, with joy.*) What's that? (*She picks something up off the floor with great excitement.*) A bug. A ladybug! You'll be my friend? Oh, I'm so happy. Look how big my cell is for you. But it's all yours. You're all dusty. No matter, when they bring my soup I'll pick out a piece of lard and when its dry I'll rub you with it and you'll get all shiny. You will be the most beautiful ladybug in the world. You can be proud of that. You see I can only take three steps in one direction and three in the other. But you can do long-distance running if you like. And I could even tie a string around one of your legs and you could slip under

342

the door and explore the surroundings . . . that way you can let me know what's happening in the corridors. And when the guard comes around at night and tosses a pail of water into my cell to keep me from sleeping, you and I will climb up on the toilet seat and stay there, huddled together, until the water evaporates. We'll have good times together, you'll see. And when I cry, don't worry, it won't be because of you, it'll be because I'm so unhappy. And when I start screaming and I look like I'm getting desperate, will you just whisper something in my ear to cheer me up? Because those are the times I want to kill myself by drinking my urine or banging my head against the bars until it bursts.

Cannon shots and violin strains.

Lights change.

LAIS (*young girl*) Teloc! Teloc!

TELOC Calm down. Calm down. I'm here waiting for you.

LAIS Make me an actress! Please make me an actress! I want to be the most beautiful woman in the world. I want to be a success, not stay the little orphan the sisters punish and whose heart is turning black and blue.

TELOC And why an actress?

LAIS Because . . . I don't know why . . . because I want to live a thousand lives I've never had, to be tall, beautiful, feminine or small, homely, and adorable, or to be able to climb a trapeze. And to know that even though I'm just me I can become all the

343

others and that gives me the power to make all the heroines of the world more human and transform myself into an ever-changing kaleidoscope.

TELOC   Did you know that objects can speak! (*Pause.*) world.

LAIS   Well then, I want to see the evening of my greatest triumph. Make me see it. Put the helmet on my head and make me see it!

TELOC   Did you know that objects can speak! (*Time.*) Why know the future? Let surprise overcome you with its stones and storms.

LAIS   No, no. Let me wear the helmet, I want to see the evening of my consecration.

TELOC   You can ask the different objects and they will answer you, it's simpler.

LAIS   No, the helmet please.

TELOC   All right . . . Look there. . . . See that boat in the marshes?

LAIS   Yes, yes, I see it.

TELOC   Did you see its unmanned oars and its lonely appearance?

LAIS   Yes, yes. But give me the helmet.

TELOC   The boat carries death, you can speak to it and ask it anything you'd like.

LAIS   I don't want to die, I want to be free and live forever and ever.

TELOC   And the river? And the street? Don't you want to speak to them?

LAIS   Give me the helmet.

TELOC *obeys. Darkness. Lights up with special effect.*

Atmosphere is particularly ominous. Bouquets drop from above stage. They are upside down and

344

*the ribbons surrounding them drift in the air. They
bear* LAIS' *name. Everything has a gloomy air. The
feeling is lugubrious.*

VOICE   Lais, believe me, I'm an experienced producer,
I know what I'm talking about. During all my years
in the business I've never seen such a smashing success. You were simply divine. No one can come close
to you, you'll have the critics at your feet. Every
celebrity who came to see you will be praising you
to the skies. I heard the best of them ecstatic about
you, there was just one word on their tongues:
"genius." You're on the top, my girl, the top.

LAIS' VOICE   Thank you, thank you.

VOICE   Don't thank me. It is I who thank you in the
name of acting. Good night and sweet dreams.

The door slams. LAIS *enters and walks back and
forth stage center, looking happy and excited.
Then she sees the flowers and is frightened. Suddenly she stops in front of the mirror and examines herself suspiciously. She makes horrible
grimaces and contorts her face. Finally she slaps
herself soundly.*

LAIS   Who do you think you're kidding, you cheap
bitch. You really fooled them all, didn't you, you
phony. (*Change of tone.*) As of tomorrow I will
give up the theater and I'll go far away. I'll go hunting in the virgin forest and I'll live alone with the
beasts. (*She dons a safari hat and wraps a boa around
her neck. She grabs a hunting rifle and appraises the
outfit in her mirror. She assumes a very military
pose.*) That's it, I'll be an explorer. I'll talk to the ani-

mals. I'll flatten my breasts, I'll wear a loincloth and I'll swing from vine to vine screaming: ah ha, ah ha, I'm Tarzan! (*She mimes this scene.*) I'll discover existentialism . . . (*Suddenly frightened she turns quickly and discovers something among some flowers: a catafalque on which lies the bust of a woman and a bit further, the legs [upside down] in a vertical position.*) Miharca, Miharca. . . . Are you dead? And your eyes? Who did that? Who could have murdered you so viciously? Miharca. It's me, Lais. . . . It's not possible. (LAIS *runs aimlessly around the room.*)

Cannon shots. Violin music. Darkness. Projections appear on screen. Breughel painting. Bosch painting. Goya painting. Prison bars. Pictures of destroyed cities. Men imprisoned. Starving children. Planes bombing. Breughel painting. Bosch painting. Goya painting. Prison bars.

Darkness. Cannon shots, Violin music. Silence. LAIS *tries to tear off the mask. She sobs.*

TELOC　What's happening?

LAIS (*young girl*)　It's not true.

TELOC　What did you see?

LAIS　Death. . . . It was a nightmare.

TELOC　My poor little Lais.

LAIS　Do you love me?

TELOC　I hate you with all my might.

LAIS　How it thrills me to hear you say it that way. I could never love anyone else but you.

TELOC　Go away!

LAIS　You're chasing me away . . . away from you?

TELOC You've got to get used to living without me.

LAIS I prefer to die.

TELOC Run toward your triumph. Go on, get out!

LAIS Put me in the pocket of your trousers, let me sit there with your change and when you buy your evening paper, you can pay for it with me.

Darkness. The action follows its "course." Lighting "normal." ZENON, *locked in his cage, suspended above stage, is restless with impatience.*

ZENON Lais . . . let . . . me . . ou . . . out.

> LAIS *takes off her shoes with great care.*

Loo . . . look at mm . . . me!

> *Without looking at him,* LAIS *sings her song softly.*

LAIS! (ZENON *roars.*)

> LAIS *is wearing a vaporous gown of tulle and over it she wears a waist-pincher.* LAIS *joins her hands together and sings her song with great feeling; she seems to be floating on air.*

ZENON Come . . . let . . . me . . . out!

LAIS You were bad.

ZENON Me . . . me . . . not bad . . . me . . . love you.

> LAIS *goes on singing as though she hadn't noticed him.*

Let . . . me . . . down!

LAIS Now I love only the sheep, I'm singing for them, I'm leaving them all my money in my will and nothing to you, and they'll get all the royalties from my records, my photos . . .

ZENON Sheep . . . mean . . . me . . . hate.

LAIS The sheep are very sweet, they're always quiet. Soon they will be able to speak as you do, on some I'll put wings so that they can fly around the house and on the others I'll put fins so that they can become sheep-sharks and be the envy of all.

ZENON Me . . . better.

LAIS You . . . terrible.

ZENON You . . . hate me . . . love . . . only sheep.

LAIS And I'll buy them each a chateau so they can contemplate the countryside from their terraces. And those who get sick I'll send to the hospital in a city with canals so that they can get well while bathing with the storks. And for you, nothing! And when I sing, it's for them.

ZENON Sing for . . . me.

LAIS No, just for them.

ZENON They . . . not listening.

LAIS Yes they are . . . (*She sings for the sheep.*) And I'll buy each of them sunglasses and a tanned boyfriend, at night they'll sleep in a bed and their little heads will rest on pillows and they'll have sweet dreams!

ZENON Sheep . . . bad . . . sheep . . . bitches!

LAIS I won't allow you to insult them. Poor little things. (LAIS *sings for sheep.*)

ZENON Sheep . . . not listening.

LAIS Yes, they are.

ZENON   Let me . . . squeeze . . . your nose.

LAIS   All you ever want to do is hurt me.

ZENON   A little bit . . . squeeze . . . nose . . . little squeeze . . . no blood.

LAIS   There, you see. I did well to lock you up.

ZENON *throws down a rope from his cage.*

What is that?

ZENON   You tie . . . rope to your foot . . . me . . . can touch you . . . when . . . rope touch . . . you.

LAIS   You're bad!

ZENON   Say . . . you love . . . me . . . mm . . . more than . . . sh . . . sheep.

LAIS   No!

ZENON   Say you . . . love me . . . more than . . . friend . . . you killed . . .

LAIS   Who told you that? (*Beside herself.*) I hate you with all my heart. I'll never let you out of that cage. (LAIS *raises the cage even higher.*) I thought that with you at least I'd have peace and you . . . you too! What's gotten into you? You're a monster. Tell me, have you ever gone out? Have the neighbors talked to you?

ZENON (*speaking very clearly*)   I killed . . . sheep.

LAIS   You killed my sheep? My sweet darlings, my angels, where are you? It's me, it's all right. (*She runs around stage looking for them, calling. She leaves the stage.*)

LAIS' VOICE   My sheep, my darlings.

Long silence. We hear a moan, a sound of pain. Then a scream.

349

You killed all nine of them! You cut their throats.
Oh my helpless creatures.

We hear nothing. LAIS *returns to the stage holding
one of the dead* SHEEP. *She kneels down with the
sheep stage center directly under* ZENON's *cage.
She seems to be silently sobbing, her face next to
the sheep's body. We hear her intermittent sobbing
and moaning.*

ZENON   Now . . . everything . . . for me.

   LAIS *continues to cry.*

Cry for . . . me . . .

   LAIS *moans. She is still in the same position next
   to the* SHEEP. *Suddenly something liquid falls from
   the cage.*

LAIS   What are you throwing down?
ZENON   Good . . . that good . . . pay attention . . .
to me . . . speak to . . . me!

   She remains next to the SHEEP. *The liquid continues to fall a drop at a time.*

LAIS   What are you doing?
ZENON   To . . . get your . . . a . . . attention . . . to
me . . . I . . . sh . . . shit on . . . you.

   LAIS *looks up with hate on her face. The curtain
   closes quickly. We hear a hysterical scream.*

Act Two

As the curtain goes up, LAIS *is on stage and as in the first act, she is singing romantically.* ZENON *accompanies her with sounds, obviously happy, but we do not see him. The song goes softly on. We continue to hear* ZENON's *sounds on stage: we see only* LAIS *who is lit with a spot. When her song is finished, she jumps with joy. Then we realize that* ZENON, *in a kneeling position, was acting as a chair for* LAIS. *The stage lights up. We seen nine trays standing at different heights, each carrying a skeleton of a* SHEEP. *Pieces of fur remain hanging from the skeletons on three of them; the skin looks rotted.*

LAIS (*following* ZENON, *looking happy*)   Even though you killed my beloved sheep, I love you, Zenon.

> ZENON *runs around happily; he climbs the columns and hangs from one of them by his feet, his head down. He puts his arms out to* LAIS *and embraces her in that position. Then he claps his hands in satisfaction.*

ZENON   Egg! Egg!

> *He and* LAIS *run around the stage in loving abandon.*

LAIS   You are my earthworm of happiness, my treas-

351

ure trove of filth and buttercups, my own heart of hatchets.

ZENON I love y . . . you, love you.

They continue to cavort. This morbid love scene should become like a hallucination of frenzied joy. ZENON *carries a huge egg on stage. Its top is cut open and it is covered with drawings by Bosch.*

LAIS No one knows that you are superior to all the men on earth and that you alone can raise me to the skies with your hands like royal eagles and giant sharks.

ZENON Egg! Egg!

They run all around the stage. ZENON *brings the egg. They both play with it, turning it, clumsily, running around it. Suddenly* LAIS *stops her mad dashing; she stands still stage center, her hands joined, in an attitude of prayer.* ZENON *watches her.*

LAIS Did you know, Zenon? . . . I prayed for you, I prayed to God for you.

ZENON (*laughing*) You . . . don't believe . . . in God.

LAIS That's true, but just the same I prayed to God for you, for you to be happy, even if I have to suffer for you, to see that you have everything you need. Prayed for you to be saved at the hour of your death and for you to go to Heaven. God and paradise must exist, they have to exist for you who are so good.

352

While she makes this speech, ZENON *raises her skirt solemnly and kisses her knees.*

ZENON   Egg! Egg!

They start chasing each other again; ZENON *finally catches* LAIS *and drags her around by her hair.*

LAIS   Zenon, you're really *hurting* me.

ZENON *laughs and continues to pull* LAIS *until he has gotten her inside the egg. They are both in it and we cannot see what goes on.*

While they remain inside a kind of lovers' ritual takes place. Flowers float down around the egg. Music. A character out of Breughel crosses the stage from right to left. It is an invalid with a limp. One of his legs, bent at the knee, seems to be held tightly by a vice to which is tied a strange splint. He pulls a rowboat which is on wheels: from the boat grows a tree without leaves or flowers but on its naked branches sits a motionless black bird. A padlock is on its beak. The stage is lighted normally and remains silent for a moment. But then we hear the phone ring. It rings insistently for a long time. LAIS *comes out of the egg. She pushes it until it disappears into the wings.*

LAIS   Hello.
VOICE OF POLICEMAN   This is the police. You know a woman named Miharca?

LAIS   Yes, of course.

VOICE OF POLICEMAN   We understand you were raised in an orphanage together.

LAIS   Yes.

VOICE OF POLICEMAN   Then you haven't seen each other in a long time? '

LAIS   Yes, it's been a long time, very long, but . . .

VOICE OF POLICEMAN   But what . . . ?

Silence.

Weren't you about to say something?

LAIS   No.

VOICE OF POLICEMAN   I had the feeling you were going to say you had seen her more recently.

LAIS   Yes . . . I . . .

Silence.

I saw her last night about an hour before leaving for the theater . . .

VOICE OF POLICEMAN   Yes, allow me to congratulate you, your opening was a smash hit. We heard about it at the station. They say you are the greatest actress who ever lived.

LAIS   (*interrupting him*)   They came to see me here . . .

VOICE OF POLICEMAN   They? Who's they?

LAIS   She came with Teloc.

VOICE OF POLICEMAN   Teloc?

LAIS   A man we met when we were girls at the orphanage.

VOICE OF POLICEMAN   Didn't you live in?

354

LAIS Yes, but we used to sneak out to see him . . . you know how girls in a boarding school are.

VOICE OF POLICEMAN You never saw him again?

LAIS No, never, until last night when I heard his trumpet as I was dressing to go to the theater. His trumpet . . . he was playing it in such a strange way.

A lighting effect changes the scene.

The action "resumes" the evening before.
Suddenly we hear trumpet playing. LAIS *runs on stage and dashes about looking for the player, she is half-dressed in her stage costume, which is very baroque. She seems very excited and happy at the prospect of finding* TELOC. *From a back lamp projection the enormous shadow of* TELOC *looms across the stage. At that point* LAIS *stops dashing and we find her on a small balcony on the second floor. From that vantage point she examines the trumpeter. She begins to sing the song of the first act but now she screams out the words hysterically. Alternate projections of the Bosch "Garden of Delights" and cartoon strips of today.*

LAIS I'm here, alone like a sunflower in smoke deep in my nightmares of butterscotch and bolts.

TELOC Where do you find the heart and the pulse?

Slowly the lights return. TELOC *is holding his trumpet in his hand.* LAIS *is wearing the same stage costume.*

355

LAIS   I'm here, huddled in a cage, between the bars of the night and crinoline petticoats.

TELOC   Poor Lais. You're alone and I can't see you or help you. Everyone makes fun of you, criticizes you, and I too abandon you. You are ridiculed and we would have all preferred that you embrace your punishment without any final fanfare.

LAIS   May I cry?

TELOC   Cry, cry to the sea and the night. But don't forget that you're wearing your finery, that you're in your stage costume and that . . .

LAIS   I can't cry. I want neither the trunk nor the rubbish. From my enchained body my soul goes out to you.

TELOC   How long has it been since we've seen each other?

LAIS   So many years! Do you remember when you showed me the stairs on your chest, and remember when you made me travel in the future and the past . . . and afterward in my bed, I'd become as tiny as solitude itself and I'd walk across the thousand and one steps of your body kissing each. Let me kiss your chest.

TELOC   No, Lais. (*He takes off his jacket and hangs it on a hook.*)

LAIS *throws herself at the jacket and kisses it passionately.*

LAIS   Love me!

TELOC   No, I don't love you. You are alone and abandoned. You are no longer the helpless little girl who would run out of the orphanage; today you are the center of a show and your concessions.

LAIS   I earned it.

TELOC   Look at my hand. I send you a thousand images of confusion.

LAIS   Listen, we can leave everything behind. Come with me. We can quit all this together. We'll take a boat and drift in it together. I'll sit up front and you'll stay in the center with your sun hat. You'll work the movie projector. See how I'm rowing.

LAIS rows. TELOC puts on his hat and works a projector which is placed on a tripod.

TELOC   Don't row so hard, you'll knock me over.

LAIS   Look, the film is projected on a screen formed by the mist on the lake.

TELOC   Be careful, you chose the route where the giant octopus congregate: they could reach in with their thousands of tentacles and grab us and pull us down into the black depths.

LAIS   Now I can see the film . . . it's the story of a shepherd girl who loves insects.

TELOC   Those are not insects.

LAIS   Oh, that's right, they're robots. Look, lying next to her is a sleeping harvest reaper in his overalls, and in his dream he sees the shepherdess naked as a statue.

TELOC   But behind her looms the shadow of death!

LAIS   I love you, Teloc.

They drop the "boat," the "projector," and the "oars."

TELOC   Lais!

LAIS   Put a string around my neck and I'll be your

357

trained flea, or put a spiked collar on me and I'll be your watchdog and protect you.

TELOC   Don't touch me.

LAIS   Oh yes, just like when I was at the orphanage. I can't touch you. I can't touch you. I know that I'm not worthy of you. But if you'd like, I'll be your humble giraffe and I'll spend the day stretched out the window so that I can tell you when the clouds form a memory and months of January.

TELOC   Did you remember me?

LAIS   I've looked for you all these years.

TELOC   You were a recluse.

LAIS   That didn't matter . . .

TELOC   Did you travel too?

LAIS   No . . . but take me anywhere you like . . . even back to those times when they persecuted me.

Lighting changes. LAIS *is stretched across a standing torture block.* TELOC *puts on a hood.*

LAIS   What do you want of me? I haven't done anything. I can't remember having done anything.

TELOC *(violently)*   Try, you'll remember!

LAIS   I don't know what this is all about. I'm just a poor young woman in a strange place. All I want is to be free.

TELOC   What do you mean by that?

LAIS   I'm not a witch, nor an enchantress. I haven't done anything wrong.

TELOC   Remember what you did!

LAIS   I swear to you that I've . . .

TELOC   By whom do you swear, hypocrite? By God or by the Devil?

358

LAIS   Why do you abuse me, what have I done?

TELOC   You're saying that we abuse you?

LAIS   I didn't mean to say . . .

TELOC   Because we arrested and imprisoned you there must be a reason, it's up to you to admit it.

LAIS   I swear I don't know why, I don't!

TELOC   That makes things all the worse. What you are clearly saying, in your sneaky way, is that we have arrested you without any motive. In other words, your presence here is proof of our "injustice," which means that our tribunal is not guided by the unique desire to discover the truth.

LAIS   No, no, I didn't want to say anything like that. You don't understand, I just . . .

TELOC   (*changing his tone suddenly*)   You are our friend, consider us as yours, open your heart, tell us everything. We are all men of honor, we keep our word. Have confidence in us.

LAIS   I'm glad to hear that. Untie me so that I may speak more comfortably.

TELOC   I cannot do that, my girl. I don't give the orders around here. I'm here to help you to seek clemency of those who will dispose of you. Speak to me as you are. Tell me what you have done and why you have perhaps committed blasphemy against us . . . if by chance that is the reason you were arrested?

LAIS   But I did no such thing, I assure you. What makes you think . . . ?

TELOC   (*angrily*)   Well then, since you did not commit blasphemy, you must have done something much worse.

LAIS   Never! But look, without free will how can there

359

be love, and if you punish me for blasphemy, how can you reward love?

TELOC   Then you admit you committed blasphemy!

LAIS   No, I admit nothing. All I'm saying is that God preaches love and forgiveness and not accusation and punishment, and yet in the name of God you . . .

TELOC   You speak words of the Devil. There is proof enough of your blasphemy. Not satisfied with insulting God, you wish also to condemn our religion and those of us who are its humble servants! You are a monster of arrogance!

LAIS   No, I repeat, I never committed blasphemy, I never committed blasphemy, I only want to make you understand . . .

TELOC   Prideful wench! Insinuating serpent!

LAIS   I beg you, I'm just a simple woman, a human of no importance, I didn't want to irritate you. Please know that I am not a monster of pride or arrogance because I'm afraid, I'm terribly afraid, and thinking of my punishment fills me with terror.

TELOC   So now you're afraid! But when it comes to insulting God, deprecating God, are you afraid then?

LAIS   How can one insult God? How can a simple mortal insult or hurt the Creator?

TELOC   You speak the words of the Devil, I say. Confess to what you have done!

LAIS   I cannot know what I have done. How can I guess why you have arrested me?

TELOC   (*furious*) Guards! Take her to the underground cells and no one is to know where she is.

The action continues "normally."

LAIS Come live with me.

TELOC *shakes his head "no."*

Do what you want with me.

TELOC *shakes his head again.*

Love me.

TELOC *shakes his head again.*

Then let me love you!

TELOC May I decapitate you?

LAIS Oh yes, yes, you may! Look, I'll lay myself down on this table and you may plunge a dagger into my breast, tear off strips of my flesh, then pour boiling wax into the open wounds.

TELOC I'll do nothing.

LAIS Drill a hole in my skull and suck out my brains with a straw.

TELOC You used to ask me for this sort of thing when you were a little girl.

LAIS Yes, yes, make me suffer.

TELOC I can't.

LAIS I'll give up the theater, I'll leave everything behind.

TELOC You want us to live together?

LAIS Oh yes.

TELOC Look at my heart.

Projections on the columns of the following images accompanied by a tic-tac beating: Photo of a crowd. An insane man in an asylum. Cartoon strips. "The Schoolchildren" by Breughel. A train. "Spring" by Botticelli.

LAIS   I love you!

She runs all around the stage, climbs to the top of one of the columns, hangs there by her feet, head hanging down. Her face brushes against TELOC's. *They kiss.* LAIS *comes down and chases after* TELOC. *She catches him and brings him to stage center, making him cross his arms on his chest in a somewhat solemn attitude. She drapes a cape with baroque ornaments about his shoulders, curtsying continuously as she does this. We see an image of what looks like a Boy Scout in dress uniform standing at attention. A serpent wraps itself around him.* LAIS *puts on a horse's harness and gives the reins to* TELOC.

My Lord, your humble servant is not worthy of uniting herself with you for eternity. Order me to wash your feet and I'll dry them with my hair, order me to bring you drink and I shall carry the receptacle on my head to you, order me to write and I shall open my veins so that you may therein dip your pen.

TELOC   Have the vehicle and the will power brought to me.

TELOC *climbs into a sort of cart (with rubber wheels) that* LAIS *brings to him. She attaches herself to it as though she were a horse. She pro-*

362

ceeds to pull the cart with TELOC *in it.* TELOC
guides her with the reins. Suddenly LAIS *stops and*
leaves the cart as she takes off the harness.

LAIS Kiss me.

They kiss.

When you begin to feel weak, I shall rock you.

TELOC You know that every night I take out my
compass and measure the distance between two
stars.

LAIS I'll measure it with you.

TELOC And now prepare me a stew with a lot of lard
and onions in it. That's the way I like it.

LAIS Oh yes, I'll make it just the way you like it.

TELOC We'll dine together.

LAIS We'll eat with our fingers.

TELOC Yes, we'll even eat the sauce that way and let
the grease roll down the corners of our mouths . . .

LAIS Did you know that was a dream I always had
when I was small: having a husband for whom I'd
cook rich, heavy food.

TELOC And we'll bathe ourselves on the terrace and
over our naked bodies we'll pour noodle soup, and
sardines in oil, and pineapple syrup, and an ointment
called pride.

LAIS You'll accept me?

TELOC Come!

LAIS I'm so lucky!

TELOC Come!

LAIS Will you caress me before we go to sleep?

TELOC Come!

363

LAIS Will you squeeze my ass in your big hands too, but without really hurting me a lot, just a little? Will you?

TELOC With the tips of my fingers.

LAIS And when we go to bed I'll say that I don't want to undress and you'll play along saying "don't you feel well?" or "does your back hurt?" and you'll be the doctor and undress me slowly, or roughly, like a drunkard, until I'm naked in front of you.

TELOC *points to the balcony and whistles.*

TELOC (*calls out*) Come up!

LAIS What's going on?

TELOC Nothing!

LAIS Who are you calling?

TELOC My companion.

LAIS You live with someone?

TELOC Of course!

LAIS *climbs to the top of a column and remains there crouched, silent.*

TELOC You're not saying anything. Are you angry?

LAIS *turns, remains silent.*

LAIS (*very sadly*) That jam jar carries my soul. Look, there it is. Lais' soul dangles in the jam jar at the end of a ribbon.

TELOC You kept it. It's the jar I gave you.

LAIS I've made so many wishes on the jar.

TELOC For example.

LAIS Not to die of starvation nor of thirst.

TELOC And no one has touched it?

LAIS No one!

TELOC But you don't believe in its power.

LAIS It was a souvenir of you.

TELOC Are you sad?

LAIS I'll stay alone with the jar and you will go back to your . . .

TELOC You don't really believe that your soul is in the jar. Can I put my finger in there?

LAIS No, don't . . . well, I guess if you want to . . .

TELOC Look! I take it. I remove the cover, do you feel anything?

LAIS (*feeling pleasure*) I feel as though a breath of fresh air has blown into my head and my life. My neck and my brain are being brushed by a thousand petals as though a thousand tiny flies without wings had just landed.

TELOC I'm sticking my finger in.

LAIS No!

TELOC A little bit?

It looks as though LAIS *is feeling pain.*

Look, my finger gets closer.

LAIS I feel a terrible pain hovering over my head.

TELOC My finger's going in.

LAIS No . . . oh, do it if it gives you pleasure.

TELOC *closes the jar.*

TELOC Yes, your soul really is in there, isn't it?

LAIS Take it. It's yours, keep it. Spread my soul on a piece of toast and if it isn't sweet enough I'll give you some honey to put on it.

365

There is a knock at the door.

TELOC   Open up, it's her.
LAIS   Who?
TELOC   Her.

> LAIS *opens the door.* MIHARCA *appears dressed in a grotesque outfit. A flood of light bathes her. A toy truck passes at great speed from stage left to right; chasing it is a midget. A drum introduction is heard. A moment of hysteria. The following images project on the wall at great speed: A rayfish. Multicolors. A giant eye. Multicolors. "La Pierre et la Folie" of Bosch.* MIHARCA *appears to be a madwoman with wild, uncontrolled gestures. She laughs hysterically upon seeing* LAIS. *Then she leaps about with great bounds. Finally she throws herself at* LAIS' *feet.*

MIHARCA   Lais . . . (*In a half mocking tone.*) . . . my sweet, my frail and faithful angel.
LAIS   Miharca!
MIHARCA   Prayer for the refrigerator. . . . Dear Father . . .
LAIS   Miharca, you remember?
MIHARCA   Don't pay any attention to me, dear Lais, heart of my heart!

> *All of a sudden,* MIHARCA *starts running about the stage wildly. During this time,* TELOC *has taken a place in a kind of armchair throne. He seems absent, and suddenly very old; he doesn't seem to be aware of what is taking place around him.*

MIHARCA Watch out for him, he's crazy. Completely crazy. He is a very dangerous man. I'm warning you out of friendship, out of love for you; he's a raving maniac. (*She is frantic, gesticulating wildly.*)

LAIS He can hear us.

MIHARCA (*screaming*) Ha! Not a word, the poor man is half deaf. (*Very softly.*) Isn't that right, darling, that you are half deaf?

TELOC (*impassive in his armchair*) Yes, that's right, dear.

MIHARCA It's so wonderful . . . who would have thought that he and I . . . it always seemed like it would be you two who would make it.

LAIS Has it been long since you and he . . .

MIHARCA Tell me confidentially, Lais, I'm your friend after all, do you really like him?

LAIS *is about to answer, but* MIHARCA *interrupts her.*

Because if you do, if you find him seductive, even if it's only physically, I'll gladly give him up to you. What do you say?

LAIS *is about to answer.* MIHARCA *interrupts again.*

Don't say anything. I know you're aware of what he's become, an impotent, half-paralyzed creature who can't utter a word. He looks as though he could speak, but he's really asleep. Come, you'll see. (MIHARCA, *with gestures of a madwoman, goes to* TELOC.) Yoo-hoo! Go ahead and spit on him, you'll see he won't say anything.

367

TELOC *remains seated, immobile.*

LAIS   Leave him alone, please.

MIHARCA   Spit on him, I said. He loves it. Give him a kick in his parts, go ahead . . . (*She laughs her mad laugh.*) He doesn't even know what's going on.

LAIS   Either he doesn't know or he's enjoying it.

MIHARCA   Aren't you clever! You haven't changed a lick, have you? So intelligent, you always were the first to catch on to things. That's the reason you've been a success in life and the rest of us have failed.

LAIS   Me, a success?

MIHARCA   Of course, come now, don't play modest. You've been a success because you deserve it, you're sensitive and clever, while he and I, we're just a couple of asses.

MIHARCA *embraces* TELOC *in a vulgar manner and covers his face with kisses. She runs her hands over his body.* TELOC *remains impassive, as though unaware of anything.*

Kiss me, my lover, kiss me. See how Lais watches us. See how she mocks us. Kiss me so we can show her we at least know how to kiss.

LAIS   What are you saying?

MIHARCA   Oh stop the kidding, I know very well that you have only contempt for us. I know it, and furthermore we deserve it.

LAIS   Don't say that. I have no contempt for you, on the contrary.

MIHARCA   Did you hear that, my love?

368

She runs wildly to TELOC, *feels him up, she is lustful and mad.*

She's sincere, she wants to show us she has real affection for us, she wants to help us. Don't take offense, she didn't mean to insult you. You understand, don't you?

TELOC *clacks his tongue.*

My poor darling, my poor sweet thing! (*She hugs* TELOC's *head to her breast, lovingly, almost maternally.*) He's like a child, he needs loving care. He's amusing and sensitive, like a child. I beg you, please don't do anything that might offend him. You promise, don't you?

LAIS But Miharca . . .

MIHARCA Don't say anything, I understand. Here, come close. It's a secret. Look, he's half-asleep . . . but his eyes are open, he hears, understands, sees nothing.

LAIS I see.

MIHARCA Listen, put your ear next to his heart, you'll hear what a strange noise it makes.

LAIS No, leave me alone . . .

MIHARCA Do it!

MIHARCA *forces* LAIS *to do it. We hear the terrifying noise of a locomotive.* LAIS *pulls back, frightened.* MIHARCA *laughs wildly.*

Did you hear that? You almost went deaf, right? Isn't he funny? You wouldn't think it looking at him, he looks so calm.

369

LAIS   Leave him alone.

MIHARCA   Look, you want to see how marvelous and different he is. Raise his eyelids and look. (*She does it. She touches* TELOC *and examines him as though he were an inanimate object.*) Raise them yourself.

LAIS *refuses.*

Oh go ahead, do it. And pull out his lips too, and look at his mouth.

LAIS *finally does it.* TELOC *lets out a scream.*

MIHARCA (*to* TELOC)   Oh now, don't be upset dear. She was a bit rough and it hurt a little, but there's no reason . . . oh look, she's made you bleed, my poor sweet.

LAIS   But I didn't mean to.

MIHARCA   Oh I know, don't bother making excuses. You pulled too hard and you made him bleed, that's all there is to it. It's not that terrible. He knows you didn't mean any harm, it was just clumsiness. (MIHARCA *whispers into* TELOC's *ear loudly.*) You see how she is, she made you bleed. You see how she treats us, she did it deliberately.

LAIS   Can't I do something?

MIHARCA   Don't worry about it. Actually, he loves it. He often asks me to beat him. Look! (*She takes a belt and strikes him a hard blow.*) Did you see his face? He loves it. He adores it.

She runs wildly around the stage and finally sits down in a corner and sobs. Her hysteria takes over.

LAIS *goes to her.* MIHARCA *calms down and seems to speak reasonably.*

Lais, I'm sorry about all this, I don't know what came over me.

LAIS Miharca, I don't understand . . .

MIHARCA Lais, I'm a hysteric, I know it.

LAIS We all get hysterical.

MIHARCA Speak to me, tell me about yourself, I'm so miserable.

LAIS It's you who should speak, it's been so long since we've seen each other.

MIHARCA We learned about your success, your triumphs, and we were so happy . . .

LAIS Why didn't you come before?

MIHARCA We belong to your childhood. You were living the adventure of your adult life.

LAIS If you only knew how much I wanted to find you.

MIHARCA Do you still remember your childhood, the orphanage, the sisters? You must have had such extraordinary experiences since then.

LAIS My childhood is more with me now than ever, and my adolescence!

MIHARCA Do you still remember the day you were locked in the cell and the sisters had taken your clothes off so you wouldn't run away, and I stole a big bathrobe for you so you could escape anyway? Remember how we laughed at the way you looked in that huge bathrobe?

LAIS How did it happen that Teloc . . .

MIHARCA Teloc was yours then, remember?

LAIS I feel like I'm dreaming. I have the feeling that something is guiding me toward my destiny, I don't know what or who.

371

MIHARCA, *crying.*

What is it, Miharca?

MIHARCA Oh Lais, I want you to be more and more successful, and that you go from triumph to triumph until you enter the garden of delights. What can I do for you? I'll do anything, and so will Teloc.

LAIS But . . .

MIHARCA I'm sure your triumph and happiness can only be guaranteed by some sacrifice, and if you wish, I'm ready to make it.

LAIS What an idea! I won't hear of it.

MIHARCA You know, when we were little I thought only of you. Let me kiss your hands.

LAIS *puts out her hands.* MIHARCA *kisses them.*

I wish I were a soldier, an officer, so you would look at me differently.

LAIS Look at you differently?

MIHARCA As though I weren't a . . .

LAIS A what?

MIHARCA Kiss me on the mouth!

LAIS But why?

MIHARCA Yes, kiss me on the mouth.

LAIS *kisses her lightly on the mouth.*

You see, you do hate me.

LAIS How can you say that?

MIHARCA Then kiss me better.

LAIS *does so unwillingly. Long kiss.* LAIS *pulls abruptly away with a little cry.* MIHARCA *laughs.*

LAIS   You bit me!

> MIHARCA *laughs wildly. At that moment* TELOC *approaches, "transformed."*

TELOC   That's very good, children, very good. Well now, let's see what else you know how to do. (*He takes a whip and snaps it in the air.*) All right, let's hear you whinny, loud and clear.

> MIHARCA *whinnies.* LAIS *remains mute and doesn't move.* TELOC *becomes furious.*

What now, you won't whinny? Grab her.

> MIHARCA *grabs* LAIS *by the hands and* TELOC *hits her with the whip. Angrily.*

And the next time, it'll really hurt. (*He sounds like an animal trainer.*) All right, my little mares, whinny together.

> *He snaps his whip and they whinny together.*

There now, that's much better. And now I want to see you trot about like a pair of mares. Go on.

> *He snaps his whip. They break into a little trot and whinny.*

Perfect! Now kiss the soles of my boots.

> MIHARCA *rushes to obey the order.* TELOC *points to* LAIS.

She's being difficult again. Hold her!

Before MIHARCA *has a chance to move,* LAIS *quickly kisses the boots.*

Perfect, that's much better.

Circus music is heard and the two women trot and whinny about the stage.

Now it gets a bit more difficult. I want you to go through the hoop of flames. (TELOC *spins a flaming hoop.*)

MIHARCA *and* LAIS *go through it. Fireworks. Projection of following images: Inquisition. Bosch. Cartoon strips. Garden of Delights.*

Darkness. MIHARCA *and* LAIS, *as young girls. Hangman's shadow looms across the stage.*

MIHARCA (*young girl*)   Poor little Lais, always being punished.

LAIS (*young girl*)   I'm very hungry and cold.

MIHARCA   How long have you been in the cell now?

LAIS   Four days.

MIHARCA   Poor little Lais. Speak lower, they might hear us.

LAIS   At night they bring me a plate of string beans and I ask the guardian to leave the plate and not take it away once I've finished the way she's supposed to do. So I let the beans sit there in their juice until they become all swollen and it seems like I'm eating much more that way.

MIHARCA   But you're not abandoned, I'm still here with you.

LAIS   There are rats here with me too.

MIHARCA   But I'm here.

Violins. Cannon shots. Darkness. Dim lights come up. Between the columns appear the heads of the SHEEP. *Bleating of* SHEEP. *A sheep's head seems to be laughing out loud.* MIHARCA *and* LAIS *as young girls appear on stage.*

LAIS   Come quickly, take all my picture cutouts and give them to all my friends. I'm going to die.

MIHARCA   Don't say that.

LAIS   Yes, yes, I'm going to die and since I've done bad things, I'm going to die a sinner.

MIHARCA   No, you're not going to die. Whatever gave you such an idea suddenly? How could you die at thirteen years of age?

LAIS   Miharca, I know I'm dying. And I haven't done one good deed. I haven't obeyed one rule this month and I took a bath without my nightdress on and oh, I looked at my body and everything.

MIHARCA   But God will forgive that.

LAIS   Sister told me that that was a very big sin.

MIHARCA   Don't worry about it. I know, put on the string of thorns.

LAIS   If I wear that will God forgive me?

MIHARCA   I'm sure of it.

LAIS   I don't have one here.

MIHARCA   I'll give you the one sister gave me for Christmas. It's for the waist and you have to tie it real tight til the thorns stick in your flesh.

LAIS   And God will forgive me?

375

MIHARCA   It's guaranteed.

LAIS   But I've done nothing but commit sins. I touched my face, and my body, its awful.

MIHARCA   Poor little Lais.

LAIS   And then I never wear the wraparound to flatten my breasts.

MIHARCA   There's still hope.

LAIS   No, I'm going to die . . . you'll bury me in the church crypt right here on the orphanage grounds.

MIHARCA   Why are you so hard on yourself? I'll tell you a secret: I happen to know that God loves me very much and I'm going to ask him to let you live.

LAIS   How do you know that God loves you?

MIHARCA   (*glancing about surreptitiously*)   Moses appeared before me while I was praying.

LAIS   Moses, really?

MIHARCA   Yes, Moses. And he spoke to me.

LAIS   What did he say?

MIHARCA   That I was very dear to him, that I should do everything the sisters ask: going to recreation in groups of three instead of groups of two, not to wash my teeth before Communion, never to speak to men who are all dirty . . .

LAIS   What luck to be able to speak to Moses, with his long beard . . .

MIHARCA   You'll see, I'll ask for your life to be spared and it will.

LAIS   But it's too late, there's nothing he can do now. I'm already dying. Please take my cutouts and give them to my friends.

MIHARCA   And how do you know you're already dying?

LAIS   Because blood is running down the inside of my legs, lots and lots of blood!

Cannon shots. Red lights. SHEEP *bleat, frightened.
One of them moves forward, laughing. Projections.*

Lights up "normal." Action continues "normally."
MIHARCA *and* LAIS, *adults, are kissing. They caress
each other. Long silence.*

TELOC   That's it, a little more.

They continue to kiss. TELOC *snaps his whip in the
air.*

Enough. That's enough!

They caress and embrace.

Did she bite you?

Silence.

I asked you, Lais, did she bite you? If she did, tell
me, and I'll punish her.

LAIS   No, she didn't bite me.

TELOC   Very good, touch her face then. Lais, caress
her face with love.

LAIS *obeys.*

Get closer to her, put your forehead to her knees.
That's right, now say something romantic.

LAIS (*feigning*)   Miharca . . . the clouds . . . the
knives . . .

TELOC *snaps his whip with impatience.*

MIHARCA (*sincerely*)   Lais, my love . . .

LAIS (*on the verge of tears*)   Let's walk together, like when we first met.

MIHARCA   Speak, Lais.

LAIS *caresses her face.*

LAIS   When I used to be punished on Sundays and had to spend the afternoons facing a tree and they wouldn't let me watch the ball game which was going on behind my back, you, Miharca, you stayed at a nearby tree so I wouldn't feel as though I was all alone.

TELOC *seems satisfied with the way things are going between them.*

MIHARCA   But one day you met Teloc . . . and then you started dreaming of other worlds and other times and you went travelling in the past and in the future and you forgot about me, Lais!

LAIS   If you want you can tie a string around me and I'll fly about at your side like a butterfly around a chicken.

MIHARCA   Your head appears in a dream as though it were cut off, your head is floating on a river.

LAIS   I imagine you nude in a park of flowers with your hair flowing and a dove sitting on top of your head, while an electric train runs at your feet.

MIHARCA   Break the spell that ties you to Teloc . . . he possesses you, you have lost your freedom.

378

LAIS Speak!

MIHARCA Free yourself of him, tear your feelings for him into a thousand pieces until you're completely free again.

LAIS Miharca!

TELOC *snaps his whip*.

TELOC (*to* MIHARCA) That's enough. Admit why you've come here.

MIHARCA What are you doing?

TELOC The game's over. Tell me why you've come to see Lais after so many years. Tell us both.

MIHARCA Because I wanted to be with her, because I always felt great love for her.

TELOC You liar.

MIHARCA Shut up, Teloc!

TELOC You came here to humiliate her, to infuriate her.

MIHARCA Don't say things like that in front of Lais.

TELOC Why, doesn't she have the right to know the truth?

MIHARCA What truth?

TELOC That you envy her, that you hate her!

MIHARCA *screams hysterically*.

MIHARCA (*lifting her skirt over her hips*) Kiss it, kiss it!

TELOC You've already said that to Lais.

MIHARCA I'm going mad!

TELOC That's right, go mad.

MIHARCA The way you insult me . . . the way you abuse me when she's here!

379

LAIS   I forgive you.

MIHARCA (*stops her hysterics and says with quiet calm and hatred*)   Who are you to forgive me? Who are you, you phony bit of fluff? You think just because you crawl around a stage jabbering silly words you've got the right to . . .

LAIS   I didn't mean to . . .

TELOC (*to* LAIS)   You should be furious with her. She's trying to run you down. She came today a few hours before your greatest opening night to jinx you, to make you fail. And everything she ever did in the past was not for your good, but that so you would fail. Even I played with your feelings the way she told me to.

LAIS   It's not possible.

TELOC   You have a right to revenge.

LAIS   No.

TELOC   What do I have to do, show you?

LAIS   Show me what?

MIHARCA   No, don't.

TELOC   Do you remember our trips in time?

LAIS   Yes, yes.

TELOC   I'll take you on another trip: you'll see what's going to take place in two hours.

MIHARCA   No, don't!

Darkness. SHEEP *bleating. Projections.*

Light changes. ZENON *cries out, his cage vacillates from above the stage. He calls down.*

ZENON   Kill . . . kill . . . kill . . .

380

*At stage center is a huge cutting blade fixed to a
slab. It is the kind of contraption used for slicing
down huge fish. It is a kind of guillotine.* MIHARCA
*is tied to the slab, her head hangs over the side
toward the audience. One touch to the huge blade
and she will be sliced in two.*

Kill . . . kill her . . . gouge her eyes . . . kill . . .

MIHARCA *is terrified, screaming.* TELOC *and* LAIS
appear on stage. TELOC *plays the horse and* LAIS,
*the rider. They are laughing uncontrollably, like
children playing a wild game. They circle around*
MIHARCA, *shouting and screaming laughter.* TELOC
passes over MIHARCA. *She howls.*

Kill her . . . gouge . . . her eyes.

TELOC *and* LAIS *fall to the floor and roll about together near* MIHARCA, *who continues to howl.*

Gouge out . . . her eyes.

LAIS *climbs onto* TELOC *as a horse and together
they trot around the stage.* LAIS *seizes an imagi-
nary "lance" and jabs* MIHARCA. LAIS *and* TELOC
scream with laughter.

Eyes . . . Eyes!

Bleating of SHEEP. *Moment of silence. We hear
only* ZENON's *heavy breathing and the insults*
MIHARCA *hurls at* LAIS. TELOC *looks as though he
is praying, all crouched into himself.* LAIS *goes to*

the hanging blade and prepares to release the mechanism which will cut MIHARCA *in half.*

MIHARCA   No, no, you bitch, you cheap phony!

LAIS *drops the blade and cuts her in half at the belly. Light turns bright red.* MIHARCA *dies. A moan comes from* ZENON *above. Bleating of* SHEEP. *Cannon shots alternate with sounds of praying in the darkness, for a long moment. Projections.*

Lights up "normal." The action continues "normally."

LAIS (*to* TELOC)   It's not possible, it's not possible.
TELOC (*to* LAIS)   You saw how the rancorous night made off with your loneliness.
LAIS   It's not possible!
TELOC   The future surprises you as it should.
LAIS   Miharca! Miharca!
ZENON's VOICE   Lais!
LAIS   Be still! (*To* TELOC.) Where is Miharca?
TELOC   She has disappeared.

MIHARCA *comes forward from the back of stage center as though she were a phantom. She speaks as though sleepwalking.*

MIHARCA   I am the adulterous princess of the serpents. Look at my breast.
LAIS (*looking*)   I don't see anything!
MIHARCA   Look at my breast and you will see the burning bonze, the naked woman, the vultures, and

if you look more closely you will perceive the futility of life.

LAIS I see also two children playing with the hoop of my thoughts.

MIHARCA You will no longer be the virgin nor the Devil.

Suddenly TELOC *pulls out his whip again.*

TELOC Tell her you hate her!

MIHARCA (*with conviction*) I hate you!

LAIS Miharca!

MIHARCA I hate you with all my gut hate. I hate you as though you were the stillborn child I never desired.

LAIS Be still, Miharca.

TELOC *snaps his whip.*

Light changes.

TELOC (*as cross-examining lawyer*) And of what are you accused?

LAIS (*defendant*) Uh, well . . . but will you agree to defend me during my trial? . . . you have such a good reputation . . . you who are the best lawyer in this area.

TELOC Well, tell me first what is the crime of which you are accused.

LAIS I, uh . . .

TELOC (*dignified*) It seems that you have committed blasphemy.

LAIS You are a lawyer . . .

TELOC Yes, I am devoted to justice.

383

LAIS Well then . . .

TELOC Is there anything more stimulating than a trial? You speak out to the country directly represented by the judge, you have the right to tell them anything you wish, to enter into dialogue with them.

LAIS How I would love for you to defend me.

TELOC My child, I do not wish in the slightest to hurt your feelings nor give you the impression that your case does not interest me, but you must understand that an affair such as yours offends my conscience to such a degree that I cannot . . . I believe in God!

LAIS But you believe in a God of love?

TELOC Yes, that's quite right.

LAIS Then how can you refuse to defend me, how can you allow the expression of a God of accusation and punishment, a God of revenge?

TELOC My girl, you are fortunate enough to appear before our judges, who are particularly just and render sentences typified by their dignity and moderation. You have no need of a lawyer.

LAIS But you . . . haven't you defended men accused of rape, of murder, theft, and embezzlement? Wasn't your conscience offended then?

TELOC Let us drop the subject.

LAIS No, on the contrary, let us go into it.

TELOC Silence, I must go to Communion.

LAIS Eat well!

Lights "normal." The action continues "normally." TELOC *finishes the installation of a kind of platform, stage center, which is covered with a cloth.*

TELOC You want to know everything?

LAIS   Go ahead!

TELOC   Miharca asked me to perform all the "roles" I played with you. She wanted to infuriate you, to show you that you're nothing and a nobody. That your only reality is the world of your childhood and that your success and celebrity today are nothing but lies and illusions.

LAIS   I know that!

TELOC   She made me hurt you.

MIHARCA *lowers the cage and tries to talk to* ZENON. *She throws peanuts at him.*

LAIS   I can't believe it.

TELOC   Her whole attitude seems empty of any meaning, except one. You remember how I was capable of accomplishing all sorts of miracles? Ha! Well, now she has managed to rob me of almost all my faculties. Look at me! Believe me! (*In a stage whisper.*) And I who love only you!

LAIS   Teloc!

TELOC   Be quiet, she will hear us, speak softer.

LAIS   She's busy with Zenon.

TELOC   She is constantly putting me through horrible tortures. Look at my arms. There's nothing left but wounds. Look at my ankles, my legs. You see those collars? They're strings of thorns she makes me wear and which she pulls and tugs on till the thorns dig into my skin and the blood bursts out. She's a monster.

LAIS   Why do you put up with it? . . .

TELOC   I'm at her mercy. She knows my life, she can do what she wants with me. With just a word she can have me locked away for life.

LAIS   Teloc, do you really love me?

TELOC   I'll do anything for you.

LAIS   Let's run away together!

TELOC   Look at her. Now that she knows how attached you are to Zenon, she's plotting to get him away from you . . . she loves only one person in the world . . . you! She is torn between her love and her hate for you!

LAIS   Let's run away.

TELOC   Listen to her.

MIHARCA *playing with* ZENON.

ZENON   You . . . bitch.

MIHARCA   Be still, silly creature.

ZENON   You . . . bitch . . . me . . . and Lais . . .

MIHARCA   Lais is the bitch. Lais locks you up. Look at me, I'm letting you out with this key. I'm setting you free.

ZENON   Lais . . . good.

MIHARCA   I'm letting you out. Lais is bad.

LAIS (*to* TELOC)   Do something.

TELOC (*to* MIHARCA)   You can stop all this, it's over, you're through brutalizing me. You're sick. Lais and I have decided it's time we put a stop to you. Isn't that right, Lais?

LAIS   That's right, yes.

TELOC   You're never going to torture either of us again, and you won't get a chance to turn Zenon against Lais either.

MIHARCA   Shut up, you're more of a monster than Zenon is. She's fed up with him and now she wants to run away with you. She's a conniving bitch and she always has been.

386

TELOC   How can you dare treat Lais like that?

MIHARCA   I'll dare treat her any way I feel like. You revealed all my secrets to her. So now tell her everything, tell her you came to . . .

TELOC   You're the one! You came to destroy her on the day of her greatest triumph!

MIHARCA   No, tell the truth. Tell her I came first to gouge out her eyes, then to kill her.

TELOC   You hate her, you want to kill her, and you prepared this whole scene so that you could enjoy torturing her before killing her.

MIHARCA   That's true, and you were in on the whole thing.

TELOC   Because you made me by threatening me, but now I'm free. (*He grabs her, throws her to the floor, and holds her hands.*) Stuff a handkerchief in her mouth so she can't scream.

LAIS *approaches. She fights with* MIHARCA, *who tries to bite her.*

LAIS   She tried to bite me. She almost ripped my hand off.

TELOC   Watch out for her! Don't get too close, she'll go for your eyes. Take that cloth off there.

LAIS *pulls off the cloth on the platform which reveals the guillotine apparatus with the enormous blade.*

MIHARCA   I'll tear your eyes out!

TELOC   You see how she fights. Your tyranny is finished, you vicious cat, now it's your turn to suffer.

Suddenly, inexplicably, MIHARCA *frees herself, runs toward* LAIS, *and bites her viciously on the ear.*

MIHARCA (*her teeth still clenched in* LAIS' *ear*) If you make one move, Teloc, I'll rip her ear off and then tear out her eyes.

LAIS Please don't do anything Teloc, the pain is terrible.

TELOC Miharca, I beg you, let her go, we'll go away, she won't do anything.

MIHARCA I'll kill you both. You because you're a traitor, and then her.

LAIS Let me go, you're hurting my ear. I can't stand your weight on me.

MIHARCA Well, you'll have to.

TELOC Kill me if you want, but leave her alone.

MIHARCA I'll kill you both and tear out your eyes.

TELOC Look at my string of thorns, I'll tighten them around my flesh if you want.

ZENON *watches the goings on and swings furiously in his cage.*

MIHARCA Go ahead, tighten them, that's good. At the same time I'll break her arm and tear off her ear.

She tears off LAIS' *ear.* LAIS *screams in agony.* LAIS *remains in* MIHARCA's *clutches as she sits on her, pinning her.*

Look, here is her ear, eat it at once, eat it if you want me to let her go. But if you come close, I'll tear out her eyes.

LAIS *moans.*

Bitch!

TELOC (LAIS' *ear in hand*)   If you let her go, I'll eat it, I'll do anything you want.

MIHARCA   You're at my feet now, more than ever before.

TELOC   I'll do anything you like.

MIHARCA   You'll never get away from me.

ZENON *throws a rock at* MIHARCA *from his cage. She falls unconscious.* TELOC *and* LAIS *grab her at once. They beat her brutally, then tie her to the chopping block. After they have finished tying her securely,* MIHARCA *comes to, moaning.*

ZENON (*to* LAIS)   Gouge her . . . eyes . . . gouge . . . eyes!

Cannon shots. Darkness. Projections: Bombs. Planes. Cartoon strips. Goya. Bosch.

The stage looks as it did at the beginning of the Second Act. Telephone rings. LAIS *picks it up. She is alone on stage.*

POLICEMAN'S VOICE   This is the police.

LAIS   Yes.

POLICEMAN'S VOICE   We have solved the Miharca incident; your friend committed suicide. She left a letter in which she said:

MIHARCA'S VOICE   With Teloc's help, I shall offer my life as sacrifice. The hand which will torture and kill me will be guided by my own voice and wishes, that way I will celebrate my death with black bottles, ecstasies, and twining vines.

LAIS *puts back the receiver. Slowly she walks around the stage, occasionally kneeling down to kiss the floor. She sings her song sadly. Numbly, she kisses the floor again. Bleating of* SHEEP.

LAIS   Zenon, where are the skeletons of my dead sheep, where have they disappeared?
ZENON   Me . . . love y . . . you.

LAIS *brings down* ZENON's *cage. At that moment, the turntable swings around bringing the live* SHEEP *into view.*

LAIS   My sweet darlings, how is it possible? My little ones have been restored to me. (*She kisses them.*) My darlings, my pretty ones, how I missed you.
ZENON   Me . . . me! Not . . . sheep.
LAIS   Wait a second, be patient. (*She brings down the cage entirely.*) Zenon, now be good, stay with me quietly and be good. Come out.
ZENON   Come . . . with m . . . me.
LAIS   Why?
ZENON   Come . . . in . . . egg.

They go into the egg through the little door.

Now . . . throw . . . away . . . k . . . key.
LAIS   Throw away the key? But we'll be imprisoned in here.
ZENON   Throw . . . key . . . Throw!

LAIS Yes, yes, I'll throw away the key. You are my light and my night and my happiness. But before, Zenon, take this jar of jam. (*She hands him the jar containing her soul.*)

ZENON (*eating with his fingers*) Jam . . . good, good . . .

When he has finished eating it, he becomes a "human being" and begins speaking "normally."

What a delicious taste !

They take places in the egg and LAIS throws away the key.

LAIS Ze . . . non . . . m . . . my sheep . . . alive !

ZENON (*speaking perfectly*) The live sheep are yours, they cry for you, you are life and hope for us. I love you desperately !

LAIS Me . . . me . . . love . . . y . . . you, Zenon. (*She speaks the way ZENON used to speak.*)

ZENON sings LAIS' song with no difficulty. The egg mounts and swings softly as he does. At that moment, TELOC comes on stage accompanying ZENON's song on his trumpet. The egg has risen out of sight. We hear the animal laughter of LAIS in the egg while ZENON sings clearly and well. TELOC stands among the SHEEP and plays the melody as the curtain comes down.

Selected Grove Press Theater Paperbacks

17061-X ARDEN, JOHN / Plays: One (Serjeant Musgrave's Dance, The Workhouse Donkey, Armstrong's Last Goodnight) / $4.95

17208-6 BECKETT, SAMUEL / Endgame / $2.95

17233-7 BECKETT, SAMUEL / Happy Days / $2.95

62061-5 BECKETT, SAMUEL / Ohio Impromptu, Catastrophe, and What Where: Three Plays / $4.95

17204-3 BECKETT, SAMUEL / Waiting for Godot / $3.50

17112-8 BRECHT, BERTOLT / Galileo / $2.95

17472-0 BRECHT, BERTOLT / The Threepenny Opera / $2.45

17390-2 GENET, JEAN / The Maids; Deathwatch / $5.95

17022-9 HAYMAN, RONALD / How to Read a Play / $4.95

17226-4 IONESCO, EUGENE / Rhinoceros and Other Plays (The Leader, The Future Is in Eggs, or It Takes All Sorts to Make a World) / $4.95

17016-4 MAMET, DAVID / American Buffalo / $4.95

17040-7 MAMET, DAVID / A Life in the Theatre / $6.95

62049-6 MAMET, DAVID / Glengarry Glen Ross / $6.95

17043-1 MAMET, DAVID / Sexual Perversity in Chicago and The Duck Variations / $3.95

17092-X ODETS, CLIFFORD / Six Plays (Waiting for Lefty; Awake and Sing; Golden Boy; Rocket to the Moon; Till the Day I Die; Paradise Lost) / $7.95

17001-6 ORTON, JOE / The Complete Plays (The Ruffian on the Stair, The Good and Faithful Servant, The Erpingham Camp, Funeral Games, Loot, What the Butler Saw, Entertaining Mr. Sloane) $6.95

17084-9 PINTER, HAROLD / Betrayal / $3.95

17251-5 PINTER, HAROLD / The Homecoming / $4.95

17885-8 PINTER, HAROLD / No Man's Land / $3.95

17539-5 POMERANCE, BERNARD / The Elephant Man / $4.25

17743-6 RATTIGAN, TERENCE / Plays: One / $5.95

62040-2 SETO, JUDITH ROBERTS / The Young Actor's Workbook / $8.95

17948-X SHAWN, WALLACE and GREGORY, ANDRÉ / My Dinner with André / $5.95

17884-X STOPPARD, TOM / Travesties / $3.95

17260-4 STOPPARD, TOM / Rosencrantz and Guildenstern Are Dead / $3.95

17206-X WALEY, ARTHUR, tr. and ed. / The Nō Plays of Japan / $7.95

Available from your local bookstore, or directly from Grove Press. (Add $1.00 postage and handling for the first book and 50¢ for each additional book.)

GROVE PRESS, INC., 196 West Houston St., New York, N.Y. 10014